The Case

Disinformati
Against a Small Nation

On the Boundary of Two Worlds:
Identity, Freedom, and Moral Imagination in the Baltics
15

The Case for Latvia

Disinformation Campaigns Against a Small Nation

Fourteen Hard Questions and
Straight Answers about a Baltic Country

Jukka Rislakki

Amsterdam - New York, NY 2008

Translated from the Finnish by Richard Impola

The paper on which this book is printed meets the requirements of
"ISO 9706:1994, Information and documentation - Paper for
documents - Requirements for permanence".

ISBN: 978-90-420-2424-3
©Editions Rodopi B.V., Amsterdam - New York, NY 2008
Printed in the Netherlands

To the memory of Nora Kūla

Physical torture is not at all as effective as influencing one's mind. That is exactly why communication is the key to power.

Manuel Castells

Contents

Prologue

9 • Misinformation, disinformation?

Questions and Answers

35 • 1. Are minorities, especially the Russians, discriminated against in Latvia? Is it very difficult for them to become citizens? Do they have political rights?

53 • 2. Are the Russians denied the right to use their language in Latvian society and in the schools?

65 • 3. Were the Baltic lands a small, underdeveloped province in a far corner of Europe, to which Germans, Swedes, Poles, and Russians brought religion, culture, and well-being and where no prerequisites for independence existed?

79 • 4. Did the Latvian Reds help Lenin seize power in Russia? Did they help murder the Russian royal family?

87 • 5. Was Latvia granted independence as a present? Was the War of Independence an exaggerated myth? Was it a series of minor skirmishes that the Latvians were able to win with foreign help?

95 • 6. Why did the Latvians not resist the Soviet army's taking over their country in 1940? Did the people carry out an anti-bourgeois, anti-fascist revolution, after which Latvia joined the legally, by means of elections?

109 • 7. Did Latvians murder their Jews in 1941? How anti-Semitic is and was Latvia?

127 • 8. Why did tens of thousands of Latvian volunteers fight in the SS troops, and why are SS veterans still allowed to march on the streets of Rīga instead of being brought to justice?

143 • 9. Did the Soviet Union occupy Latvia? Were the Latvians victims of genocide?

157 • 10. Did the Latvians succumb to Soviet power, cooperate with the Communist authorities, and start their independence movement only after the Lithuanians and Estonians had begun theirs?

173 • 11. Has Latvia always belonged to Russia and benefited from it? Is it a strategically indispensable area for Russia?

181 • 12. Shouldn't Latvia be grateful for factories, houses, schools, roads, and harbors built during the Soviet era? Shouldn't she pay compensation as well?

193 • 13. Has Latvia been unwilling to establish good relations with neighboring Russia? Does Latvia champion an intransigent, hostile line toward Russia in the European Union, and did she decline a border agreement with Russia? Does she demand that Russia hand over some border areas to her?

205 • 14. Have the new leaders of Latvia privatized state property for their own use and are they guilty of massive corruption while the majority of the people live in poverty?

211 • Acknowledgements: How and Why This Book Came to Be

221 • Basic Facts about Latvia

225 • Notes

275 • Bibliography

287 • Index

Prologue

Misinformation, Disinformation?

Eiropa mūs nesapratīs (Europe will not understand us).

A favorite song on Latvian radio in 2004

Who owns the past owns the future.

George Orwell

The first time I set foot in Latvia, at the center of Europe[1] in the autumn of 1988, the changes had already begun that would lead to regained independence for this Soviet republic three years later. I came as a journalist for the *Helsingin Sanomat*, Finland's largest newspaper. I knew little about Latvia then, except that it was situated between Estonia and Lithuania, that its capital was Rīga, and that many of its words and names ended oddly with the letter "s" I had, of course, at least heard earlier in school courses in geography and history about the Baltic countries—that they had been united with the Soviet Union in the upheavals of World War II, and that they were its most western and most highly developed republics.

As the poet Ivar Ivask wrote in 1986: "Strange to hail from almost anonymous shores / in overexplored Europe where the Baltic / still hides a lunar side, unilluminated / except for subjugations, annexations / which continued unabated for centuries."[2]

I soon came to the same conclusion as many other visitors to Latvia: that this was a nation of poets, gardeners, and singers. "Every Latvian is a born poet, everyone makes up verse and songs and can sing," Johann Kohl wrote of Latvians in 1841.[3] I would add, "and a nation of soldiers". I don't mean that the people are bloodthirsty or violent, but that circumstances—both geographical and historical—made them soldiers.

In many places I encountered people who had never met a Western foreigner. The language difficulties were huge. Once the initial problems were overcome—once I had crossed the language barrier, had time to get acquainted with the land and its history, and had made friends—a normal reaction followed: I saw everything in a positive light. Everything was fine, interesting, and exciting. Only gradually did I realize that there were problems and defects in Latvia just as in any other country.

I learned to speak Latvian, even published a book that dealt with Latvian history, and wrote a factual book about Finland for Latvians.[4] As a professional journalist, I naturally read a lot that others said about the Baltic countries. I could not help but notice that Latvia had an image problem.

A decade after my first contact with the country, I became our newspaper's chief correspondent for the Baltic countries. An experienced Finnish foreign correspondent tutored me for the task: "I wish you luck, but it is the unfortunate truth that the Baltic countries won't remain independent for long. But that is no tragedy. These days Russia is a democratic nation".

And lately Anatoli Chubais, Russia's energy czar, has also said that Russia's new empire would be liberal, since it could be created with money and not armored divisions.[5] Insofar as the Kremlin's foreign policy has a guiding principle, it seems to be a return to its position as a great power. According to Foreign Minister Sergei Lavrov: "It would be childish to expect Russia to be content with playing a minor part instead of assuming its role as one of the world's leading nations."[6]

The commentator on international politics Simon Araloff relates that the Kremlin and Russian companies are doing all in their power to get control of the big energy-related firms, the Latvian Ventspils Nafta and the Lithuanian Mažeikiu Nafta. "One sees clearly in this Moscow's long range strategy, the intent of which is to lay the groundwork for the future conquest of the Baltic economy."[7]

Continuing these thoughts (and remembering that Russia's Gazprom is also an important media owner), nowadays it is not absolutely necessary to conquer territory with traditional weapons, for "wars" are waged on multi-level information battlefields with the aid of propaganda, public relations, and rumor. With these, one can conquer minds and destabilize governments. The winner in an information war is the one with the greater resources, skill, and information. In the present age of technology, it can also be a lightning war, inasmuch as propaganda can be spread throughout the world in a moment.

The widespread conspiracy theories about 9/11 show how powerful a source of misinformation the internet can be. According to press reports, five years after the 2001 terrorist attacks in New York and Washington, 36 percent of Americans believed that the US government was somehow guilty of the attacks or at least knew about them. In the middle of the year 2004 some 40 percent of U.S. citizens still believed that Saddam Hussein and Al-Qaida cooperated and that there were weapons of mass destruction in Iraq.

This, according to Manuel Castells, shows that "manipulation is possible without censorship or orders to publish disinformation."[8] He writes that insults and rumors become art, because a negative message is five times more effective than a positive one. Everybody takes part in this game; "facts" are manipulated and fabricated.

Only Bad News is Good News

In its tenth anniversary issue in 2006, *The Baltic Times* wrote perceptively: "The world is a big place, and the population of the three Baltic States barely matches that of New York [City]. So it is not surprising that after the euphoria of the Flower Revolution, stories about Lithuania, Latvia and Estonia are often relegated to the 'news of the weird' section in the American press."[9]

If anything was written or related abroad about Latvia after the initial enthusiasm, it was largely negative, biased, and riddled with errors. In the worst cases, it is difficult to say if the matter was one of *mis*information, the publication of faulty, untrue or incorrect information, or of *dis*information, a concoction of factual distortion and lies, deliberately spread at home or abroad for specific reasons.

Those who believe in misinformation are said to be misinformed but not lying. Disinformation, on the other hand, was used especially as a cold-war tactic and in the context of espionage, military intelligence and propaganda; the aim was to mislead an enemy.

Since "only bad news is good news" to the international press, one might think it good that little is written about Latvia. The writer Pauls Bankovskis testifies resignedly and clearly realistically:

> I don't think that many people in Latvia have heard anything positive about the decent folks in Rwanda, whereas the systematic mass slaughter is probably common knowledge. Latvia and Rīga are likewise normally mentioned in the international media only when something has gone awry once again. The Prime Minister Einārs Repše has owned up to being an extraterrestrial alien. The British heir to the throne has been given a thrashing with a carnation. Jews have been murdered, Russians humiliated. Women sold into white slavery.[10]

In my opinion, the hostile campaign against Latvia really began, or rather, rose to a new level of intensity when, in the spring of 1998, a group acting in the

name of oppressed Russian retirees clashed with the police in downtown Rīga.
The same spring serious attacks against the Latvian war veterans' commemorative events began both at home and abroad.

Many journalists and photographers were present when the police forced
the participants—many of them Russian ex-officers—in the illegal pensioners'
demonstration off a traffic lane. The news film of this action has been shown
in many contexts since then. Even in 2006 it still served the makers of a documentary: a Russian TV channel showed it then in an inflammatory film on
"Baltic Nazism," many scenes of which had nothing to do with Latvia.[11]

The problem was not, however, new to me, since I come from a small
country between the East and the West. Finns know how difficult—if not nearly
hopeless—it is when one tries to correct old and stereotyped misconceptions
abroad. Official Finland was worried about how little was known of the country
and people: for a very long time elsewhere in Europe, even in encyclopedias,
Finns were thought to be Mongols, or in any case an uncivilized Asiatic nation,
a part of Russia, and not really Europeans.[12]

Since the early 1930's, the Finnish Foreign Ministry has been trying to
correct wrong and insufficient information about Finnish history in the
schoolbooks of other countries. In the autumn of 2005, a researcher became
acquainted with the schoolbooks of Finland's western neighbor Sweden and
discovered the gloomy picture of Finns given in them, according to which
they are poorly educated, use drugs and alcohol, and die young of
violence.[13]

In 2005, on hearing that Finland wished to be profiled as the land of the
tango, ice hockey, and Lapps, Professor Matti Klinge wrote: "I would have to
work and struggle for the rest of my life if for my part I should wish to profile
Finland as a cultured land, an old European cultural state, such as it appeared
at the World Fair at the end of the nineteenth century. ... Rich barbarians—
within a hundred years?"[14]

I don't believe that official state propaganda has much influence on opinion
abroad. The most significant and influential shapers of opinion are chance
acquaintances, friends, and relatives, as well as internet, TV programs, movies,
newspaper stories, and products that intrigue consumers—even such as Nokia
cell phones.[15]

The government of Finland funds institutes in many different countries,
but their offerings reach only a thin layer of the educated who are actively
interested in such matters. Latvia made a large and expensive cultural assault
on France in 2005; but at the same time riots broke out in the French cities,
and the French had something else to occupy their minds.

A well known Latvian poet recently found out the hard way, how difficult it is to tell fellow Europeans about Latvia. She agreed in 2004 to write a children's book, "New EU Countries and Citizens, Latvia," for a Dutch publisher. Later, to her dismay, she heard of gross mistakes in the translations (in Holland, Britain, Norway, Serbia, Estonia…) that seemed to become even wilder from one version to another: that only one third of the inhabitants speak Latvian, that most of them are Russians, that wine making has been an important branch of the economy… Pine trees became junipers, Latvian holy oaks turned into birches, Latvian school kids wear red pioneer scarves from Communist times, Latvia became independent in 1991 after long domination by foreign powers, and the President is elected for one year. Even centuries changed, and so Latvia was supposed to be occupied by Germany at the beginning of the 19th century…[16]

The Latvian Institute, which is under the Foreign Ministry, tries to polish the image of Latvia abroad, but its resources are limited and its task is not an easy one. However, in the age of the internet, in principle one surely can reach a large number of people, especially if the offerings are easy, enticing, and ingenious. In the opinion of Net users, the Estonian Institute's home pages, for example, are just that. I have also been able to follow closely how well the Estonians deal with foreign journalists (a skill probably learned from the Finns): they are flown to Tallinn; housed in mid-city luxury hotels, and taken to meet young, dynamic, English speaking politicians, officials, and businessmen.[17]

In 2006, with EU support, Latvia opened an official internet portal Latvia.lv. A private company was hired to do the job. What followed was, according to the press, a very ordinary, modest, and unassuming result for a very big sum of money. Both the appearance and the content of the portal were criticized.[18]

The Latvian Institute published at the end of 2007 an "optimistic" book, *History of Latvia. A Brief Survey*, that tries to show foreigners the positive side of the country's past and avoid "negativism." If people want to know more about the Holocaust and the Latvian legionnaires, they can look for it else-where, the author of the booklet said.[19]

No matter what the Latvian Institute does, individual experience and first impressions are what decide the issue. It was thus that a British travel reporter described his arrival in Rīga in the year 2001.

The first sight of Rīga was a culture shock. If Tallinn had been on the Baltic periphery, Rīga was at the heart of Eastern Europe. There were old tower blocks, crumbling apartments, dead-looking shops and drinking holes, old women at the side of the road selling piles of turnips. We seemed to travel miles through this type of thing, past derelict factories, kids sitting at the side of lifeless industrial ponds dangling crude sticks and twine into the greenish murk. Finally we approached central Rīga along the river and its one remaining Stalinist 'wedding cake' building … The bus pulled into the chaotic looking Rīga bus station … full of circling Gypsies and tough-looking blokes with crew cuts.[20]

The *New Statesman* published in November 2006 an article that was headlined "The Scars of anti-Semitism and the Soviet Past are All Too Apparent in Lithuania and Latvia." It purported to be a travel story, and had nothing good to say about Latvia and Latvians. One could ask, did the reporter really see the museums she writes about, or did she try to understand what she saw? Also: how is it possible that she did not see the Holocaust memorial that stands in the former Rīga ghetto?

Opposite the town hall, cuboid Museum of the Occupation of Latvia contains a catalogue of terror from the two Soviet occupations [also the German occupation and the Holocaust—J.R.]. However, the display skates over Latvia's pro-Nazi past. Any mention of the murder of Jews by collaborators is minimal. Fifteen minutes' walk away, Rīga's Museum of War shows images of Latvians welcoming the Nazis as liberators. Today elderly former SS Latvian volunteers still parade, which embarrasses a government eager to show its shining EU credentials. … No sign marks the Rīga ghetto, which housed 30,000 Jews.[21]

The director of the Latvian Institute, Ojārs Kalniņš, a former refugee and a former ambassador to the United States, says his point of departure is that 80 percent of the people in the world know nothing about Latvia, nor do they wish to know. Americans, "who know nothing about war and foreign occupation," know the least, but Kalniņš is often astonished by the lack of knowledge among close neighbors. "I never say that Latvia returned to Europe, since we never left Europe. Europe, which abandoned and forgot us in 1940, has returned to us."[22]

The example from schoolbooks mentioned above indicates that even Finland has problems with its closest neighbors, who, to top it all, were part of the same state as Finland for 700 years. Over and over we are forced to admit that

Picture 1. Latvian history: "Just look at you now! We can't show you to
Europe looking like that." Gatis Šļūka, Lauku Avīze, January 2004.

Swedes know very little about Finland and do not understand Finland's culture, history, and its language.

Of course it is true, as some sage has pointed out, that we do not become
more Europeanized by what others know about us, but by what we know about
them. Nevertheless it seems that Latvians, like Finns, consider the view others
have of them to be very important. It seems that Latvians have learned to think
that they must surely be inferior to others, or at least different from them.
Eiropa mūs nesapratīs (Europe will not understand us) has in recent years been
one of the favorite hits on Latvia's airwaves. Latvians find it very hard to praise
themselves and their country (if one excludes the supporters of their national
hockey team). Professor Aivars Stranga recently told a researcher who considered Latvia's becoming independent in 1918 an error and a misfortune: "Let's

not paint ourselves black; there are so many others who will do it for us." There
really do seem to be.

Nationalist, Anti-Semite, Criminal, Prostitute?

It is not easy to name names—to accuse any individual, group, or communication medium of distortion. We all make mistakes and we all have prejudiced
attitudes. I will, however, call attention to a few.

I can already note problems in the coverage of the Baltic countries by the
mass media of Latvia's western neighbor, Sweden. I have sometimes had occasion to ask a bit sharply: "Is there a Swedish journalist who can report on
Latvia without turning over every stone to find at least one violent nationalist,
an anti-Semite, a criminal, or a prostitute?"

When the Baltic countries regained independence in 1991, the intention
was that Sweden should "adopt" Latvia in the same way as Finland adopted
Estonia. The plan did not work out well; at some point its development went
astray and the relationship soured. Diplomat Lars Peter Fredén said Sweden
was practicing "duck politics" in dealing with the Baltic countries: "Smooth
and unruffled on the surface but paddling like hell underneath." Then even the
surface became rougher.

 Just a few examples: Sweden brought to an international court the case of
an old ship lying in the Rīga harbor, which the Latvians had cut up for scrap
iron. Also brought to court were disputes between the Latvian state telephone
company and the Swedish-Finnish company Telia-Sonera, disputes from
which Latvia ultimately withdrew. Swedish politicians want to put an end to
cod fishing in the eastern Baltic with EU help; this would hurt Latvian fish-
ermen in particular. In 2004 Latvia protested to Sweden and lodged a complaint with the European Union because trade unions and officials prevented
Latvian construction workers from working in Sweden. A school building site
had been blocked off as "a demonstration of solidarity with the Latvians." They
worked "too cheaply" and were forced to go home; the building company's
Swedish branch went bankrupt.[23]

In another case, Sweden would not surrender to Latvia a Swedish businessman who in July of 1997, while exceeding the speed limit near Rīga, killed
two policewomen and fled from Latvia on the following day. What would
Sweden's reaction have been if a Latvian had done the same in Sweden?

Latvians were deeply offended by a documentary film, *Buy Bye Beauty*
(2001), by the Swedish director Pål Hollender, a film which received high
praise and awards in Sweden. Hollender brought to his room in Rīga three

women of the trade, paid USD 200 to each, and filmed himself having sex with and humiliating them. According to Hollender, 50 percent of Latvia's young women sell their bodies for money, and every other policeman uses their services. In the same breath, he presented another obvious lie—that in every bar, restaurant, and hotel there is a list of at least 15 available prostitutes.[24]

And so forth—examples abound. A journalist of *Dagens Nyheter* began a recent report on Latvians thus: "One can kill them and escape without punishment. One can buy their bodies, call it art, and win praise. One can summon them as cheap labor—and then shout: 'Go home!' Why shouldn't Latvians be thankful for the care Swedes take of them?"[25]

According to Professor Andrew Ezergailis, the German newspaper establishment's attitude, especially that of "progressive journalists," is a problem for Latvia. He conjectures that with the fall of the Berlin wall, there arose for many German historians and journalists another barrier, a mental one, between Germany and Eastern Europe. "Is this a wall of ethics and values. as German journalists seem to say, or one of knowledge and understanding?" Ezergailis speaks of the easy habit of unfounded assertions and *a priori* claims of ethical superiority and asks: "How is one to confront and overcome the clichés, stereotypes, and shibboleths that appear with metronomic regularity in major German newspapers and magazines?"

In the United States and Canada, the public is not really interested in the small and distant Baltic countries, although tens of thousands of Baltic refugees have long lived there. Latvia is a "non-subject," as Jānis Peniķis, who teaches in Indiana, said to me. "Latvia does not evoke *any* image, does not incite *any* emotions, or call up *any* stereotypes, good or bad."

In the West, the Baltic countries are often confused with the Balkans, and Latvia and Lithuania are almost as a rule confused with one another. The French State Senator and anti-EU campaigner Jean-Luc Melenchon wrote on his Web site in January 2006 that Lithuania, an EU member, had refused to issue "identity cards" to 400,000 Russian-speaking persons and that Lithuania's parliament paid pensions to former SS members. Although he spoke of Lithuania (*Lituanie*), Latvia (*Lettonie*) demanded an apology. Melenchon asked pardon of Lithuania.[26]

Often "it is known" that these countries have always belonged to Russia.[27] If anything is recalled from history, it is most likely that "the Baltic countries are anti-Semitic and fought on the side of Nazi Germany." With the Google search engine in less than a second one can find 282,000 hits with the key words *Latvian Fascism* (and *Latvia Fascism*—246,000 and "*Fascism in Latvia*"— 366 hits). The first of these begins thus: "Fascism has been spreading

in Latvia for a long time, causing anger among more or less sensible citizens."
(On the other hand, *Fascism Sweden* and *Fascism Russia* yield more hits.)

Ten years ago the Oxford University Press published an interesting and
readable 1,365-page book, *Europe, A History*, by professor emeritus of London
university, Norman Davies. It covers Eastern Europe unusually well. Still there
is only one reference to Latvia in the index: that page tells how the Latvians
helped the Germans to murder Jews and joined the Waffen-SS troops as
volunteers.[28]

In 2003 the German publisher Taschen published a book about the world-
renowned artist Mark Rothko (Marcus Rothkowitz) who was born in 1903 in
the old Latvian city of Daugavpils (in Russian Dvinsk, in German Dünaburg),
a city on the banks of the Daugava, Latvia's largest river. According to the
book, Rothko was born in *Dvinsk, Russia*, the name of which was *changed in
1990 to Daugavpils*, which now belongs to *Lithuania* and is located on the
banks of the *Dauga* River.

The American Time-Life Books large *Europa Encyclopedia*, published in
Finnish in 1989, states that *Lithuanians* gather in large numbers every year in
Rīga for a national celebration. One news agency recently reported on
Georgia's conflict with South Estonia (properly South Ossettia).[29] In 1997 a
Finnish university press published a history of Latvia which begins with this
assertion: "Latvia is bounded on the west by the Baltic Sea, on the east by
Estonia, and on the south by Russia and Belarus." The correct borders are the
Baltic Sea in the west, Estonia in the north, Russia in the east, Belarus (for-
merly Poland) in the southeast, and Lithuania in the south.

On the few occasions when newspapers do write of Latvia, they easily
blunder. Their articles reek of prejudice. It is especially so when the correspondents travel to the Baltic countries from Moscow. In the Western press, Russian-speaking correspondents stationed in Moscow have traditionally covered
the affairs of these countries. Probably the best known new book about this
area, *The Baltic Revolution*, was written by Anatol Lieven, who is the former
Moscow correspondent of *The Times* and a descendant of an old and important Baltic German family. Most of the Lieven family properties in Latvia were
donated by the Czar. One cannot help noticing how sympathetic Lieven is
towards Russians, as compared to Latvians—not towards communists, though,
but towards the imperial and aristocratic Russian tradition.[30]

Interesting pieces of writing about Latvia can be encountered any time and
anywhere. After President Bush's trip to Europe in May 2005, *The Daily
Freeman* from Kingston, New York, published a commentary condemning the
visit, entitled "Overlooking Nazi Past."

Since the departure of the Russian military and bureaucracy, 'free' Latvia and Estonia have annual public parades of their SS-veterans … The Freedom Monument where Bush gave his FDR speech is the cemetery where Latvian SS officers are buried with national honors. Surviving Latvian SS veterans get a government pension. Ninety six percent of Latvia's Jews were killed in the Holocaust, mostly on the spot, by special Latvian SS security forces and an enthusiastic local population. Today the surviving 14,000 Latvian Jews are officially 'stateless' non-citizens who can't vote or hold teaching or civil service jobs. Another stateless class in Latvia are the half-million Latvian-born Russian speakers, 20 percent of the population, a hated minority.

In addition, the writer enlightens readers with the following information: Bush is "overlooking the Baltic States' Nazi past and present." Anti-Semitism is a sentiment "about which we can all agree, except Latvians, Estonians and Lithuanians. For them, anti-Semitism, the church, and anti-communism are the embodiment of their national spirit." And, "Unlike U.S.-occupied Germany and Austria, there never was a denazification process in Soviet Europe."[31]

Ten sentences about Latvia—and the facts are not quite right in a single one of them. I shall return to all these themes later in this book.[32] However I will at this point assert that as I see it, branding certain peoples as anti-Semitic and criminal is in itself criminal and racist.

I am told that the Israeli media do not tell us much about Latvia, at least not much that is positive. I wonder if this is because of the continuing propaganda and publicity campaign and the criticism of the Baltic countries carried on by some Russian Jews and the Simon Wiesenthal Center, especially its Jerusalem bureau director, Efraim Zuroff. The Wiesenthal Center was established in California and received permission from the now deceased Simon Wiesenthal, who had operated out of Vienna, to use his name. His motto, however, was *Recht, nicht Rache* (Justice, not revenge), and he did not find the Baltic peoples collectively guilty.[33]

Writing in the Finnish press is matter-of-fact, and relates to the Baltic peoples with understanding. However, taking into consideration that the Baltic countries are as close as Sweden, have almost as many inhabitants and are in many respects already as important to the Finns, it is hard to understand why Sweden gets so much more coverage; the slightest movements in Swedish politics, economy, culture and press are reported "real-time" by, for example, the biggest Finnish newspaper *Helsingin Sanomat*.

Factual errors do occur in the Finnish press, but that is normal in the rush of newspaper and radio work; I, for one, am always ready to admit having made errors, also when writing about Latvia. There is no glossing over of the truth in the Finnish press, however. Its journalism is normally objective and critical. It is true that there are journalists in Finland who have admitted publicly to being friends of Estonia. That sounds odd to me. I believe that a journalist cannot promise anything to anybody unconditionally, not even friendship.

I recently had a chance to give a lecture to a group of Finnish historians visiting Latvia on a bus tour. Their first questions to me were the following: "Why are Latvians so militant and violent? Why did Latvians butcher their Jews during the war? Is it really true that Latvians were more anti-Semitic than the Germans?" Then again recently in Helsinki a Lutheran minister came to me to ask: are not the Latvians [with their Language Law] taking revenge on their Russians the same way as the white Finns on their red prisoners after the civil war of 1918?

Latvia—Enemy Number One

Since Latvian independence was renewed in 1991, its relations with Russia have never been especially good. At this writing they are, if possible, even worse than before. The relations reached a critical point in the spring of 2005 during the Moscow celebration of European Victory Day, in which the President of Latvia took part. More of that later in this book. Official Russian propaganda has not found much good to say about Latvia of late, and even the independent media – as much of it as still exists in Russia – follows its example.

"In a society where information is lacking, it is very easy to sustain images of enemies," says the Russian historian Grigorij Amnuel. According to him, the present information vacuum is even more dangerous than what prevailed during the Soviet days of the 1970's, for then there were at least the *samizdat* (underground publications), foreign radio stations, and "people could read between the lines." In contrast, nowadays there is no alternative to propaganda, Amnuel says.[34]

The Latvian Ambassador to Moscow, Andris Teikmanis, says that it is the Russian television channels, practically all of them under government control, that are responsible for Latvia's bad image and the hostile atmosphere. They air mainly negative news about Latvia.

When a simple inhabitant of Russia, who does not have other sources of news, hears that kind of information, he concludes that Latvians

really love to eat Russians for breakfast. … In fact, Russians can sin-
cerely think that here [in Latvia] an SS-battalion marches through Rīga
every day and everybody greets it with flowers.[35]

The greater part of the Latvian Russian language press follows a blatant anti-
Latvian line. Some papers call Latvian politicians "fascists." They gladly make
note of Soviet and Red Army holidays; Latvian national holidays they either
ignore or defame.

It seems as if Russia can say publicly anything at all about Latvia. A few
years ago, Juri Luzhkov, the Mayor of Moscow, announced that genocide was
going on in Latvia, and compared its government to the Pol Pot regime of
terror in Cambodia[36] – an extraordinary statement about a country where
there are no extremist or racist parties and organizations, and where during its
independence there have been no violent clashes or racial or political murders.
And an extraordinary statement from the representative of a country that is
carrying on a war in Chechnya.

One should note that Freedom House – an American organization that
measures political freedom in 150 countries – shifted Russia from the "partly
free" to the "not free" group in 2005. (Latvia has a pretty good position in the
"free" group.) In October 2006 *Reporteurs sans frontières* listed Russia as
number 147 in world press freedom. (Finland was number one, Estonia 6th,
Latvia 10th, Lithuania 27th.) As to Russia, this organization added that since
Vladimir Putin came to power, 21 journalists have been killed practically
without repercussions.[37]

Hundreds of thousands of Russians have been forced to flee to Russia from
the former Soviet Union's Central Asian states. No one is known to have
escaped Latvia, at least not in fear of violence. Eleanora Mitrofanova, the
Director of Russia's International Center for Scientific and Cultural Cooperation, said at a press conference in February 2006 that it was clear to her that
"Russians do not want to leave the Baltic countries: they are already in Europe,
the countries are peaceful, and they have higher living standards. Russians
want to leave Central Asia, above all, Turkmenistan and Tajikistan." Russia has
launched a voluntary repatriation program for compatriots living in Latvia to
remedy a critical demographic and work force shortfall, the embassy in Rīga
said in April, 2007. The embassy started registering volunteers and informing
people about the program. So far the results have been meager.[38]

The sowing of hate and propaganda has borne fruit. An opinion poll
among Russian officers in 1994 showed that Latvia was considered Russia's
enemy number one (49 percent of those answering) – a country of a little over
two million people, with only nominal defense forces, thirty percent of whose

inhabitants were Russian. Afghanistan was second. Sociological research conducted in Russia in May 2006 revealed that Latvia was again "enemy number one" – 46 percent of the respondents considered her their worst enemy. Latvia was followed by Georgia (38 percent) and Lithuania (42 percent).[39]

In 2007, Finns studied the opinions of Russians living in St. Petersburg and its surroundings. The result was that also in this big, "European," and relatively well-to-do city the most negative attitude of all was towards Latvia.[40]

A representative of the Russian government stated at the end of the year 2005 that "Russia is the Jew among the world's nations."[41] He meant that Russia was ignored in the international arena and that malicious and negative information was circulated about it. Only a bit earlier the Russian state had established an international English-language TV station, *Russia Today*, to distribute "correct" information to the outside world around the clock. Later the Kremlin also paid the American PR firm Ketchum to help it; the intent is to upgrade Russia's public image in the Western media.[42]

"The Western press is today dominated by such anti-Russian frenzy that we did not see anything like it even in the cold war period," said the deputy director of the Russian foreign ministry press and information section A.A. Sazonov in Helsinki in 2005.[43]

In March 2007, there was on Russian TV a discussion *Are Western media waging an information war against Russia?* Historian Valentin Falin spoke of Russophobia and said that the campaign against Russia began centuries ago.[44] Finnish Ph.D. Johan Bäckman, who has written a number of books about Russia, believes that propaganda against Russia is fanned much more aggressively than against Latvia.[45]

A mere check on today's Russia is not sufficient for our purpose. For decades the Soviet Union spread a picture which was stereotyped to say the least. First the Latvians were called fascists, and then, with the collapse of the Soviet Union, it was recalled that they were also among the most enthusiastic of Reds, and helped Lenin to come to power. Aleksandr Solzhenitsyn wrote in his *Gulag Archipelago* that he did like the Lithuanians and Estonians, but not the Latvians. "They actually started it all."

But that isn't all. The Germans also were only too willing to insult the Latvians. As will be demonstrated in this book, both Russians and Germans have been masters in accusing Latvians of crimes of which they themselves were guilty. "The two imperial powers of the past century disagree on many things, but, judging from their writings, they agree that the people in the disarmed occupied countries between Germany and Russia were the real criminals, worse than Cheka or the Gestapo," writes Professor Ezergailis.[46]

It was to the advantage of both to brand the Latvians as violent fascists and anti-Semites, bigots, "different" kinds of Europeans. Often this propaganda has been absorbed by the international public and sometimes even Latvian scholars have swallowed the claim as truth.

In 1999, *Walking Since Daybreak*, the work of Modris Eksteins, a Latvian-born Canadian professor, was awarded a prize as the best historical text of the year in Canada. According to the commendatory review in *The Washington Post*, Eksteins "with his book placed Latvia within the world's imagination."

However, as a person who left Latvia in childhood and has lived all his life abroad, Eksteins seems to have used his own imagination boldly. He generalizes about Latvians and other "East Europeans" – whomever that term may include. In his work, they are stereotypes of violent and bloodthirsty human beings.[47] The notion among some book reviewers in the West, that "the Latvians slaughtered a large part of the country's Jewish population before the Nazi killing machine could be set up,"[48] stems from that book.

According to Eksteins, in small East-European countries, "radical sentiment, especially of a fascist stripe, was widespread. ... Patriotism and national pride easily shaded into xenophobia and hate."[49]

Regarding Latvia, Eksteins writes, with no particular grounding or indication of sources, that "Holocaust was a state of mind here before it was Nazi policy." According to him, Latvians were in the grip of a monstrous hatred; in Eastern Europe "fear and hatred were a way of life." Why was it so? Eksteins offers an explanation: "This was a frontier land where borders and peoples had fluctuated throughout history and where the Jew and the Gypsy were symbols of transience and instability." Further: "Moral feeling had been blunted again and again in this part of the world. ... extermination was the only answer."[50]

One can reply to this that, if any land, Finland has always been a frontier land, and seldom has any country's border fluctuated throughout history as much as Finland's. And Jews and Gypsies have long lived in Finland, too. However, they were not murdered during the war; and furthermore, Finland did not surrender its Jews to Germany.[51] Why not? Obviously because Finland was not an occupied country.

It almost seems as if some curse follows Latvians and the books written about them.

Agate Nesaule's book, *A Woman in Amber*, like Ekstein's book, a depiction of childhood in Latvia, of war and refugee life, achieved widespread distribution in the West at the same time as *Walking Since Daybreak*. Nesaule's book was published in Great Britain by Penguin, and was the American Book

Award winner in 1996. It has been translated into several languages, and there have been plans for a big-budget film. The book has been praised as "a broad portrayal of Latvian history." No other book by a Latvian writer has received as much attention in recent years.[52]

Nesaule's book is marketed as memoirs, but it also contains fantasy, and indeed the writer has stated that she originally planned it as a novel. According to experts, there are "historical errors and fabrications about Latvia and Latvians" in the book.[53] Even a lay person can wonder, for example, that a violent Latvian was supposedly destroying a jewelry store owned by a Jew in Rīga when the Germans arrived in the summer of 1941. (As we know, the Soviets had already nationalized all businesses in 1940.)

Many of the countries I have mentioned – Germany, Russia, Sweden, Poland – have been Latvia's occupiers. How fittingly the Latvian historian and diplomat Arnolds Spekke wrote in the 1950's of the conquerors' psychology: "Our country's, our fateful shores' charm is so great that its conquerors, at the moment they must leave these shores, are seized by such an animal rage at having to relinquish power that only fire and ruin – *terra bruciata*, scorched earth – can even partly extinguish it."[54]

"What the Latvians Really Are Like"

There are deep roots to the myth about "what Latvians really are like." Adolf Hitler is known to have first mentioned the mass murder of the Jews on July 22nd, 1941, when killings in the Baltic countries had been going on for weeks. Then, according to the minutes of the conversation with Croatian Marshall Sladko Kvaternik, he specifically blamed the inhabitants of the Baltic countries for beginning the bloodbath. First he related what he had heard of atrocities by the Bolsheviks and Jews in Lithuania. Then he went on: "*Die Juden seien die Geissel der Menscheit. Sowohl die Litauer als auch die Esten und Letten nähmen nun blutige Rache an ihnen.*" (Jews are [in the opinion of the Balts] the scourge of mankind. The Lithuanians, as well as the Estonians and Latvians, then set about taking a bloody revenge on them.)[55]

The disinformation began before the killing.[56] From the very beginning, the German plan was to destroy the Jewish population of the areas conquered in the East. But they said they could do nothing about the Baltic peoples' blood lust when they took revenge on the Jews. From the start, the Germans were careful that the murders in the East not be linked to them, but to the "natives." They were already thinking of their future reputation, and, as is well known, they were careful to avoid committing the most sensitive material to paper. Even Hitler did not sign the death orders.

Rudolf Höss, the German commandant of the Auschwitz death camp,
wrote self-justifying memoirs in a Polish prison after the end of World War II,
before his hanging. He wrote that he first encountered and became inured to
frenzied violence when fighting in Latvia in 1918–1919 in the ranks of the
German voluntary *Freikorps*.

> The battles in the Baltic were more wild and ferocious than any I have
> experienced. … There was no real front; the enemy was everywhere.
> And when contact was made, the result was butchery to the point of
> utter annihilation. The Letts were especially good at this. It was there
> that I first encountered atrocities against civilians. … I could not
> believe then that this mad human desire for annihilation could be
> intensified in any way.

According to Eksteins, Höss was horrified by just those "gangster-types" to be
found in Latvia in 1941.[57]

Party ideologist and race theorist Alfred Rosenberg was a Baltic German
by birth. Long before he became Hitler's minister in the occupied Eastern
areas, he wrote this: "In Russia, **Latvian and Chinese** [bold in the original]
battalions with the help of machine-guns forced the Russian worker to obedi-
ence. … It gave the Latvians and Chinese the greatest joy to mow the striking
German comrades down" with shrapnel shells. Hitler had done his homework,
for in one of his written monologues from wartime, he said: "For executions
the Russians were not ready to conduct, Stalin resorted to ethnic Chinese and
Latvians; they were also the executioners of the old Czarist State."[58]

One could add here: for executions the *Germans* were not ready to conduct, Hitler resorted to Latvians. Such was the picture presented, and many
still believe it.

There is much testimony to the atrocities of the groups Höss belonged to
in Latvia. With regard to the same time and place, there is the highly praised
novel, *Le coup de grâce* (1939), by the French academician Marguerite
Yourcenar, which has been translated into many languages and shown as a
movie and a stage play. According to the author, it is based on actual happenings, and in the opinion of some analysts, she is successful in portraying
accurately the 1919 war in Latvia, the misogyny and cold emotional violence
– and also the claim that Latvian women participated in the violence, which is
a favorite theme. This kind of legend has had a long life among the Russians.
In the 1980's the Soviets circulated incomprehensible rumors about "Baltic
Amazons" decked out in white tights, supposedly fighting on the side of the
Afghan rebels.

In Yourcenar's despairing tale, neither side takes prisoners, and everyone is killed, women as well as men. Epaulets are nailed to the shoulders of White officers. Regarding the Latvians, there is this claim: "As for common cruelty, the highly specialized Letts who served the Reds as hangmen had perfected the art of torture in a manner truly worthy of the most celebrated Mongol traditions." In 1919 certain German war leaders in fact branded the Latvians as "half-Asian," and the point of view prevailing in this novel as well is close to the German.[59]

In other respects, too, Latvia and Rīga have often been seen in literature through the German and Russian prism. Richard Wagner, in his memoirs, was "the more agreeably surprised, on reaching Rīga, to find myself surrounded by the familiar German element which, above all, pervaded everything connected with the theatre." In Jules Verne's novel about Mikhail Strogoff, everything about Rīga is automatically Russian. In Ian McEwan's novel, *Saturday* (2005) "a Russian Tupolev cargo plane on its way from Rīga to Birmingham" has its own vital part to play.

The way that Latvians have traditionally been used as villainous and suspicious types in the lightest adventure and spy stories is worthy of a study in itself. When Ivars and Ingrida Alksnis from the University of Geneva spoke about this subject in Rīga a few years ago, they pointed out that Latvians are usually depicted in foreign literature as dark, crude, freakish people, culturally closely associated with Russians. As examples they used *Peter the Lett* by

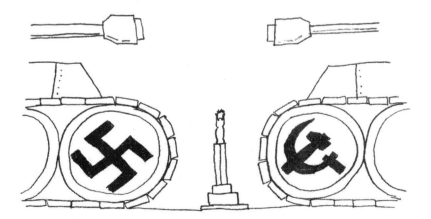

Picture 2. Ernests Kļaviņš' view of Latvia's occupation with the Rīga Freedom Monument in the center. Diena 16.03.2006

Georges Simenon, *They Fell From God's Hands* by Hans Werner Richter, and *Russian Hide and Seek* by Kingsley Amis.

In Simenon's book the main character is a drunk, an opium user, a passport forger, and a murderer who commits suicide in the end. It remains unclear, however, if the criminal is a Latvian, Lithuanian, or Estonian; but at any rate, the title in different languages is a variation of *Maigret and the Enigmatic Lett* or *Peter the Lett* (*Pietr-le-letton* in the original).

Forest of Gods, the concentration camp memoirs by the Lithuanian writer Balys Sruoga, recently published in English, gives its own distinctive picture of Latvians.[60] He writes that no other national group in the Soviet camps liked the Latvians, and that they were arrogant, stuck to their own circle, and constantly sang their own strange and monotonous songs. Finally the other prisoners became so exasperated by the singing that they began to throw stones at the Latvians.[61]

Henning Mankell, Sweden's most popular writer at present, paints an extremely dark, cold, and violent picture of Rīga in his novel, *Hundarna i Riga* (1992, in English *Dogs of War*, the movie *Dogs of Riga*). On the other hand, the most positive character is a Latvian woman with whom the Swedish policeman, having traveled to Latvia, of course falls in love.

The book (Len Deighton, 1966) and the Hollywood movie (Ken Russell, 1967) *Billion Dollar Brain* spread some very unfavorable comments on Latvians. They speak Polish, wear some kind of rags and live with their domestic animals in shacks in Rīga, which is situated next to Finland – in place of Estonia. The film was made partly in Finland. One passage, for example, tells about a meeting in Luna Cafe on Soviet Boulevard facing the Freedom monument that "was something of a milestone in municipal graft." The speaker is Coloner Stok, an erudite poetry-quoting KGB officer.

> This is a land of losers. … You've no idea what awful things have happened here. The Latvians had Fascists who were more vicious than even the Germans. In Bikernieki Forest they killed 46,500 civilians. In Dreilini Forest five kilometers east of here, they killed 13,000. In the Zolotaya Gorka, 38,000 were murdered … the old, the pregnant, the lame, … They killed them all, sometimes with the most terrifying and prolonged torture.

According to Stok, the Germans were so pleased to find such enthusiastic and effective murderers that they sent trainloads of people from "all over Europe" to be killed in Latvia. He says that now Latvian war criminals are living "all over the world."

> We have dossiers of hundreds of such Latvians … You would imagine that people guilty of such terror would remain quiet and be thankful they have escaped justice, but no. These scum are the foremost trouble-makers.[62]

Let us remember that in Soviet war movies Rīga generally "played the part" of Berlin and that Latvian actors were "Germans". This helped to strengthen the stereotypes among the Russian audiences.

Harrison Salisbury, former *New York Times* correspondent in Moscow and a prolific writer on the Soviet Union, published his acclaimed best-seller *The 900 Days* in 1969.[63] The 15th chapter of the book tells about the Baltic countries, especially Latvia, during the Soviet occupation and before the German attack in 1941, and presents an blatantly grotesque description, based exclusively on the memoirs of KGB officers. It is impossible to repeat the whole story here; what follows are only a few of the "facts" that I have never seen or heard anywhere else:

The Balts were celebrating and having a good life, but peace was an illusion; danger lay below the glittering surface; Russian officers had to walk always and everywhere armed to the teeth. (Fact: According to the military base treaty of 1939, Russian soldiers were not to carry arms outside the bases. President Ulmanis asked Latvians to treat Russians well, and they were never attacked by Latvians. Everything was completely peaceful.)

"Many Russians hesitated to enter the Baltic area, fearing the general state of insecurity. Some wives of naval officers refused to accompany their husbands to Rīga. They had heard too much about the Latvian nationalists, about terrorists, snipers and bombings." (Fact: The treaty said nothing about sending naval forces to Latvia, and *nothing of the families* of the military; Latvians were, against their will, *forced* by the Soviets to let in both.)

The Balts had a hostile attitude, a chauvinist hatred for Russians, and they willingly cooperated, in secret, with German agents. The dissident Balts were encouraged by the overt Nazi preparations for attack. (Fact: Germans were traditionally the most hated nationality in Estonia and Latvia. This is not mentioned in the book. Another fact: The Soviet Union and Germany were allies at the time.)

The Perkinkrusts (correctly: *Pērkoņkrusts*) and Aisargi (*Aizsargi*) in Latvia and Kaitzelites (*Kaitseliit*) in Estonia plotted with networks of German agents against Russians, and all kinds of fiercely anti-Soviet nationalist and military underground organizations were active. There were mysterious forest fires, "interference with spring sowing, and growing reluctance on the part of poor peasants to join in Soviet agricultural projects [collective farms – J.R.]." There was sabotage in saw mills, and from the pulpits priests were giving "voice to their antagonism to Soviet power." (Just one fact: The Pērkoņkrusts – that incidentally was also anti-German – had been outlawed and disbanded many years earlier, and its activists and leaders sent to prison or exiled.)

The Soviets tried to purge the dangerous elements by deporting tens of thousands of Balts to Siberia in June, 1941 – kulaks or well-to-do farmers, politicians, former military and police officers, priests, ministers … The purge was "far from complete." What is more, "secret members of the Latvian underground, who protected their cohorts … managed to send to prison persons either neutral or inclined to the Soviet cause. The underground was not seriously damaged; many bitter opponents of the Soviet power were left untouched." (This is really something 'far out'; for once I am almost speechless. Those clever, untrustworthy Balts! – J.R.) In fact in the big 1949 deportation, some wrongly chosen persons were really sent mistakenly from Latvia to Siberia; frightened Communist officials had to fill the quota given from above, so they hastily detained people at random, as "enemies of the people."[64] Just one more detail: land was nationalized by the Soviets in 1940, taxes for farmers rose to the heavens, and it was forbidden to use outside labor; there were no longer any "kulaks" in Latvia.)

In August 2005 *The New Yorker* magazine published a short story by the prize-winning writer Gina Ochsner, in which the action is apparently presented through the eyes of a Latvian girl, but the content of which is not flattering to Latvians. The scene of the action is an imaginary small town near Rīga, inhabited by, among others, "Russian Jewish émigrés." The homes of people who have come from elsewhere are beautiful and neat. The Latvians relate to them with prejudice and arrogance, and there are many suicides among the foreigners. In the end, the Latvian main character becomes aware that she must apologize to her neighbors so that life can become "normal." Such character surnames as Brkic, Cosic, and Iossel lead one to think that the writer may be a member of the large group to whom the difference between Baltics and Balkans is unclear.[65]

Latvia – the Jew among the nations? I wish to avoid exaggeration and the cheaply dramatic, so I will not resort to such terms. Perhaps this is better: Latvia – a small, solitary and unknown sparrow on the shores of the Baltic Sea.

Questions and Answers

1

Are minorities, especially the Russians,
discriminated against in Latvia? Is it very difficult for
them to become citizens? Do they have political
rights?

*The best propagandist is the one who believes his own lies, ensuring that he
can't leak his deceit through nervous twitches or self–contradictions.*

EVOLUTIONARY BIOLOGIST ROBERT TRIVERS

I will begin with these questions, since they are the ones most frequently heard
nowadays and also since the manner of their phrasing contains some inherent
errors and misunderstandings. To put it briefly, according to relevant international organizations, Latvia does *not* oppress its minorities, it is *not* especially
difficult to become a Latvian citizen, and Russians are *not* excluded from politics; they participate fully both within the Parliament and the political parties,
as well as outside them.

But of what use are explanations if – according to the Russian television
channel RTR – "dogs have more rights in Latvia" than the Russians? In the
winter of 2006, this channel carried a story that Latvian dog owners could
register their dogs for trips to Europe, while noncitizens could not travel there
(without visas, as was still the case at the time with all who were not European
Union citizens – J.R.)[1]

President Vladimir Putin declared in October 2006 that Latvia and Estonia
should start "observing common European juridical norms" in treating their
national minorities. He said that it is "our [Russia's] moral duty" to defend
"compatriots" (*sootetshestvenniki*) in the Baltic States and asked the Russian
diaspora to cooperate actively in this effort.[2]

A little earlier the Latvian-Russian Party PCTVL, which emerged from the
Interfront anti-independence movement,[3] conducted an unofficial inves-

tigation into the exclusion of the Russian minority. The work was done out of "love for the truth." The researchers announced having found "over 100" examples of discrimination, and claimed that the situation was steadily getting worse, with the further assertion that it could not really get any worse, for then an "apocalypse" would follow. "Latvia is a country in which Russophobia and a double standard prevail."[4]

PCTVL declares that Latvia is "a unique country" in the sense that it has "massively and artificially denied minorities' citizenship rights"[5] – as if Latvia had special laws for minorities. In fact everybody is eligible for citizenship on the same terms, as I will explain later.

The Foundation for the Study of Independent Social Ideas spreads "information" on the Net that Latvian Russians "suffer various forms of discrimination, of which the most important involves eligibility for citizenship." Furthermore: "Language is the principal factor on which citizenship is denied to ethnic Russians, even those who were born in Latvia or Estonia, where they have lived all their lives."

The foundation reminds us in one of its articles that the government of Boris Yeltsin justified the presence of Russian troops in the Baltic countries by pointing to the need to protect the rights of the Russian minority. "If a strongly nationalistic regime should come to power in Moscow, continuing discrimination against Russian speakers in Latvia and Estonia could provide a pretext for a new threat against Baltic independence. (Purported mistreatment of Sudeten Germans was, of course, the rationale Hitler claimed for invading Czechoslovakia.)"[6]

Outsiders resort to very strong language in condemning Latvia, but bend over backwards in their effort to understand Russia. In February 1996 a Swedish social scientist wrote in the *Göteborgs-Posten*: "It is to Europe's advantage to stop Latvia's new proposal for the citizenship law, for it may lead to aggressive counter-measures by Russia … and to a conflict among the great powers."[7]

Anatol Lieven wrote in his book *The Baltic Revolution*, that if Estonia and Latvia did not completely integrate their Russians, violent clashes would follow, which could bring about chaos in Europe.

Ted Galen Carpenter, vice president of the Cato Institute, warned the U.S. in 2007 of what dangerous NATO partners Estonia and other tiny Baltic States can become in the future. "All it would take to trigger a crisis is a Russian president who tires of the Baltic republics' continuing treatment of their Russian inhabitants as second-class citizens and decides to rectify that situation by force if necessary. For example, Moscow's anger might reach the boiling point if Estonia continues to insist on proficiency in the Estonian language for citizenship – a requirement that disenfranchises hundreds of thousands of Russian speakers. Or the Kremlin could tire of the pervasive discrimination against Estonian citizens of Russian descent in employment – especially in government ministries. Although the Russian government would probably first use economic pressure to force a change in policy, nationalist emotions inside Russia could lead to an adoption of military measures."[8]

"Something Nazi-like is arising"

In an article I wrote in March 1993, I surveyed articles dealing with the Baltic countries that had been published in the previous weeks' Western newspapers and journals.[9] In my opinion, they indicated that although the world had followed the Baltic nations' campaign for independence with sympathy, viewpoints had changed within a couple of years, and now the Baltic peoples were being accused of all sorts of things – chiefly of oppressing the Russians. So, the victims do change, as Graham Greene once pointed out. ("The writer … stands for the victims, and the victims change.")

The following were among my examples:

• *The Guardian*, under a headline "Something Nazi-like is arising," wrote that the Latvians are preparing for an ethnic cleansing. According to the article, anti-Semitism and Russophobia are the main political currents in the land, that seeks its model in South Africa. (My comment: A strange comparison – in South Africa the more recent immigrants discriminated against the original population).

• *Life* captioned a big pictorial report: "SOON THEY WILL COME FOR US." The sub-caption read: "Five decades after the Nazi massacres, a resurgent anti-Semitism is forcing the Jews of Latvia to run for their lives." Among other things one can see photos of crying women who say they are fleeing Latvia to Israel, to Russia, even to Germany. The captions say: "Forced out of her country for the second time in her life, [M.B.] says a final goodbye;" "At the Rīga airport, hundreds of Latvian Jews converge for seats on the flight to Israel." There are photos of old home guardsmen wearing their uniforms whom the *Life* photographer had inveigled into the woods, and some of these dangerous, militant nationalists are even waving guns. (My comment: Not a single Russian or Jew has *ever* been wounded or killed for political, nationalistic or racist reasons during the new independence of Latvia.)

According to the writer of the *Life* article, hatred and ethnic prejudice have become mainstream political thinking. He makes incorrect statements alleging a system of ethnic separation, the disenfranchisement of 95 percent of the nation's Jews, and about laws making it illegal for roughly half the population to own property or open a bank account, as well as it being all but impossible for them to hold a job. To prove this, he gives completely misleading information on the regulations for granting citizenship.

He also writes that "carpets decorated with swastikas hang openly in downtown stores." The store in question was a shop of traditional Latvian folk handicraft. (My comment: As many Europeans know, the swastika is a loan from Sanskrit and is an age-old symbol in Buddhism and Hinduism, even in Judaism. It was known in European folk art long before the Nazis started to use it. In Latvia it was and is *ugunskrusts*, cross of fire.

U.S. authorities later stated that asylum seekers, in their applications for admission to the country frequently included this material from *The Guardian* and *Life*. But, as they said, "We have seen no evidence that these allegations are justified. Leaders of Latvia's Jewish community at that time reported that anti-Semitism was not a major problem in Latvia."[10]

• The prestigious German *Die Zeit* article on the Baltic States ended with this demand: "The Balts must be told firmly that apartheid cannot arise in Europe." According to *Die Zeit* "The Baltics are going beyond reasonable bounds in order to insure their independence;" the atmosphere has changed, Russians are treated badly and insolently and scare tactics are used against them. According to the paper, it is unreasonably difficult for Russians to become citizens. "It is painful for the friends of the Baltics to see that the previously wise political leaders have worked themselves into a blind alley ... Anti-Russian furor does not create jobs."

• *Der Spiegel* had a moving piece about an old Lithuanian Jew who collects information about Nazi war crimes, since Lithuania "is not concerned about their actions but intends to pardon their perpetrators." *The Washington Post* published a resentful Russian writer's piece about how he no longer felt at home on his vacation in (Latvian) Jūrmala. He waited for the "time bomb" to explode. The reader was enlightened with the "information" (disinformation) that "in Estonia, automobiles of ethnic Russians are equipped with a different kind of license plates."

• *The New York Times* published the stern warning by an American scholar that ethnic segregation in Estonia and Latvia could lead to a crisis like that in Yugoslavia. The paper also published on the front page a series of interviews with Estonian and Latvian Russians who said they would probably lose their homes, places of employment, and their pensions (none of this happened). The paper also headlined the news that Russian troops still staying in the Baltic countries told of being harassed.

• At about the same time *The Moscow News*, generally thought of as a liberal paper, had a headline: "Estonia On the Way to Dictatorship."

This kind of "information" seems to have a strong influence on public opinion abroad. Just one example. When Prince Charles was visiting Rīga a few years ago, a young Latvian Russian woman, a member of the National Bolsheviks, hit him with a bunch of carnations. The girl was detained (and soon freed), and at once a strong international solidarity campaign spreading mainly on the internet was born to defend her; she was, after all, a repressed Russian. Later she went to jail in Moscow for hooliganism.

Every Nation Has the Right...

First of all it must be remembered that after 1945, as Brits, French, Belgians and Dutch streamed *out* of their colonies, Russians started to stream *into* theirs. The 1949 Geneva Convention prohibited settling civilians in occupied territories. After that time the russification of Latvia was intensified, and the flow of immigrants was organized by the CPSU and the Soviet government.[11] Therefore it can be said that when the country regained independence in 1991, the Soviet era newcomers were in Latvia illegally. The Russians today are being granted citizenship *as a humanitarian measure* by the Latvian government and *not as a right*.

One should note that citizenship is not an inherent human right; every nation has the right to decide independently upon what conditions it will grant – or refuse – citizenship to foreigners living on its land.

According to the Charter of the United Nations, normal citizenship laws belong to a country's internal affairs, and other countries cannot meddle with them, not even the UN. A country need not explain why it refuses citizenship, nor do countries normally do so. Nevertheless, such explanations are continually demanded of Latvia, and those few Russians to whom citizenship is refused take the matter first to the Latvian and then to international courts.

Just one recent example: A Russian military family, whose members took out secretly, without informing the Latvian authorities, Russian citizenship and a Russian passport but demanded noncitizen status in Latvia, fought the state of Latvia in courts for more than ten years. Finally, in 2007, they lost in the European Court of Human Rights, although the state of Russia backed them. Latvia did not have to pay them the sum they demanded. They were allowed to stay in Latvia, however.

It is also entirely normal throughout the world to require that applicants for citizenship have lived in a country for several years, that they demonstrate a reasonable ability to use the language of that country, and in addition, that they be loyal or at least not hostile to it.[12]

Efforts have been made to deny the Baltic countries this right that belongs to all others. Appealing to "oppression," Russia has waged a propaganda war against Latvia and Estonia during the entire period of their new independence; and such organs as the Organization for European Security and Cooperation (OSCE), the Council of Europe (CE), and the EU have monitored and "advised" – or rather given orders – on these issues. That, perhaps more than anything else, has increased the anti-EU sentiment in the Baltic States.[13] It is interesting to note that every time Russia and Latvian Russian europarlamentarians begin a new anti-Latvian campaign, some western news agencies and newspapers join in telling how Latvia has "tightened" her laws and how minorities are repressed.

Let us examine this question more closely by way of a recent article in an American publication.

At its founding in 1865, *The Nation*, an American magazine considered to be left-liberal, took as its motto the statement: "We will … wage war upon the vices of violence, exaggeration, and misrepresentation by which so much of the political writing of the day is marred." In May 2005, the journal published an article with the title "Bush's Bitburg?"[14] The article was written by a journalist stationed in Moscow. According to him, "official discrimination" against Russian minorities in Latvia and Estonia is one of post-Soviet Russia's greatest ongoing grievances, leading to repeated official protests and demands that these countries "prove in actions their respect for human rights." The writer goes on to say that the Russian minority in Latvia is "disenfranchised" and that roughly one half of Latvia's Jews share their stateless fate. (As a matter of fact, 63 percent of Latvia's Jews and one half of Latvia's Russians had Latvian citizenship in 2005 – J.R.) "Latvians' contempt for Russia is deeply ingrained."

The caption "Bush's Bitburg?" refers to the fact that President Ronald Reagan caused a minor scandal in the 1980's by visiting a German military cemetery where Waffen-SS soldiers were buried along with others. The implication was that President Bush erred in visiting Rīga before Moscow's victory celebration in May 2005 (sixty years after the end of World War II in Europe); or that he offended the Jews, the Red Army veterans who had fought against fascism, and the Russians in general.

The fundamental idea of the article collapses, however, when it is known that contrary to *The Nation*'s claims, Bush neither visited, nor planned to visit any of the Latvian military cemeteries ("blunder his way to a controversial cemetery site"). Instead he visited a conference and concert hall in downtown Rīga.

A reader can see why Bush's visit to Latvia had to be condemned in the sin list which the article offers. This tirade, with all its errors and insinuations, is

Picture 3. "Our homework." (In Russian.) The Latvian foreign minister points, and the president and ministers listen in the classroom. Latvia was given a set of instructions by the EU, the OSCE, and the Council of Europe on the treatment of the Russian minority, among others, before the country was allowed to join the EU in 2004. Ēriks Osis, *Lauku Avīze*, 2003.

so expressive and inclusive that it is worth outlining here.

First, the writer is apparently indignant on behalf of President Vladimir Putin because early in the year 2005, the Latvian president had given him a hot-off-the-press book, *History of Latvia, The 20th Century*.[15] The writer goes on to say that the Russian minority is "officially discriminated against" and "disenfranchised." Further: The Russian minority manages to obtain Latvian citizenship only "through grueling tests and requirements."

The Holocaust in Latvia "was made possible only by enthusiastic local collaboration." Latvia "also had one of the highest per capita recruitment rates into special SS legions, whose veterans are revered as 'freedom fighters.' " Latvia is "the only country in Europe to host annual SS-veteran processions." There was "never a process of denazification," and "not a single Nazi collaborator has been tried." And still further: "Tens of thousands died at the Salaspils concentration camp in Latvia, most of them Jews." The writer also presents a wild and libelous generalization without stating any grounds or sources for it: "Most ethnic Balts … view the defeat of the Nazis as their own defeat."

All of this reminds one of the *Life* photo reportage mentioned above. The idea there was to show that the home guards were ready to repress the Russians even violently – in the same vein as they or their comrades killed Jews during the war.

I will deal later with the book that the Latvian President presented to Putin. The accusations of joining the SS and of murdering the Jews will be treated in other chapters. What of *The Nation* article's claim that Latvia slights its Russian minority?

Horoshij Gorod

As background, one must note that Latvia already had significant minorities during its first period of independence from 1918 to 1940, the largest being Russians, Jews, and Germans.[16] Nevertheless 75–77 percent of the inhabitants were ethnic Latvians.[17] Beginning in the autumn of 1939, Germans moved out of Latvia at Hitler's invitation, and almost all of the Jews were executed or fled during the period of German occupation that started in 1941. Under the first period of Soviet occupation, a significant number of the Jews was deported to the east.

When Soviet rule was solidified after the war in 1945, a powerful, planned, and organized immigration began. People were encouraged as well as pressured to migrate to the Soviet republic of Latvia where they were offered a higher standard of living, employment, and housing – much of which was either confiscated from Latvian deportees or refugees or left vacant by murdered Jews. Some immigrants supervised the process of occupation, some were sent to work in Latvia, some were seeking a better life, and some practically fled from other parts of the Soviet Union to a somewhat freer and quieter life in the Baltic republic.

As a result, in the postwar decades, as many as two million people arrived in Latvia – Russians, Belarusians, Ukrainians, and others. Not all of them stayed, and there was also migration in the other direction; but those coming to Latvia and staying exceeded those leaving during the Soviet period (from 1940 on) by 941,000 people.[18] Most were Russians. These, together with the 194,000 ethnic Russians already living in this small republic, constituted 34 percent of Latvia's population.[19]

The newcomers never had to learn the local language, and Latvian traditions and culture were totally strange and even *repugnant* to them. The Soviet policies achieved what no enemy had achieved before: the total separation of people from their country, birthplace, home, and property.[20]

To the Soviet Union, Latvia was the most important part of the Baltic area – a wedge between Estonia and Lithuania. People connected with the military and security services flooded into the land – they were privileged at all times, in all circumstances; they got apartments without waiting in queues, and they had their own special stores. Along with them came workers to build and staff new factories that produced goods for the giant empire, using raw materials imported from elsewhere. Russian became the only language used in government and economic affairs. The holders of power saw to it that the immigrants settled into strategic positions and in strategic areas. It was especially Latvia's big cities, its harbors, its maritime traffic, its railroads, and its militia that became russified.

During that period, up to a thousand Russian families a month moved into Rīga's large new apartment suburbs. In a closed session in July 1959 the Latvian Communist Party leadership stated that Rīga had received almost 700,000 new inhabitants after the war.[21] Rīga became a city of almost a million inhabitants, and an appreciable part of the housing was reserved for the military.[22] Rīga was one of the designated cities in which retired Red Army people could settle without restrictions when they completed their service – sometimes as early as the age of 45.

All told, in Latvia's seven largest cities, there were as many as or more Russian speakers than Latvians. In 2004, the inhabitants of the capital, Rīga, were 43 percent Russian, 42 percent Latvian, and 15 percent other nationalities.[23] As the Russian saying goes, *Riga – horoshij gorod, no tam slishkom mnogo latyshej* (Rīga is a good city, but there are too many Latvians there). Like many witticisms, this has a serious side.

Over 22,000 retired officers (with their family members, some 50,000 people) were allowed to remain in the country when in 1994 the Russian army finally withdrew from Latvia, which had by then been an independent country for three years. These military families have guaranteed rights to property and housing, to social services, to civilian and military pensions, and to education. A settlement of this kind is unique in history.[24] Those who have remained in Latvia continue, with the support of Moscow, to demand more privileges. Military officers have always been particularly devoted to the Soviet cause. They and their family members are among the most bitter and unrelenting enemies of the new Latvia, a strange example of people who debase and reject the people and the land in which they have settled to live. Soviet loyalists are unable to adjust to a new era; they have no home anywhere – not in the Baltics, nor in Russia, nor elsewhere in Europe.

Let's try this scenario: Norway was occupied by the Germans during the Second World War. When they left in 1945, the Norwegians sentenced to death several collaborators sympathetic to the Germans. What would the Norwegian reaction have been if the outside world had demanded that German officers were to remain in Norway as retirees with full rights, and that they were to be addressed everywhere in German?

Almost a Minority in Their Own Land

Toward the end of the occupation the Latvians were on the verge of becoming for the first time a minority in their own country. In the last Soviet census of 1989, only 52 percent of the country's inhabitants identified themselves as Latvians, and in all of her largest cities, Latvians were in the minority.[25] Of the Soviet Union's fifteen republics (excluding the Russian Federation), only Kazakhstan had proportionately more Russians – 44.4 percent; but there, in contrast to Latvia, the number of Russians was decreasing. The Latvian language had also declined to a secondary position. One might well say that in Latvia the oppressed minority was the *Latvians*.[26]

For a number of reasons, Latvia lost about a third of its population during World War I. World War II was almost equally fateful: historians and population experts have estimated that during the 1940's (1939–1950) as well, Latvia lost about one third of its prewar population when one includes among victims the inhabitants jailed and murdered during the German and Russian occupations, those mobilized for war and fallen on both sides, the missing and the prisoners of war, those who fled or were evacuated to the east or west, those taken by force to Siberia and Germany, those who left at Germany's invitation, and those who were shifted to Russia with the cession of the Abrene area.[27]

Some of those who wound up in the east or west returned, and many survivors in prisons and in camps were freed, as well as those in the armies, so that now the loss is usually estimated to be at about one fourth of the pre-war population.[28] The results of one new investigation (the calculations of population experts Pārsla Eglīte and Ilmārs Mežs) have concluded that most likely Latvia lost violently about 325,000 inhabitants from 1940 to 1959. That would be 17 percent of its prewar population. Of those whom Latvia lost during that period, 267,000 were ethnic Latvians.[29]

Present-day Russian historians' estimates of the number of Latvian victims of "Soviet political repression" vary from 140,000 to 240,000.[30] The precise number is not known. Records were taken to Moscow, and not many Russian archives are open to Latvian researchers. Many people were simply lost or were executed without a paper trail.

In terms of percentages, Latvia, which declared itself neutral in WWII and did not take part in the war as a nation, lost more of its population than countries that *did* take part in the war. The only comparable losses are those of

Poland and Belarus. The instigators of the war lost proportionately no more or even fewer people: the Soviet Union lost about 27 million civilians and soldiers (17 percent), and Germany 6.3 million (9.5 percent).[31]

About Latvia's Latvians we can say that they are the only nation living in an independent European country whose number has not reached the level of the 1930's. As a matter of fact, despite the abnormally large immigration of the Soviet era, in Latvia taken as a whole has *fewer inhabitants than before WWI*. During the same time, the population of Finland has grown from three million to 5.3 million. Latvia's Latvian population today is approximately what it was at the end of the 1800's.[32]

One should add that in the last decades, the birth rate has declined and the death rate risen. A Latvian man's life expectancy is only 65.6 years; in Europe, the figure is lower only in Moldova, Belarus, Ukraine and Russia. During her childbearing years, a Latvian woman bears on average 1.2 children, which is one of the lowest figures in Europe.

Free Choice

In Lithuania, which has a much smaller Russian minority,[33] all who wished to do so received automatic citizenship when the country became independent in 1991. In Latvia, many have demanded the same treatment. A further proposal has been that non-citizens be allowed to vote in municipal elections (as in Estonia), and that an official switch to bilingualism be made (Latvian *and* Russian, Latvian now being the only official language). Only citizens can vote in Latvian elections. In municipal and EU elections, naturally, the citizens of other EU countries living in Latvia can vote.

Some scholars are of the opinion that if the number representing "foreign" citizens as compared to the "native" citizens exceeds a certain limit, the state no longer can function normally – especially if an appreciable number of the "foreigners" are loyal to another state. The suggested limit is 30 percent. European sociologists write that in big tenement houses "the crisis point" is reached when one fifth or more of the tenants are immigrants; then the "old" inhabitants start to move away.[34]

In Latvia the number of "aliens" exceeds those limits; for example, 40 percent of its inhabitants are Russian-speaking and nearly 30 percent are Russian by nationality (ethnicity). Almost 400,000 inhabitants are "non-citizens" or aliens.[35] They have residence permits, or the old Soviet passports, or they are citizens of other countries, mostly of Russia (Russia has never disclosed how many have Russian passports). Hardly any other country in the world has proportionately as many permanent residents who are non-citizens without

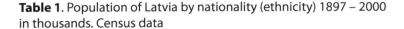

Table 1. Population of Latvia by nationality (ethnicity) 1897 – 2000 in thousands. Census data

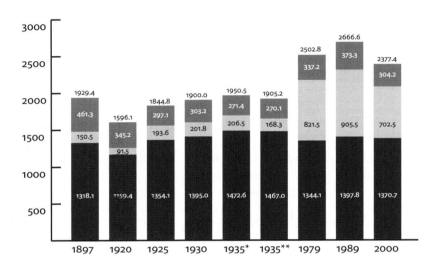

* Within the borders of Latvia in 1935 – Compare to previous years
** Within present state borders – Compare to subsequent years

the right to vote.[36] Those who choose not to learn the Latvian language retain their permanent resident alien status with full rights to health care, social services, and economic opportunity as in any other country, including the United States.

The uninvited guests were given a free choice. They could go back to Russia; they could stay and adopt Russian citizenship; they could take local citizenship (if prepared to learn Latvian); or they could stay on as non-citizens, able to work but not to vote.

So, they were asked to choose. When the preset time limit was reached in the spring of year 2000, there were in Latvia still almost 40,000 persons with only an old Soviet passport that was not recognized anywhere. They had not bothered to apply for a residence permit and an alien passport.

At first the Latvian state even used financial inducements in an attempt to encourage Russians to move back to their mother country, but it soon became clear that very few wanted to go. No one was waiting for them there, nor was there housing for them. Life in Latvia was peaceful, and the standard of living was higher.

According to Russian information, from 1992 on, the return migration to Russia from Kazakhstan – in fact, a forced departure or an actual flight – amounted to about 1.5 million people, and 36 percent of the Russian schools there were closed. 200,000 Russians left Tajikistan.[37] Nevertheless Russia accuses only Latvia and Estonia of trampling on the human rights of Russians. "No other diaspora issue was accorded so much space in the Russian media or provoked so much bitter and incensed comment," as one observer writes.[38]

Some six million Russians live outside the boundaries of Russia in Europe, and the mother country declares that it defends the interests of these "compatriots." For example, President Putin maintains direct contact with them. The Russian ambassador in Latvia attends local Russian events, where he speaks of Russians as "we" and of Latvians as "they."

In the autumn of 1991, Latvia's Russians were certainly placed in an extraordinary and psychologically difficult position. At one moment they were the privileged citizens of a superpower; at the next moment they were the minority in a small, independent state, confronted with demands that they considered humiliating.

In 1991 Latvia restored citizenship to all those who were inter-war citizens (before June 17, 1940) and their direct descendants. They were citizens automatically if they registered, even though they had been living or even been born abroad. All aliens, including those born in Latvia before August 21, 1991, had to take a test to qualify for citizenship.[39] Children of aliens born in Latvia after 1991 receive citizenship automatically at the age of sixteen upon completion of school if they want it.

There were some 740,000 non-citizens in the country, almost a third of the population, when Latvia began to naturalize them on the basis of petitions in 1995. They were in legal limbo, not fitting any category – citizen, alien, or stateless person.[40] At first there were annual naturalization quotas, but they were given up on the advice of international organizations. Soon on an average a thousand applicants per month passed the test, and by the summer of 2007, citizenship had been granted 125,000 applicants.[41]

A number of Russians do not want citizenship (1) because then they might have to serve in the Latvian Army, and (2) because their visits to Russia would become more difficult. (Actually, Latvia has just done away with compulsory service and is switching to a professional army.) A number will not seek citizenship as a matter of principle – they feel that citizenship belongs to them automatically and to apply for it would be humiliating. Some have an antipathy toward the state of Latvia. Latvian authorities estimate that some 120,000 will never apply for citizenship.

Some complain that the citizenship test is difficult, and that the Latvian language is impossible to learn. However, Latvian is not a particularly difficult language; some, who are in the position to know, say that it may be the easiest language in Eastern Europe. Many foreigners learn it at a level sufficient to pass the citizenship test in a short time.

I learned to speak Latvian when I was over fifty, and for linguistic reasons it should be even easier for Russians. The crux of the matter seems to be that they do not *want* or will not *bother* to learn it. Some say that the language is not impossible to learn nor the test impossibly difficult, but that it is a question of a "psychological barrier" now that the Latvians insist that the citizenship applicants learn the language.[42]

Russia and Latvia's Russian politicians demand the "zero option," – that all those living in Latvia at the renewal of independence should receive citizenship unconditionally. A lesser demand is that all who voted for independence in the 1991 referendum be granted citizenship – however their vote might be verified. Indeed, before the voting, vague informal promises to that effect had been made.

Since the percentage of voters was 87.5, and the "yes" votes were 74 percent of the total, it is evident that many non-Latvians really *did* vote "yes."[43] Even in Daugavpils, the most Russian among Latvia's cities, the majority, 66 percent, voted for independence.

As a result of anti-Latvian activity, some Russians have been refused citizenship and even denied entry from Russia to Latvia. They have complained of their treatment to international agencies. The most radical of anti-Latvian factions fan the flames of hatred and are stockpiling arms. If their demands are not granted, they threaten to "resort to alternative battle tactics."

Latvia's Security Police warned in 2006 that "extremist organizations have recently very actively used not only all the protest forms allowed in a democratic country but also radical methods, for example calls to overthrow violently the state power or attack violently certain social and ethnic groups."[44]

"Grueling and Strict"

Are the citizenship tests Russians are required to take (not just Russians, but everyone! – J.R.) "grueling," as *The Nation* claims? Another American magazine, *Newsweek*, wrote of the matter during the same year, and characterizes the Latvian citizenship laws as "strict."

As a Finn who has lived in Baltic and some other countries, I would say, rather, that the test is normal, among the most liberal in Europe, and that the Latvian citizenship law is certainly more liberal than the corresponding Russian law of 2002. Compared to those of the United States, where the periodicals in question are published, the Latvian requirements are ridiculously easy.[45]

As to participation in politics in Latvia, all citizens can vote and be nominated for office. Latvia has not, however, permitted resident non-citizens to vote in municipal elections. There is no simple solution to that problem. Municipal voting sounds harmless, but has potential for troubles in a society where tensions exist over language and ethnicity. Universal suffrage *might* further integration and solidarity (although it obviously has not done so in Estonia). On the other hand, as one can infer from information given above, Latvia's large cities could again become totally Russian in character if everyone had the right to vote, and their schools would start moving away from Latvian language teaching.

Also, there would be even less motivation then to learn Latvian and get citizenship, if everybody would be allowed to vote anyway. The motivation was lessened already in 2007, when EU countries decided to allow visa-free travel for non-citizens from Estonia and Latvia.

Many Latvians are already frightened by the behavior and actions of some Russian representatives in the Latvian parliament. The latter organize anti-Latvian events even in parliamentary quarters, use school children to participate in illegal demonstrations, go on trips to Moscow and Brussels to complain about Latvian abuses and refer to themselves as "second-class citizens." They even say mockingly that no test in Russian language and history was demanded of Latvians when they joined the Soviet Union in 1940.

The reality in Latvia today is that a person speaking only Russian can manage his life in his own language, but a person speaking only Latvian cannot. Russian is heard everywhere; Russians generally speak only Russian to Latvians, and will not respond even to greetings or questions in Latvian – they go so far as to criticize the interlocutor. At the workplace, knowledge of Russian is a must; the employment advertisement page in newspapers tells the story.

International organizations have agreed that Latvia and other Baltic countries do not oppress the Russians or other minorities, either in the application of laws or in other ways. If this were not the case, Latvia could not even have become a member of the OSCE, the EU, and NATO. The OSCE and the Council of Europe have long since ceased to monitor the human rights situation in the Baltic countries.

Picture 4. Oh you bad, bad, bad Latvia. Māris Bišofs on Russia and Latvia in Diena, 2005.

Rolf Ekeus, the OSCE Minority Commissar, visited Rīga in 2006 and said that Latvia had made such great strides and achieved such results in social integration that she could begin sharing her experiences and advising other countries. There already are Latvian experts in Georgia, and, in Ekeus' opinion, they could also assist in Kazakhstan, Kyrgyzstan, and Tajikistan.[46]

The pace of naturalization has now slowed again. Some observers believe that Latvians could do more to teach its Russians their language, to integrate them into society, and to speed up their attainment of citizenship; they have been especially urged to ease the path to naturalization for children and the old.[47]

It is clear that many of Latvia's Russians will never become *assimilated*. The question is whether they will even become *integrated*. In a survey of Latvia's residents conducted in March 2006, only 9 percent of respondents agreed with the statement that "the society can be considered to be consolidated and integrated."[48] Most respondents, however, considered ethnic relations to be satisfactory.

When Latvia regained independence in 1991, only 29 percent of Russian respondents said they considered Latvia to be their "homeland." In 1993 only 15 percent of Latvia's Russians supported the idea of withdrawing Russia's armed forces from Latvia, and in 1997, 20 percent of non-Latvians still believed that Latvia would eventually become part of Russia. In 2001, when asked with what they most closely identify themselves, only 3 percent of non-Latvians gave "with Latvia" as the first choice. Not only the first-generation immigrants but also their children born in Latvia were weakly integrated into local society and had a poor command of Latvian and little knowledge of Latvian history.[49]

In 2007, only 66 percent of citizens and 37 percent of non-citizens say that they are proud of their country – a considerable drop in a few years. Only 44 percent and 28 percent, respectively, would be ready to defend Latvia with weapon in hand.[50]

Scholars say true integration cannot occur as long as a common conception of history (and of a future) is lacking. In Latvia, two completely different concepts of history exist side by side, and there are actually two separate school systems – the Russian and the Latvian. Some books for the Russian schools come from Russia, and the students and teachers remain isolated from the mainstream within their own Russian cultural sphere, which includes the media. The most important Russian press publications in Latvia "continue repeating old totalitarian myths" about Latvian history.[51] Fifty-two percent of non-Latvians say that they watch news broadcasts and political programs on Russian Television almost every day, while only a minority watches such programs in Russian on Latvian TV.[52]

It is strange to spend New Year's Eve in a Latvian town: at 23:00 a noisy celebration begins and rockets explode; people are watching Moscow television (one hour ahead of Latvian time) to see the festivities begin there, and some of them may really believe that the year has changed.

Shortly after the above-mentioned article appeared in *The Nation*, the British BBC article service carried the articles "Latvian Lessons Irk Russians" and "Citizenship Row Divides Latvia." In them, Latvia's Russians related how difficult their lives were.

I wrote to the BBC that, surprisingly, both stories on the same subject had a similar bias, and asked: "Should the Latvians now send a newsman to Ireland to interview Sinn Fein members on the subject of what Englishmen are like, and then have him write articles about England? (More to the point historically would be to have newsmen interview Englishmen and then write articles about the Irish.)

"The general problem seems to be that western newspapers and news agencies send journalists to the Baltic countries who have worked in Moscow and speak Russian. Could you imagine one of us with no knowledge of English going to work in London? To save its reputation the BBC should now send somebody here who would interview Latvians and also foreign correspondents and diplomats – the British, too! Maybe they should interview a person like me, a Finnish journalist who lives in the Baltics and knows their languages and history."

There was no response. Already in November of 2000, when President Vaira Vīķe-Freiberga made her first official visit to London, I was astonished to see how aggressive the BBC *Hard Talk* interview with her was. All the questions Tim Sebastian asked her were about Nazi criminals, SS veterans and oppression of the Russian minority.

Unfortunately Latvian officials overreacted and "dealt with" the 2005 articles in exactly the wrong way: they began to put pressure on the people who had spoken to the BBC journalist. Naturally the BBC journalist wrote about this in his subsequent article.[53]

Russians in Latvia are not oppressed, not even in the sense of being poorer than the Latvians; there are numerous millionaires among them. Poverty does not have a Russian face. An official survey, conducted in 1999, showed that ethnicity was not play a role in explaining the risks of poverty in Latvia.[54]

In certain matters, however, Russians do differ from other ethnic groups: in crime and unemployment. Latvian Russians are 2.8 times more likely to be charged with manslaughter or murder than Latvians.[55] In a 2006 survey by the Russian-Latvian party mentioned above, it is claimed that "unemployment among 'speakers of Russian' is 30 percent higher." In fact, according to official statistics, the difference in employment rates between Latvians and non-Latvians is only 3 percentage points.[56]

2

Are the Russians denied the right to use their language in Latvian society and in the schools?

This question is also often posed "backwards:" Has Latvia done its best to teach Latvian to its Russians and to integrate them into society?

President Putin, in his radio speech on Christmas Eve 2001, urged Russians and Russian speakers to demand official status for their language and numerical quotas of representation in governmental bodies in the Baltics. The objective would be a society officially divided along language and nationality lines. In 2006[1] the *Helsingin Sanomat* also seemed to favor the same notion by proposing the Belgian plan for the Baltic countries – that is to say, for all practical purposes, a country sharply divided into two, the halves of which are downright hostile to one another, although the minorities have lived in the countries for centuries (unlike the Russians in Latvia).

Moscow zealously defends the position of the Russian language in the Baltic countries, because it is declining everywhere else in the former Soviet Union. Among the former Soviet republics (in addition to Russia), it is the official language only in Belarus.

A total of 164 million people speak Russian as their mother tongue, and 114 million know it as a second language. In some forty years, Portuguese will surpass Russian as the world's fourth most spoken language.[2]

In January 2006, the conservative British newspaper Daily Telegraph wrote:

In those Baltic States, now members of the European Union, there are Russian minorities (and in the case of Latvia an only-just minority). There, the Russians are meant to learn Baltic languages that, with the best will in the world, Russians cannot take seriously as cultural vehicles (and the Europarliament is strangely silent as to the linguistic oppression that results, whereas there is jumping up and down about Kurdish in Turkey).[3]

I will not comment on this British view.

Russian Spoken More Widely

The language question may be considered a fateful one for Latvia. Hardly anything else has been debated as much as language, its use, and its future. That has been the case for sixteen years already. If politicians, officials, and scientists had used a part of this time and energy in pondering economic development, perhaps Latvia would have gone far in that area. But we must understand the psychology of a people whose language has repeatedly been the target of oppression and threatened with downright extinction. As a matter of fact, the status of the Latvian language has shown astonishingly small improvement, if any, during the years of independence, and recently public expressions of belittlement of and scorn for it have increased.

My home country Finland has two official languages, Finnish and Swedish, although only about six percent of the inhabitants are Swedish-speaking.[4] Russia and Latvia's Russians have repeatedly proposed the Finnish model to Latvia as well: two official languages with equal status, Russian and Latvian. The Latvian language law of 1989, one of the first and most important laws relating to independence, decreed that Latvian was the country's only official language. The law makes the knowledge of Latvian a prerequisite for many posts in government and in state and private sectors of the economy.[5]

If Russian were to become Latvia's second official language, it would also become, for the first time, one of the EU bureaucracy's official languages. Tunne Kelam, an Estonian member of the European Parliament, says that it is in the interests of Russia to make Russian, either through Latvia or Estonia, a language of the EU.[6]

No one forbids the speaking of Russian in Latvia in private and public places, in courts, in advertisements, in places of business, in offices, in the media, on athletic fields, in schools, hospitals, and at various events, and it is probably the most used language in the country – simply because there are many more courteous, bilingual Latvians than there are Russians of analogous skills and motivation. All Latvians were forced to learn and use Russian during the years of the occupation, while the Russians did not have to know Latvian. Does one dare speak of language oppression in the manner of *The Daily Telegraph*?[7]

Of Latvia's inhabitants, 96–98 percent are counted as knowing Russian. 94 percent claim they know Latvian; that percentage should actually be less than 80, because the language many speak is so elementary and faulty.[8] The Latvian language was corrupted by "Soviet" Russian, and Russian is still affecting Latvian. According to expatriate Latvians, the "language ear" of the Latvians who live in Latvia has been ruined. Moscow's objective was the *homo sovieticus* and one means to that end was to make the languages spoken in the Soviet states closer to Russian, even imposing the Cyrillic alphabet on some.

Latvia's bilingualism has already been realized in practice, and in daily life, that means russification. Usually Latvians bow to their predicament and speak Russian to "their" Russians.

According to research, non-Latvians feel more comfortable in the cities than Latvians. Still the Russian ambassador said, incredibly, at the end of 2006, that "a concerted attempt is being made to squeeze out the Russian language from all spheres of Latvian society." The fact that one can manage with Russian anywhere in Latvia is not enough for some politicians, but they continue to demand more rights for their language.[9]

Russian visitors are astonished when they arrive in Latvia: they are not treated with hostility, Russian is spoken to them, and Russian is even used in the schools. At home they had been given entirely different information about Latvia.

Russian is still dominant, especially in technical areas, in manufacturing, in transport, in business, in construction, in banking, and in the information technology field. Sixty two percent of Latvia's factory workers were non-Latvians at the end of the Soviet era, and at one point it was estimated that 64 percent of the country's doctors did not understand Latvian.[10] Russian-speaking minorities controlled economic life, having been favored by the Soviet government for 47 years. According to the country's Language Center, Russian dominates the private sector at present, with the exception of agriculture, and it is also indispensable for state and municipal office workers.[11]

Businessmen and employers are often Latvian Russians and view Latvia as part of Russian-speaking Europe. They expect a good knowledge of Russian in those seeking employment. That cuts off the possibility of employment, at least in the big cities, for many young Latvians, for the majority of them no longer learn Russian in school. Instead, they study English, just as was the case in Latvia in the 1930's.[12]

The language situation not only annoys and offends some Latvians, it oppresses and humiliates émigrés returning from the West, who are often treated with distrust and discourtesy when they naturally speak Latvian and explain that they do not know Russian.[13] If a Latvian dares comment on the violation of some edict (such as "Latvian should be spoken here," or "No smoking here") a Russian speaker may well snort: "Those are *your* laws!" At the residents' meetings in large apartment buildings, the Russian participants, no matter what their number is, may very well threaten to walk out if Russian is not chosen as the language of the meeting.[14]

Russian speakers have their own newspapers, their own radio and TV channels, in addition to which some 70 different Russian papers are sold or can be subscribed to in Latvia; on the other hand, *no* Estonian *or* Lithuanian publications can be bought *nor* subscribed to in Latvia. TV programs and movies are often dubbed or subtitled in Russian. Sometimes Russian speech on TV is not translated at all – on the assumption that everyone understands it. It is not uncommon to have four Russian-language programs on four of the five Latvian channels at the same time. In general, however, Latvia's Russians watch Russian television and get quite a biased impression, to say the least, of the land in which they live – if they get any impression at all.

According to the laws and statutes, the practitioners of many professions and trades should know at least a certain amount of Latvian; especially officials, teachers, doctors, nurses, judges, secretaries, bookkeepers, taxi drivers, sales people, and other workers (altogether 70 out of 3,500 occupations) in state institutions, enterprises, business firms and organizations, who are "in contact with the general public." The nominal penalty – rarely enforced – is a fine and dismissal. There are three different levels of the language test, depending upon the position the person taking the test wants to qualify for. But persons who have passed the test are not always able to speak Latvian at the required fluency, nor do they want to. There are taxi drivers in Rīga who will not consent to speak a word of Latvian, and if one comments on it, at best they will laugh, at worst, they will fly into a rage.

The Finnish Model?

During the Christmas season of 2005, *The New York Times* wrote that nowhere else in the world is a small language minority as spoiled as in Finland. Let it be noted that in Sweden, for example, Finnish has no official status, although a half-million Finnish speakers live there, or more than there are Swedish-speakers living in Finland. Finnish is not taught in the schools, nor can Finnish be used anywhere. The protests of Finns have not really changed Swedish linguistic politics. An example of the double standard applied to Latvia is that representatives of countries like Sweden are quite ready to pressure Latvia to change its linguistic politics.

Picture 5. In 2004 Russian speaking politicians marched schoolchildren onto the streets and Latvia experienced its greatest protests during the period of independence when a new law decreed that Russian schools should shift in part to Latvian language instruction. Ilmārs Znotiņš, Diena. Picture taken 23.01.2004.

Picture 6. "No to the reform!" The Latvian language: "Good heavens, all this for my sake!" Gatis Šļūka, *Latvijas Avīze,* 2004

What is more, there are four million Turks living in Germany. Why does that country not have several official languages?

The *New York Times* article inspired Finnish commentators to suggest that Finland make "an exportable commodity" of its "linguistic peace," send its expert assistance to aid countries where there are linguistic quarrels, and internationally propagate the linguistic equality prevailing in Finland.[15]

Finnish language legislation is in fact already an exported product: Canadian Prime Minister Pierre Trudeau once saved his country from breakup and perhaps even from violence, through bilingual legislation, the model for which was taken from Finland.[16]

Finnish "linguistic ambassadors" have also been seen in the Baltics. International organizations have chosen Swedish-Finnish politicians as researchers and reporters for Estonia and Latvia, who have advised these countries to study the Finnish model and adopt bilingualism. One really cannot congratulate them on their sense of history and psychology. I also wonder if the Russians, who receive them so enthusiastically, know that Finland's Swedish-speaking minority must by law learn to speak, read, and write Finnish, the language of the majority, in school, and that all immigrants must learn to speak both languages well if they plan to serve in municipal or state offices or functions in Finland.

One must make something clear at the start. Finland Swedes are *Finns*, whose mother tongue is Swedish (or rather a dialect of Swedish) and whose native country is Finland. They are an old minority; they have "always" lived in Finland, mainly in the south. There was some Swedish immigration to that coastal area from 12th century. Finland Swedes are all Finnish citizens, they have Finnish passports, they are patriotic, and in wars they have fought and will in the future fight on the side of Finland.

How Latvia's minorities came to be established was the subject of the preceding chapter.

Let us speculate again. If there were proportionally as many Russians in Finland as in Latvia, there would be some two million. Currently there are some tens of thousands of Russian immigrants in Finland, but the number is growing every day. Then, when their number is "large enough" they may demand an official position for their language – as a matter of fact, there has already been talk of it. Are the Finnish politicians who now advise Latvia ready to make Finland a trilingual country?

Amnesty International shocked many in the Baltic States with a quite negative report entitled "Linguistic Minorities in Estonia: Discrimination Must End," which they drew up at the close of 2006, promising to do the same in the near future for Latvia. Amnesty called on Estonia to recognize Russian speakers as an official minority language group and to view their concerns as a human rights issue. According to Amnesty, Russians in Estonia "enjoy very limited linguistic rights." It recommended radical changes to language and citizenship laws. It also criticized the cost of Estonian language courses and recommended that lessons be free of charge. *The Economist* heard echoes of Kremlin propaganda in all this.[17]

The Battle Over Schools

Latvia inherited from the Soviet Union a segregated system of education in which virtually all Latvians went to Latvian language schools and all Russians and other minorities attended Russian schools. This system produced bilingual Latvians and monolingual Russian-speakers.

For a long time the most disputed law in Latvia has been the 2004 Education Law, which called for a transition to instruction primarily in Latvian in state-funded Russian secondary schools starting that same fall. The law even stated that some 60 percent of the instruction be in Latvian and thus 40 percent in Russian. The regulation does not, of course, apply to such subjects as Russian language and literature. Estonia was planning the same kind of law, but decided to postpone its introduction.

The matter is, of course, sensitive, for one's language is a person's most delicate and personal affair; one cannot impose a language on anyone, coercion merely gives rise to resistance. On the other hand, as a multilingual friend of mine says, "Learning another language has never hurt anybody's physical or mental health. Swiss children normally learn three languages. I have never heard a word about children suffering there."

By the same token, one can understand the Latvians as well. They live in their own country where their ancestors have lived for millennia, whereas the Russians are uninvited newcomers who arrived as conquerors/colonial masters at most a few decades ago. Most small nations take special steps to maintain the primacy of their language and culture, which otherwise might become extinct in a few decades. Why must Latvians always hear accusations, why must they always be thinking integration, whom and how to integrate and how they are perhaps to be integrated to something?[18] They already feel themselves to be strangers in their own land, and new concessions are continually demanded of them. Some experts have asked whether integration in Latvia already means that the Latvians, who are generally more prudent and adaptable, will adapt to a Russian-language culture and environment.[19]

My home town of Jūrmala, a seaside resort town, is in principle one of the most pleasant places to live in the Baltics. Yet some of my Latvian friends have said lately that they no longer feel at home here, and are thinking of moving away. Their houses have been surrounded by the palaces and concrete castles of the Russian *nouveaux riches*. The huge holdings of many of these strangers are undoubtedly the gains of crime and money laundering.

Of late, many researchers have accused the Latvians of being slow in integrating. Already in 2004, the Baltic Institute of Social Sciences affirmed in its research project *Ethnic Tolerance and Social Integration* that the Latvians' constrained and reserved identity was an obstacle to the country's development. The opinion survey firms, Baltijas Forums and SKDS, conducted an inquiry in 2005 and concluded that Russians were more open and the Latvians more suspicious and prejudiced, which hindered integration significantly.

In 2006 the Department of Sociology of University of Latvia, with the aid of the EU and the Social Integration Fund, carried out an expensive research project on the reasons for resistance to integration. Advance information from the results tells us that "cultural trauma, the dramatic loss of meaning and identity, and historical memory," which is a "heavy burden" to Latvians, impede the development of trust among different ethnic groups. According to the authors, the Latvians dwell upon past sufferings and wrongs, because politicians and newspapers will not let them free themselves of them, but fan the flames "artificially." Latvians also "expect too much" of non-Latvians, for example, that they should adapt to the prevailing circumstances. The worst, the study says, is that they see their country's independence as a continuation of the first Latvian republic, while the immigrants do not think of it as such.[20]

I do wonder why only the Latvians, of all nations, should forgive and forget. Also, I dare say that my fellow countrymen's Finnish identity is quite "reserved" and that their "historical memory" is particularly strong. I don't dare even to think what would happen if as many aliens came into Finland as into Latvia – whether it be Americans, Zimbabweans, Swedes, or Russians (that is to say two million, if there were comparatively as many as in Latvia).

"Worse Than Nazi Rule"

Be that as it may, the OSCE (Organization for Security and Co-operation in Europe) has announced its support of the Latvian school reform.[21]

When the law took effect, some politicians and even some teachers threatened to strike and riot, marching groups of their school children out onto the streets to demonstrate. The protests in Rīga were the most sustained Latvia had witnessed since independence. Someone even set fire to the Ministry of Education's front door.

Feelings seem to have cooled a little now. Schoolchildren are adapting to the required Latvian, but it is true that only about half of the pupils in Russian schools know Latvian – that is, the language of the country in which they have lived their entire lives![22] In the parliamentary election of autumn 2006, the language question in the schools was no longer a primary issue, and the quarrel, according to researchers, is apparently receding into the background, although some of the parents still complain that the children are suffering from the reform.[23] Many of the young understand that to succeed in the workplace, a knowledge of Latvian is good for them, and often they know the language better than their teachers, which is a problem. Nowadays many Russian parents put their children into Latvian kindergartens and schools. The difference in mentalities, however, causes such a group of children to become russified easily, even if there are only a few Russians in it.

The most heated opponents of school reform are organized into "headquarters" (*Shtab*), a military term which reflects the idea of its activity. It uses the education issue as a tool for a populist criticism of Latvian democracy in general. The *Shtab* works in conjunction with the Russian parties (and apparently with Moscow): it distributes leaflets on the streets, demonstrates, and maintains a web page. On this home page, one of its members, Aleksandr Gilman wrote that "Latvia is worse than Nazi rule, but luckily it is weak and fearful;" so it is easy to fight against this enemy. The founding of the Latvian republic was in his opinion, a misfortune, "and it would be best to liquidate it."

Gilman is also of the opinion that "we [Latvian Russians] have to be grateful to those who gave this land to us" – meaning the Red Army.[24]

On Latvian national holidays, when flowers are placed on monuments in the presence of visitors and journalists from abroad, these politicians have a habit of organizing noisy protests in the same places, in which, dressed in striped prison garb, they shout anti-Latvian and anti-fascist slogans. A photo of these "prisoners" is the only picture of Latvia published, for example, in a new Italian encyclopedia.[25] The cameras of Russian TV channels are always on hand in the hope that the audience may be provoked into attacking the protesters, and that the police will arrest them; neither ever happens. One has to admire the forbearance and toleration of the Latvians; they endure an astonishing amount of provocation. And nevertheless the demonstrators' message is that this is a neo-Nazi nation.

Picture 7. During national holidays, demonstrators dressed in prison garb try to interfere with proceedings, at the Freedom Monument in the center of Rīga among other places. Their claim is that Latvia is a neo-Nazi state. Uldis Briedis, Diena 17.03.2005.

Picture 8. The Russians often organize demonstrations at the statue of Latvia's national poet Rainis. In the picture, a Latvian woman is strangling a Russian "negro". Jānis Buls, Diena 03.02.2006.

The newspaper *Vesti Segodna* wrote in February 2007, when a small right wing party was founded in Latvia, "In Latvia, a new Nazi generation is striving for power, which aims at the physical destruction of the Russians."[26]

A party named the PCTVL (Par Cilvēktiesībām Vienotā Latvijā; For Human Rights in United Latvia) is the most active in opposition to school reform. In surveys of support from 2000 to 2006 this party has often been the second most popular. It recommended in 2006 that Latvia stop downgrading "their" holidays. For example, Christmas is observed with free days only in December (Orthodox Russians observe it in January). They also recommended that May 9th, (Victory Day in Russia) be declared a national holiday, or that "Europe Day" should also be "Victory over Fascism Day" in Latvia.[27]

The outside world is continually concerned about the situation in Latvia although its society is much more stable and peaceful than those of many European states. In a newspaper interview of January 2006, an anti-terrorist special agent of the US State Department wondered at the criticism directed at Latvia and added: "To the best of my knowledge, Russia is the country with the largest number of neo-Nazis, neo-fascists, and skinheads."[28] At about the same time, Professor Leo Dribins wrote that the "strengthening of anti-Semitic tendencies" could be noted everywhere in Europe, and that the spread of this idea must be considered most dangerous in Russia, where many writers and publishers specialized in it.[29]

Amnesty International criticized Russian officials for closing their eyes to national hatreds and racism in the spring of 2006 when in four months, over a hundred people had been attacked, of whom at least fourteen were killed. Russia has some 50,000 neo-Nazis, and a full ten percent of the people seem to support fascism, according to some polls. *Le Monde* wrote of foreigners and non-Slavs being afraid to walk the streets of Moscow and St. Petersburg because of these attacks, of how xenophobia is spread on the internet, and of how new ultra-nationalistic groups are being born.[30]

The leader of the Social Democratic Party of Latvia, Juris Bojars, who is a professor of jurisprudence and a member of the Academy of Science (and who worked for the KGB in the past), warned at the start of 2006 that Latvia was a "soft state" in which all sorts of forces could operate freely. "Here everyone can do whatever he wants." Bojars wonders that no one cares about the subversive activity in which the Russian newspapers, the Russian language channel TV5 and to some extent Latvian television take part. "They are not only critical, they are openly hostile to Latvian state politics." The government is regularly and consistently painted black.

"It is a very serious matter. I have warned that one or several people direct it knowingly. … It happens systematically that a big part of Latvia's population – we are speaking of some 800,000 people – are worked on to develop an antagonistic and tendentious spirit toward Latvia. … It is dividing Latvian society, whipping up hatred and in some cases chauvinist thoughts, for example, such lies as that there was no occupation here. It is ideological destabilization." In Bojars' opinion, all this can continue because Latvia is a free country and its people are peace-loving.[31]

Martiņš Kālis, who is writing his doctoral thesis at the University of Lund, wonders that although a law forbidding the incitement of racial and national hatreds is in effect in Latvia, no one who has attacked a Latvian without verbal or physical provocation has ever been brought up on such a charge. There are many known instances from recent years in which gangs shouting abuse have assaulted children and young people speaking Latvian on the street. Kālis conjectures that Latvians have an inferiority complex; they have internalized the notion that their nationality is not worth defending.[32]

Some Russian organizations demand free instruction in Latvian and exemption from compulsory study of the language for certain groups. Latvia has received financial aid from abroad in order to make the language teaching more effective. One can, of course, ask whether all the money has been used properly and effectively. The Russian-Latvian research referred to in Chapter One claims that the state used only 32 santims per person per year for language teaching to adults.[33]

It is undeniable that for adults who can speak only Russian learning Latvian may seem difficult. It is especially difficult for the infirm aged and the ill to take part in the study, and one may ask if the linguistic demands of the law might be made more flexible in their case.

The lack of discussion, collaboration, and mutual understanding pose a danger in Latvia. Small but vociferous radical groups on both sides oftentimes set the tone in public debates and the newspapers fan the flames. Perhaps hope may lie with the younger generation whose thinking is not burdened by the heavy weight of the past.

3

Were the Baltic lands a small, underdeveloped province in a far corner of Europe, to which Germans, Swedes, Poles, and Russians brought religion, culture, and well-being and where no prerequisites for independence existed?

Thus far the world extends, and this is the truth.

TACITUS OF THE BALTIC LANDS

He works like a Negro on a plantation
or a Latvian for a German.

DOSTOYEVSKY

The proto-Balts or early Baltic peoples began to arrive on the shores of the Baltic Sea nearly 4,000 years ago. At their greatest extent, they occupied an area some six times as large as that of the present Baltic peoples. Two thousand years ago, the Roman Tacitus wrote about the *Aesti* tribe on the shores of the Baltic; according to him, its members gathered amber and were not as lazy as many other peoples.[1]

In the area that presently is Latvia, grain was already cultivated around 3800 B.C.[2] Archeologists say that agriculture did not reach southern Finland, only some 300 kilometers away, until the year 2500 B.C. About 900 AD Balts began establishing tribal realms. "Latvians" (there was no such nation yet) were a loose grouping of tribes or cultures governed by kings: Couronians (Kurshi), Latgallians, Selonians and Semigallians. The area which is known as Latvia today was also occupied by a Finno-Ugric tribe, the Livs, who gradually merged with the Balts. The peoples were further commingled in the wars which Estonian and Latvian tribes waged with one another for centuries.[3]

To judge by findings at grave sites, the ancient inhabitants in the area of Latvia were a prosperous people, tall in build. They practiced agriculture and kept slaves. Their relatively high degree of development shows in the number of Finnish words with a Baltic origin, among them words relating to sea travel, agriculture, and tools.

The Lithuanians and the Latvians were "the last of Europe's pagans." They did, however, have their own animistic, pantheistic religion. Innocent III, the most aggressive and violent of the medieval popes, declared a crusade "against the barbarous peoples" of the Baltic in 1199. The subjugation of the eastern shore of the Baltic Sea was of interest for economic and trade reasons, and the Order of the Sword (*Fratres Militae Christi de Livonia*), later the Teutonic Knights, took on the task assigned by the Pope. The new arrivals founded the city of Rīga in 1201. The Livonians were the first "natives" that they encountered, and they named the area Livonia (Livland).

The Balts were baptized as Christians during the 13th century; the last to convert were the Couronians and the people of the island Oesel. The conversion was accomplished by force, even by violence, if old chronicles can be trusted. Many Balts at first tried to wash off the baptism in sacred rivers. "They deserve to be killed, rather than to be baptized," wrote the German chronicler Heinrich (Henricus de Lettis) in frustration.

The crusaders did not need many soldiers; they were superior in arms and also resorted to a policy of divide and conquer and to the use of local allies – they turned the Balts against one another. The Balts retain a collective memory of this. The conquerors used the fears and hatreds prevailing among the tribes to their advantage. The Livs and the Latvians became the trusted weapons-bearers for Germans in battles against Estonians. The Lithuanians successfully resisted the German conquerors, but their king chose the Christian religion voluntarily.[4]

Churches were built in places sacred to the Balts. As had happened in other places, pre-Christian and Christian practices blended into a unique new tradition. Many "pagan" beliefs lived on, even for centuries. Many of them live on in Baltic folk customs, festivals, and songs.

The Balts had received influences from both East and West, but as a result of the conquest, the greater part of the Baltic area became part of the Western cultural sphere, the Roman Catholic community. It came to be known as the Confederation of Livonia, a state attached to the Holy Roman Empire. In the ensuing struggle, the Slavic principalities of Novgorod, Polotsk, and Pskov were defeated. The Baltic peoples have generally been labeled Central Europeans, and the Estonians and sometimes even the Latvians have also been called Northern Europeans. During the 16th century, Luther's reformation found its first supporters outside Germany in Rīga – initially among its Germans. Nowadays in the Baltic States the majority in the north are Lutheran and in the south Roman Catholic, so that the dividing line runs approximately through the middle of Latvia. The Greek Orthodox are mainly in the east.

The Knights ruled Livonia as a feudal confederation, which meant that the Latvians gradually sank into serfdom. The population was divided into two entirely different social groups: the German masters and non-German (*undeutsche*) serfs. Livonia was situated along an important trade route, and the Daugava River was especially important. Eight cities in Latvia joined the German trade association, the Hanseatic League.

By the beginning of the 17th century, the Latvian tribes had coalesced into a single people called the Latvians. They spoke an old Indo-European language, which belongs to the East Baltic language group and is closer to Sanskrit than are most other Indo-European languages. Latvian and Lithuanian have remained the national languages of the respective nations, whereas the other eastern Baltic languages became extinct after the conquest of their native lands by Slavs or Germans.

The first Latvian-language books, written by German clergymen, date from the 16th century, and the entire Bible was translated into Latvian in the 1680's. For centuries, literacy remained virtually a German monopoly, as few Latvians received any schooling. Thus Latvian indigenous culture lived on as oral traditions. Not until the Enlightenment did growing numbers of Latvians acquire higher education, and some of them turned their interest to folklore. An example of the deep roots and the vitality of Latvian culture are the folk songs or *dainas*, most of which Krišjānis Barons gathered and wrote down among the people at the end of the 1800's. To date, more than 1.2 million texts and 30,000 melodies have been identified. The daina collection now forms part of UNESCO's world heritage. The *dainas* give a remarkably detailed picture of the lives of Latvian country folk: their joys, sorrows and customs; their views of religion and clergy; Germans, Jews, and Russians, even Finns; virtue and sin. They also contain many adages and sage insights.

Hardly any respect was accorded the common people and their cultural heritage. A German publication printed in Rīga in 1746 described the songs like this: "Their music is crude and undeveloped." The Germans considered Latvian a barren and vulgar language which would be incapable of engendering a literature. It reminded them of the "barking of dogs."

J.G. Herder, the German philosopher of the Enlightenment, compared the Germans' behavior toward and effect on the Baltics to those of the *conquistadores* in Peru. The Polish Nobel Prize winner Czeslaw Milosz characterized the people of the Baltic area as Europe's redskins. Garlieb Merkel enlightened his fellow Germans 250 years ago by announcing: "Latvians are humans, too!"

This was not a joke. As recently as at the beginning of the 19th century foreigners viewed Latvians in their writings as poor, dirty, and uneducated, just like humble slaves, "not a spark of life in their eyes." They were stupid or at least acted as if they were.[5]

The peasantry became gradually tied to the land and to the manors. Although nowadays people speak of the "good old Swedish times," feudal serfdom did not disappear even then, although it was not known elsewhere in the Swedish-Finnish great-power area. In the 17th century, Rīga was the Swedish states' largest city and (northern) Latvia was Sweden's breadbasket. In the Great Northern War (1700–1721), Russia conquered Livonia, and later, in 1795, the Duchy of Courland was also annexed to Russia as a province.

Through the centuries, even under Russia, the ruling and privileged class in the Baltic provinces was the German nobility, and their language had a privileged position. A Latvian could become educated only by switching to German, for higher education was in that language.

Latvia has been compared to a small stone being ground between two large millstones. Wars have often rolled over the Baltic lands, and throughout the course of history, the attacks have come more frequently from the west than from the east. It has been calculated that from the 1200's up to 1945, the area of Latvia has been a battlefield for more than 170 years. For every year of war, there have thus been just a little over four full years of peace.

Historian Edgars Andersons has written: "Because of their geographical location, the Baltics have not been able to stay out of European wars, and a declaration of neutrality only whets the attacker's appetite for them."

In the 16th, 17th, and 18th centuries, long wars between Russia, Sweden, and Poland destroyed the Baltic area, and the population fell sharply time and again. The attackers adopted a scorched-earth policy and took civilians as prisoners-of-war and slaves. Violence, hunger, and the plague took a terrible toll.

The Duchy of Courland and Semigallia (1561–1795), nominally subservient to the Polish-Lithuanian Commonwealth, flourished especially in the 1600's during the reign of James (Jacob) Kettler until envious neighbors destroyed it. Sweden delivered the death blow.

The kind of progress and well-being that prevailed under Jacob has seldom been repeated in the Baltics. The duke was ahead of his time in seeing his land as a bridge between the East and the West. The dukedom had factories and shipyards, a large merchant fleet, colonies in Gambia and Tobago and mines in Norway. Serfdom in the Duchy, however, amounted to near slavery for the peasants.

Nor did Napoleon's Grande Armée bring the freedom to the Balts in 1812 they had been led to anticipate by a French propaganda campaign against serfdom. The Latvians made the mistake of rebelling against Russia, the end result of which was the occupying French general's order for all to remain loyal to their former masters.

Serfdom meant that people were sold like cattle or commodities. The peasants were heavily taxed and were forced to labor. By degrees the Czars ended this system from 1817 to 1861; thus slavery in the USA lasted longer than serfdom in the Baltic provinces.

Nevertheless the rule of the barons and the privileged nobility continued. "If the barons were the most privileged of the Czar's subjects, the Letts whom they oppressed were the most wretched," wrote Hubert Butler. "Their very existence was denied, the name of Latvia was abandoned, and the Baltic lands divided into Russian provinces in which racial differences were carefully ignored."[6]

It is often forgotten that among Baltic Germans, the owners of manors with their families numbered only 2,000; the rest were craftsmen, officials, teachers and other "ordinary" people.[7] The German-speaking Lutheran population in the Baltics never exceeded eight percent of the population, but nevertheless it controlled economic, political, religious, and cultural life. In Lithuania and in the southeastern part of Latvia, Latgallia, the upper class was Polish. The only organs of government in which (well-to-do) Latvians could participate were the country district governments and certain municipal councils.

After the "liberation" peasants had the freedom to move, but no land. Land was to be rented or purchased from the *muiža* (manor). The rent was paid in work at a nominal wage. The change was from serfdom to indentured labor. Life in Livonia and Estonia continued in a kind of postfeudal state longer than it did in most of the western European cultural sphere, and a large number of their landless poor lived in rural areas.

The situation in the Baltic provinces differed from that of the Finns, who also belonged to the Russian empire, but who had extensive autonomy in the 19th century. During the time of Czar Alexander II, the position of the Finnish language was strengthened, the economy flourished, Finland got her own money, and a parliament was called into session. Finland remained peaceful, a remote corner of the empire which caused the Czar no worries, while there were rebellions in the Baltics. It was precisely in the Latvian provinces that the

1905 revolution assumed its most violent form and claimed the most victims in the whole Russian empire.

According to some "revisionist" historians, the accounts of "slavery and a 700-hundred-year struggle against the German masters" are a myths or a fantasy with its roots in Heinrich's chronicle, almost the only known historical source that describes those times. To them, "Germany" did not even exist then, and Livonia was owned by the Pope, who governed it with a small group of crusaders.

On the other hand it is, according to the same historians, a great exaggeration to say that the Germans brought culture to Latvia. Before the arrival of the crusaders, the Latvian tribes already knew pottery and masonry, the dyeing of cloth, the forging of metals, the making and use of tools, constructing large buildings, seafaring… They were advanced in the art of war and their soothsayers were famous far and wide. The Baltic peoples were no savages.[8]

The Estonian author Andrei Hvostov writes in his controversial book of a still extant corrosive relationship with the Germans. He believes it to be a myth that the Baltic tribes were non-violent, democratic, and relatively advanced and that it was only others who killed, betrayed, and robbed them. According to Hvostov, the Estonians were awakened in the 1900's, molded into a nation, and a history was created for them based on fomenting hatred against the Germans. According to him, the time has now come to make peace. He finds it ironic that in WWII the Balts found themselves in the same trenches as their German enemies.[9]

Historians Jānis Krēsliņš and Detlef Henning remind us that the leaders of Latvia's and Estonia's national awakening had received a German education and that the language spoken in their homes was often German. Henning writes: "Painting the Germans black, which is still characteristic of many Latvian intellectuals, is on one hand, a consequence of socialist Marxist historiography and on the other, of the petit-bourgeois nationalistic history culture of the Ulmanis era."[10]

Let us remember that this is a German view.

The director of the Rundāle Castle museum, researcher Imants Lancmanis speaks of the Baltic Germans' tragedy: their lives were difficult and full of worry, they could seldom be happy. Lancmanis deplores the fact that the Latvians did not come to understand the lords of the manors, but considered them strange and laughable, "and did not see their human side." According to Lancmanis, the Latvians envied them and in 1905, during WW I, and during the land reform of 1920, treated them so mercilessly that they left the country embittered and brooding on revenge. More recently their descendants

Picture 9. A rarity in the countryside, where the decaying concrete colossi of the kolkhoz is typical: a well-preserved and cared-for old Latvian farmhouse. Jukka Rislakki, June 2007.

– according to Lancmanis, extraordinarily likable people – have been received with open arms. The Latvian *diaspora*, those Latvians who fled the country after the last war, have still not got over their feelings of hatred, he claims.[11]

The revolution of 1905–1906 was both a popular uprising and a national revolution. The kindling was socialist agitation rather than poverty, for the Latvians were then living better than ever before. The rebellion was directed not only at the German manor lords, but also at the rule of the Czar, against russification, and all forms of oppression and exploitation. Its extremism and violence were learned largely from the radicalism of the Russian opposition.[12]

The outburst of rage, the unsuccessful rebellion, was severely avenged by Russia. "The Latvians have gone crazy," wrote the Czar to his mother. In the rebellion and its aftermath Latvia lost 15,000 residents who either emigrated or were murdered, executed, or exiled. Manors, castles, churches, and farms were burned, cultural treasures and irreplaceable archives and libraries were robbed and destroyed. It was a prelude to this country's trials and population losses of the 20th century. As early as 1910 the plan was born in Russia to direct such a flood of migration from the interior of Russia to the Latvian provinces that Latvians would become a minority there. In fact this was accomplished a half-century later.[13]

National Awakening

Modern, as opposed to traditional indigenous, Latvian culture, has its roots largely in eighteenth and nineteenth century German bourgeois culture. Latvians became conscious not only of their common language and cultural bonds, but also of their status as an economically and culturally oppressed majority in their own country. Squeezed between the Baltic German upper crust and the Russian bureaucracy, they slowly became a third, ever more insistent and persistent, presence.

The national awakening in Latvia began after the mid-1800's, just as in Estonia and Finland, and took its cue from German national romanticism. It was during the awakening that a golden age began for literature, journalism, art and music, and when a Latvian intelligentsia was born. This was an astonishing ascent; only a little earlier had foreign observers had asked if Latvians were people at all.

Neither the German ruling class nor the Russian administration wanted to see a strong, independently-minded national force in their midst.[14] The Young Latvian nationalist movement declared that Latvians must be educated and prosperous in order to compete with the Germans and Russians.

The Baltic Germans were especially loyal subordinates of the Czar, and they had an important position in Russia's diplomatic service, its army, its government, and its educational system. They modernized and Europeanized the empire. Because of their sense of superiority and their powerful class consciousness, they did not integrate and did not voluntarily surrender their privileges. The opposite was true for the Swedish-speaking minority in Finland.

Because of widespread dissatisfaction, the Czar sent an investigative commission to Livonia and Courland in the 1880's. It received tens of thousands of letters of complaint, especially from the rural poor, demanding limitations on the rights of manor lords, land for the landless, the reduction of land rents, schools, and rights for the language of the people. Alexander III responded by announcing a policy of russification in Latvian and Estonian areas, so as to bind the population more closely to Russia. At first the Estonians and Latvians did not hinder the progress of russification; the Baltic German landowner was a common enemy.

Russian took the place of German as the official language. The teaching of foreign languages and Latvian ceased, and Russian became a compulsory subject. Compulsory military service was extended to the Baltic countries. Religious imperialism spread – the people were pressured to join the Orthodox Church.[15]

Independence – Against All Odds

The idea of the country's independence was born in Latvian social democratic circles at the start of the 1900's, but at that time their demands for democracy and autonomy bore no fruit. For years during World War I the Baltic lands became a battleground for the great powers. At the right moment the three Baltic countries – Estonia was the first – dared and were able to seize the opportunity, using the collapse of dynasties and the weakness of Russia and Germany to their advantage. The impossible became possible and like many other small states at the time they fought and gained independence. Outside observers, however, for the most part, did not predict that their independence would last.

Even after the collapse of the German and the Russian empires, the West found it quite fitting that German troops remain in Latvia. The Western Allies were above all interested in stemming the tide of Communism in Russia, preserving the Russian empire intact, and protecting their financial interests and investments without getting directly involved.

Even to many Latvians, independence came as a surprise. Some "dissident historians" still claim that in fact it was unfortunate that such a weak country became independent. In a book published by the University of California at Berkeley, Stephen Dunn, an American historian who uses primarily Russian sources, affirms that the Baltic nations' becoming independent is "a model example of how and when countries should *not* do so." According to Dunn, Baltic culture before World War I cannot be investigated "because of a paucity of sources." This brings to mind what *The New Yorker* wrote of Lithuania in 1944: "Probably because of its long history of war and oppression, Lithuania hasn't much native literature, music or art."[16]

Judging by his books, the well-known Finnish historian, Professor Matti Klinge, seems to be of the opinion that the small Baltic countries have been some sort of annoying obstacle, a disturbing element, in between the larger ones (Russia, Germany, and Sweden). He writes that in Eastern Europe, "in place of the empires there arose new national states, some larger and some smaller, with all their minority problems and reciprocal antagonisms. *Klein-staaterei.* The distressing triumphal progress of nationalism in place of the old imperial identification." And "the system of small states is a particularly destructive idea."[17]

In the beginning, Kārlis Ulmanis' government did not really have land, people, or power, and there were only a few hundred men in its army. But together the Latvians brought their war for independence to a victorious conclusion, although at first the enemy seemed overpowering.

General Rüdiger von der Goltz, who fought in Latvia in 1919 to extend German power in the Baltics, was horrified that there were plans to give democracy even to "uncivilized, half-Asian Latvians." To him Latvia was an "operetta-like, makeshift state unfit for existence." According to von der Goltz, Latvians were slaves by nature, guileful and treacherous – they cowered but were "always ready to betray." And they were "psychotically hostile to Germans."[18]

A Finnish acquaintance of the General complained that the German government was so unfamiliar with conditions in the East that it "promised a democratic constitution even to the Latvians, which must perforce lead to socialism and probably to bolshevism because of their immaturity and lack of any machinery of state."

A Finnish general who in his day had also fought in Latvia writes in his memoirs that the Latvians were slavishly obsequious. "Centuries of slavery have slashed ugly scars in the faces of the vulgar and made their backs pliable before all whom they view as belonging to the upper class. Their demeanor is repulsive and repugnant." According to him, "Latvian types are gloomy, impoverished, taciturn, shy, and sour-faced."[19]

It is indeed ironic that only a short time before, it was generally believed that a Finno-Ugric people like the Finns could not establish their own state. Few had believed that Finland would become independent. Because the Swedes had "raised the Finns, who belonged to an inferior race, to a higher level and taken care of them", independence from Russia could hardly succeed except under the Swedes' guidance, and that arrangement was not advisable (for in an independent Finland Swedish qualities would retrogress).[20]

In the large neighboring countries, Latvian culture was despised. One Russian politician in the Duma said that if the Latvians were given autonomy "it should also be given to the Samoyeds." Alfred Rosenberg, who was born and had gone to school in the Baltics, wrote: "The *Ostland* nations did not have their own independent cultures, but rather only derivatives of German and Russian culture." During his tenure in Hitler's government, the Germans demonstrated by the use of maps and records from the 1200's that the Baltics belonged to them. The Teutonic Knights and the Baltic baronial system were endlessly invoked by the Nazis, and served as a model for colonization and Germanization of the East.[21]

Although Latvia gained independence from Russia in 1918 through her own efforts, the Latvians often proclaimed during the war for independence and later that it was the war that freed them from the "700-year rule of the [German] barons and manor lords." In the same spirit the Latvian epic, *Lāčplēsis* (*The Bear Slayer*), tells of the battle against the "black knight," that is, the Germans.[22]

World War I was a great tragedy for the Baltic countries. Russia drained them of resources and people. The Germans established concentration camps there and planned to introduce up to a million new settlers in Latvia, the Red and the White terror afflicted the country, local residents became cannon fodder for both sides, and both sides stole from and executed Latvians…

A European State

Despite the enormous losses, Latvia, Lithuania, and Estonia were able to build thriving liberal democratic states in a relatively short time. Land reform created a prosperous farming sector. Exports flourished. Latvia had a sizable army which had demonstrated its desire for independence and its fighting ability in the war for independence.

Latvia was and is in all respects a European state. Its cultural and educational level was exceptionally high when measured by the number of students and books published. Even in rural areas people could read and write already during the 1700's – for this the Germans deserve some credit. The provinces of Livland and Estland had the highest level of education in the Russian Empire: 95 percent of those in Livland and 88 percent of those in Courland were literate at the end of the 1800's. Russia's figures cannot compare with these. Almost all of the Russians called into the army in 1917 were illiterate.

The Baltic countries' foreign policies and alliances failed, and when World War II began, they lacked security guarantees, including any amongst themselves. It was, of course, impossible for these small countries to raise armies which could match the German and Russian war machines. Their trade policy also failed during the era of the first republic: The isolation of Russia and the cooling of relationships with her left Duke Jacob's model of a gateway and transit between East and West a dream which was only to be fulfilled many decades later.

The worst was still to come: during World War II the slaughter of Baltic civilians, the use of soldiers as cannon fodder, and the robbery of natural resources reached a peak. The destruction of the Latvian language and culture was also an objective.

When Hitler's army conquered Rīga in the summer of 1941, it was decided to make it the capital city of *Ostland*, since it had always been such a German city. A guidebook was distributed to the soldiers according to which the Latvians had *kaum eine eigene nennenswerte Literatur und Kunst* (a literature and art of their own scarcely worth mentioning), and the worst of all, of course, was the Jewish effect on the city.[23]

Both occupiers, Germany and the Soviet Union, falsified and distorted the history of Latvia and Latvia's traditional ties to Europe. Both sought to suppress national self-awareness and culture. Use of the word "Latvia", the Latvian flag and other national symbols were discouraged or altogether forbidden. Both Soviet and Nazi ideology treated Latvia and Latvians as historical objects and excluded any notion of Latvian independence or Latvians as sovereign subjects of history. Latvia was separated from the humanistic cultural foundations of Western civilization. Yet part of the population, some in Latvia and some who had found refuge abroad, nevertheless kept the hope of independence alive through decades. In 1943, *Ostland's* cultural commissioner, Doctor Erich von Stritzky, wrote a memorandum on the research into and teaching of history in occupied Latvia. He taught that the Latvians had glorified their history and had actually fabricated a history for themselves, in which they had an important role. The doctor emphasized the significance of Germany in the history of Latvia throughout the centuries, asserting that the Germans had always defended the Latvians against the East and linked the country to the Western world. The Latvians' "two-facedness" and false assumptions had brought tragedy on them, but once again Germany had liberated the country.[24]

On the other hand, the November 1942 report of the German Ministry of Occupied Eastern Provinces on the situation in Ostland states, with a rare insight, that the Baltic peoples were in no way an indifferent mass of oriental-type people, but had in their twenty years of statehood developed and consolidated a thoroughly Central-European Germanic sense of national unity which was even "out of proportion" in some intellectual circles. "From the very outset Latvians have been the main force against the German aspirations for domination in the Baltic area."[25]

The fate of all Europe has often been decided here on the banks of the Baltic rivers, as the Latvian historian and diplomat, Arnolds Spekke has testified. He wrote, as I mentioned before, that the conquerors who were forced to give up Latvia often resorted, in their fury, to scorched earth tactics.[26] An acute observation, to which one may add that not only the land but the people's mind set and world picture have been left in ruins.

At the end of the 1980's, the Latvians demonstrated decisively to the world that nothing less than independence would satisfy them. The outside world, and to a large extent the Western world, did not give them full support even then. One should not "rock the boat" in the era of Gorbachev; there were fears of a violent break-up of the Soviet Union.[27]

The ingrained suspicion of the outer world has survived; Latvia has too often been left alone, and too often the great powers have settled matters behind her back – not the least being Germany and Russia. That was why the Latvians were so eager to become EU and NATO members in the early 2000's.

In her Independence Day speech of 1999, President Vaira Vīķe-Freiberga said: "Latvia is not the waiting room of a station. Latvia is not a corridor one walks through. Latvia is a country with its own rich traditions."

That same year, shortly after having been elected, the president was interviewed on BBC television, where in response to the interviewer's accusation that Latvians were Nazi-minded and violated human rights, she had this to say on the Germans', Russians' and Latvians' relationships:

"Did you know how they (the Latvians) were treated? They had to listen to abuse constantly. The Soviet army came with its tanks in 1940; they shot, arrested, and deported people who had a profession and property in independent Latvia. They were told: 'Nothing is satisfactory here! You don't know how to live! We'll teach you!' " Then the Germans came with their weapons, their organizations, and their theories, and announced: 'You can't do anything!' And in turn they shot people. ... Then the Russians came again – and shot those who had worked with the Germans. And now, when the Soviet Union has collapsed, and there are again people who say, "We are accused of working with the communists. But what could we do? We had to live, and we had no alternative."[28]

Addressing Baltic friends in 1991 just after the decision of their countries to declare independence, Russian journalist Lev Anninsky wrote:

"You're not rejecting Tolstoy or Pushkin, not the great Russian culture, not even modern Russian culture, however far it may be from the classical tradition. You're rejecting our boorishness, our vulgarity, our brashness, our way of doing everything *en masse*, all together – or more often, all together doing nothing. You're horrified by the migrant workers flooding into your countries: those towns with standard, nondescript five-storey apartment blocks, another five-storey mast on the roof, with their windows that get smashed on holidays, with their dented fences, with their barracks mentality that eats into people's souls. To your mind, these are the Russians, and they block out Pushkin and Tolstoy.[29]

4

Did the Latvian Reds help Lenin seize power in Russia?
Did they help to murder the Russian royal family?

As the Introduction has made clear, the notion that the Latvians were the best Communist enforcers and executioners is at least partly a Nazi stereotype, but they certainly played a role in the Communist victory. Alexander Solzhenitsyn wrote in his book, *Gulag Archipelago*: "I like the Estonians and the Lithuanians, but not the Latvians. When all is said and done, they started it all."

Ambassador Viktor Kalyuzhny said in a newspaper interview in 2006, in answer to a question about Russian responsibility for Stalinist crimes in Latvia: "I too could blame the Latvians for what they did in Russia after the October revolution, but I won't stoop to that."[1] In another interview, the ambassador also said that mainly "Latvians and Jews were behind the atrocities of the Cheka secret police – so why were Russians always blamed for them?"[2]

There is some truth to claims that many Latvians were important early supporters of Lenin's revolution – before anyone knew what horrors lay ahead. Particularly in Russia, the reputation of the Latvians has gone through many phases and changes. The Czarist government considered them unruly and thankless troublemakers, and early Soviet Russia viewed them as cats-paws of the Western imperialists. After the takeover it was "commonly known" in the Soviet Union that they had a Germanic mentality and that they lived in the Soviet Union's most suspect, almost "European" republic. During the time of perestroika in the 1980's, the Latvians were accused of being supporters of Lenin and the Bolsheviks, who had brought a curse lasting seventy years upon the Russians. Now in the new Russia, publicity presents them as the epitome of fascism and racism; the common derogatory name Russians call Latvians is *gansi*, (from the name Hans), which attempts to equate them with the Nazis. On the other hand, those who yearn for the era of Russia's greatness accuse the

Latvians and other Baltic peoples of breaking up the Soviet Union. Russians have always been envious and suspicious of the Latvians: how could such a small republic with no natural resources have managed to do so well?[3]

Branding opponents as fascists is jargon from the Soviet era. The Carnegie Center researcher, Dmitri Trenin, said recently in Moscow that Russians regard the Baltic peoples more and more as followers of Hitler. "And one cannot devise a worse image for people."[4]

Earlier, Latvia was considered a revolutionary country, and to their critics the vaunted Latvian riflemen or *strelki (streļķi)* were "Lenin's landsknechts" (mercenary soldiers). Along with the Jews and Chinese, Latvians came to be blamed wholly for the Russian revolution In recent years it was said: "The Latvians and Chinese have betrayed and stolen Russia."[5]

It has also been said that in 1940 Latvia was occupied by precisely that Bolshevik power which the Latvians themselves had helped to set up in Russia, and that was justice, for it was Russians who suffered most under the Soviet regime. According to the polls, over half of the Russians think so.

The Social Democratic party was the most significant political force in Latvia even before independence – as a matter of fact, it was the largest of its kind in the Russian empire – and here too the Bolshevik wing got the upper hand. Lenin and the Bolshevists promised independence, Kerensky and the White generals did not, and therefore many Latvians decided to support Lenin – even with gun in hand.

In the Russian elections of 1917, in the Latvian part of Livland (Livonia), which Germany had not yet occupied, the leftists won a clear victory. According to researchers, in these last elections before the October Revolution, voter support in Latvia for the Social Democrats (which included Lenin's wing at the time) was larger than anywhere else in the Russian empire – 72 percent voted for them in the rural areas of Livland, and in all, 57.8 percent when the cities were included.[6] Beginning in the autumn of 1917 Latvian Livland experienced a brief dictatorship of the proletariat, which some historians view as the first Latvian state.

The German historian Detlef Henning writes that upon this single – in his opinion wrongly interpreted – result of an election, Latvians have been generally branded as extreme leftists.[7] This interpretation had horrible consequences when the White terror began to reap a harvest in the Latvian areas taken by the Germans in 1919. Henning testifies that the same kind of myth about the majority of Latvians supporting and collaborating with the Nazis became popular after World War II on the grounds that some hundreds of Latvians took part in the bloody deeds of the German SS and SD. Both of these claims are repeated when one wants to affirm the extremism of Latvians, their supposed anti-democratic leanings and nonconformity with European values.

As Germany advanced in the Baltics at the end of 1917, the Latvian rifle regiments in the Russian army withdrew to Petrograd (St. Petersburg). They were the best-organized military force in all Russia, comparable to the Red Finnish military school students in St. Petersburg. In addition, Lenin's personal bodyguard was made up of Latvian volunteers.

Lenin is said to have thanked Latvian revolutionaries earlier, and said that they were well suited for bank robberies and guerrilla strikes because they were fiercer and more determined than others. "Let their achievements be an inspiration and an example to all social democratic workers throughout Russia!" In the spring of 1900, Lenin had visited Rīga secretly to establish ties with the Latvians. In 1905, he developed an enthusiasm for Latvian fighting tactics and in the following year he presented the "proposal for a tactical program" for his party. In February of 1906, a group of Latvian revolutionaries robbed the Russian State Bank office in Helsinki. A number of people were killed and wounded in the robbery.[8]

In Moscow during the summer of 1918, Latvian soldiers may possibly have saved Soviet power when they were rushed from the countryside to put down an opposition rebellion. In all, 8,000–9,000 Latvians joined the Red Guard in Russia. The Latvian Red Riflemen believed that only a Bolshevik victory would free Latvia.[9]

The Role of the Red Latvians

The Irish Times wrote in March 2006 "another aspect of Latvia's past is frequently ignored" [in addition to their helping the Nazis during the war]. The newspaper borrowed from Evan Mawdsley, who in his book on the Russian civil war wrote: "The saviors of Soviet power in Moscow, and perhaps in the country as a whole, were the Latvian Riflemen." Without these Latvians there might never have been a Soviet Union, the paper concluded. Frank Gordon writes that the Latvian regiment guarding Moscow was the Bolsheviks' only trustworthy support and saved their rule from almost certain destruction.[10]

Ilgvars Butulis writes that the Red Latvians' role has been exaggerated – so small a group could not have decided the fate of all Russia. He is of the opinion that it is only an unproven hypothesis that the monarchy would have returned without them and that Latvia would not then have been able to preserve its independence.[11]

On the other hand, Latvian historians from the Soviet period lead us to understand that Latvians saved Lenin's rule.[12] However, historian Vairis

Reinholds says that the conclusion according to which the Bolsheviks would not have won in Russia without the Latvian *strelki* is a myth created by Latvian communists. During the civil war there were about a million soldiers in the Red Army, and among them only one division's strength of Latvian soldiers.

We know, however, that coups are decided not by the total size of the army but by the troops at the site of the coup. When both sides have troops on location (as they did in Moscow), fighting spirit, discipline, and training are often more important than numbers.

Reinholds asserts that the myth of Red Latvians has been taken into the arsenal of the "Great Russia chauvinists."[13] Soviet rule approved this myth and spread it effectively. When a museum was built in Rīga during the Soviet years, it was named *Sarkano strēlnieku muzejs*, Museum of the Red Riflemen. The statue still standing in front of it represents Red soldiers.

In 1994 a historian wrote in the newspaper *Latviešu strēlnieks* that these Latvian Petrograd troops have been unjustly blamed for the dispersion of the Russian Constituent Assembly. As a matter of fact they remained in their barracks in January of 1918, when soldiers were firing into a crowd of demonstrators.[14] As has been stated above, Alfred Rosenberg claimed in his 1929 book that the Latvian Reds shot the strikers "with the greatest joy."

General Rudolfs Bangerskis writes that some of the Latvians' "atrocities" are propaganda. Historian Jānis Krēsliņš affirms that too much brutality has been ascribed to the Latvians, because in Russia other foreigners who supported communism were quite generally called Latvians, among them Austro-Hungarian prisoners of war.[15] Latvians were indeed harsh when need be, but mainly toward thieves and deserters.

There is no denying that Latvian Rifles were tough, battle-hardened, fierce fighters. They have occasionally been accused of brutality and atrocities during the Civil War, but no archival evidence has come to light that would support this charge. Latvian historians conjecture that this is a myth arising later, which is not unusual in Russian history writing.

At the Mäntyharju front of the Finnish civil war in February 1918 Red Latvians took "White" prisoners but refused to help the Finnish Reds after seeing how the latter immediately shot the prisoners. In May 1918 in Moscow 202 Latvian soldiers were fired from the Red Army for not obeying orders and for refusing to fight the Finnish white guards in the fortress of Ino.[16]

Still, on the Latvian president's first state visit to Finland in 1926, one of the Latvian officers accompanying him sensed that all was not well: "Patriotic Finns will not easily forget the role played by the Red sharpshooters in Russia, and there is a certain coldness in the relationship of the soldiers."

Couldn't Finland or Poland also be partly blamed, just as the Latvians are, for the victory of bolshevism? Both countries knew that the White generals, having won, would not approve any other kind of state but an undivided Russia, to which Finland, Poland, and the Baltic countries would belong. So it was in vain that General C. G. E. Mannerheim in 1919 recommended to the Finnish government the capture of Petrograd from the Bolsheviks. Lenin's government had, after all, acknowledged Finnish independence at the end of 1918. Mannerheim wrote in his memoirs: "The Polish statesman's [Josef Pilsudski's] reasoning was understandable, and the chief cause of the defeat of the White Russians was [their commander] General [Anton] Denikin and his advisors."[17]

The Latvian colonel Jukums Vācietis, who led the *strelki* away from the path of the Germans, writes in his memoirs: "We Latvians must support any party in Russia which supports our independence and sovereignty. And that is the Bolshevik party. The other Russian parties did not want to hear of independence for the small nations."

When Russia's old army was demobilized in the spring of 1918, those who wished to were allowed to become civilians. Vācietis, however, succeeded in getting his Latvian regiment reorganized immediately after the general demobilization and joined the newly established Red Army as its first organized fighting unit, the heart of the new army.[18]

Vācietis was for a short time at the start of 1918 the first commander of the Red Army. Stalin had him executed in 1938, like many other *strelki* who remained in the Soviet Union. The commander of the Soviet Air Force Alksnis was also a Latvian. Many other Latvians served Soviet Russia as ministers, high-ranking officers, political officers, and in leading posts in the secret police Cheka. Jēkabs Peters was the second-in-command to the head of the secret police, Feliks Dzerzhinsky. Jānis Bērziņš (Pēteris Ķuzis), also executed in the 1930's, was the Soviet Union's military intelligence (GRU) chief.

Some Latvians have a tendency to blame the Russians for all the evils they have experienced. It would surely be well to remember that Russians too suffered during the Stalinist era, and that in the ranks of the rulers and oppressors there were many others besides Russians – from Georgians all the way to Latvians.[19]

In April of 1918, Lev Trotsky informed the Politburo that percentage-wise, the largest groups among the Cheka employees were the Latvians and the Jews. In the autumn of 1918 there were 781 people involved in the chief Cheka apparatus, of which 35.6 percent were Latvians. Of the Cheka commissars, over half were Latvian. In 1921 of the Cheka's 5000 employees, 1,770 were Latvians.[20] In

Russia after the revolution, the quip was: "The Soviets stand on three props: Latvian bayonets, Jewish brains and Russian stupidity."

In the Russian October revolution and the civil war, Latvians fought on both sides, the White and the Red, and for this reason: there was no going home for the refugees. Youngsters living in poverty and hunger were lured into becoming soldiers, who at least got something to eat. On the side of the Whites, in the troops of Yudenich, Denikin, and Kolchak, some 9,500 Latvians served, many of whom were not volunteers. The Latvians were treated badly by the White Guard: if Red Army men were taken prisoner, only the Bolsheviks and Latvians were shot immediately. The German general von der Goltz considered almost all Latvians to be Reds, and executed Latvians who tried to desert the Reds and join his ranks.

Historian Uldis Ģērmanis has ascertained the following: the Latvian *strelki* were not communists – to be more precise, some 90 percent of them were not party members – nor did most of them fight for Soviet power but for a free Latvia. The "Red" Latvian soldiers were more interested in breaking up the Russian empire than in world revolution. They were nationalists.

"We travelled the bloody road of battle from Moscow to Courland chiefly for our country's sake, with only our conscience to spur us on," wrote one old officer in *Padomju Jaunatne* (Soviet Youth) in 1989. "During all the long years at the front, we never stopped thinking of Latvia."[21]

There are at least two sides on every issue in Latvia. Let the fate of one family stand as a reminder of how the people were torn apart: Arvids Pelše is buried in the Kremlin walls; he was a Latvian communist who had risen to a high position in the Soviet Union. His brother Julius, on the other hand, was the chairman of the New York Latvian Lutheran congregation.

Solzhenitsyn wrote in the *Gulag Archipelago*: "Back in the twenties all the jailers were Latvians from the Latvian Red Army units and others, and the food was all handed out by strapping Latvian women."[22] The director of the Siberian Kolyma camp in the 1920's was the Latvian Eduard Berzins, but he treated the prisoners "too well" in order to keep them in condition to work effectively. He wound up being executed. Apparently the first Soviet commandant in occupied Berlin, Lieutenant-General Nikolai Berzarins, who may have been of Latvian origin, was also "too humane." According to rumors, his death in an automobile accident was arranged by the Soviet counter-espionage agency.[23]

Nor did other Latvians receive thanks for their role. Stalin's persecutions of 1937–1938 were also directed at Latvians who remained in the Soviet Union. Tens of thousands were imprisoned, thousands were executed, and thousands perished in the Gulag.[24]

The peace treaty of 1920 allowed World War I evacuees, refugees, soldiers, and farmers to return to Latvia. About 216,000 former residents of the territory of Latvia were repatriated. According to the Soviet census of December 1926, 151,410 ethnic Latvians were still living in the Soviet Union. Some did not want to return, the Soviets did not allow many to leave, and some the Latvian government would not admit. Of those who stayed more than 15 percent were later liquidated in the Stalinist repression.[25]

Aivars Stranga seems to understand the hatred directed at the Soviet Latvians at the end of the 1930's. "To a great extent it can be said that the Latvian communists brought on themselves the events of 1937 by their blind and fanatical service to Lenin and Stalin."[26] The Russian people "did not love them" because of the brutality they had shown in the civil war and in the secret police, and the fate of these victims aroused no sympathy. Perhaps "only" 5,000 were executed then in Stalin's persecutions, not as many as had been thought, Stranga writes.

Latvians received some benefit from their legendary military reputation in Russia. In 1940–41, Stalin recalled that the Latvians were good soldiers, and they also did their best to remind him of the *strelkis'* loyalty and heroic deeds two decades earlier. Perhaps partly owing to that, Stalin allowed part of the army of Latvia to remain intact as units in the Baltic military region and did not scatter them around the Soviet Union, as was originally recommended.

In their popular works, Eduard Radzinski and Modris Eksteins have recently resurrected the old myth that the Latvians had murdered Czar Nicholas II and his family in Yekaterinburg in 1918, or that they had at least constituted the majority of the execution squad (seven Latvians, four Russians).

Historians, however, had long ago shown that on the published list of the execution squad no "Latvian" name is to be found, but instead one Hungarian – Imre Nagy. In fact, among those that were killed with the Czar and his family was one Latvian – the servant Aloizs Lauris Trūps[27]

5

Was Latvia granted independence as a present? Was the War of Independence an exaggerated myth? Was it a series of minor skirmishes that the Latvians were able to win with foreign help?

Even some Latvians think so. In November of 2003, the newspaper *Rīgas Balss* published a long article in which it asserted that the army's November 11th holiday marks a "mythical victory," merely a "fairy tale about a victory," in which, as a matter of fact, a defeat was concealed.[1] The newspaper complained that school children are forced to celebrate this ridiculous holiday, which is based on a misunderstanding of history. Ridiculous or not, on that day in November the Latvians commemorate their victory over the German-Russian army of Bermondt at the gates of Rīga in 1919, an army that bought together the interests of the Baltic barons and the Russian aristocracy.

According to the newspaper, the Latvians themselves made certain of their fate – the occupation of 1940 – by resisting the Bermondt army with the support of the Allies, and "forcing" it to fight. The writer conjectures that the attacker was merely "scaring" the Latvians, and that as a matter of fact, it considered the destruction of the Russian Bolsheviks its primary objective, which the Latvians should have supported. Further, according to the article, the attackers were so "demoralized" that it was easy for the Latvians to win ("no longer a serious battle") and that therefore this was no cause for celebration.

Still further we read that the state and the government that Kārlis Ulmanis had established were so weak that one is forced to ask how he finally managed to succeed. "On the other hand, one needs to ask if he did succeed at all – wasn't the catastrophe of 1940 made inevitable by the events of 1918–1919?"

Some claim that Latvian independence was a "catastrophe" and that the country deserved little credit for it. In the autumn of 2004, the Latvian historian Āris Puriņš asserted that independence was a misfortune and that there were many people who did not want it. A "mass psychosis" had swept the Latvians along with it. Independence was an "error – an error imposed from without. How did the first independence end? In a terrible tragedy. Have you counted the number of corpses? Where are the best of the Latvians? And who lives in Latvia now?"[2]

Puriņš is of the opinion that Latvia ought not to have fought against the monarchist occupation in 1919 because if the monarchists had won in Russia, Latvia would have received a "model autonomous status."

In my opinion this is wishful thinking. Puriņš might also be informed that independent Latvia, be it authoritarian or democratic, has never started a single war, bloodbath, or "tragedy," neither at home nor abroad. It is the enemies of freedom who have always been guilty of them. For the most part, Latvia has defended herself if she has been attacked. Latvia was certainly as ready for independence as any other small European country born in the wake of the Great War. It had its own flourishing culture, as well as its own army, and furthermore, its economy soon prospered.

One might ask the writer of the article mentioned at the start of this chapter, who seems to be an admirer of "alternate history," why it was an error to be on the side of the Allies, i.e. the winners, and not on the side of the Germans or losers? And would the "militarily incompetent" and motley army of Bermondt have been able to overthrow the Bolshevik state if it had been permitted to march through Latvia to the east in November – without winter equipment? What would have happened to Latvia then if the Red Army had counterattacked? Or if the Germans had won? In either case, Latvia would at best have become the vassal of a great power. And further: what would have happened to Rīga if Bermondt had conquered it? "Serious battle" or not, Bermondt's army was nevertheless stronger than the Latvians'. And it was truly "demoralized" – it broke many of the rules of war.

The Long and Winding Road

What kind of war was it?

The Latvian War of Independence, 1918–1920, was more truly a war for independence against foreign occupation than the Finnish civil war of 1918 – a war between brothers, where Finnish Reds and Whites killed one another. The former was a long and confused struggle. For example, in the spring of 1919, Latvia had three governments at the same time: the provisional Latvian government led by Ulmanis, the Bolshevik government supported by Lenin, and Andrievs Niedra's puppet government, supported by German bayonets. The Red and White terrors were raging and many civilians were killed. The following is a brief summary.

During World War I, Russia mobilized 120,000 to 150,000 soldiers in Latvia, proportionally a larger number than in Mother Russia. In addition, over 800,000 residents were evacuated or became refugees elsewhere in the Russian empire.[3] Factory machinery and all else of value were skipped from Rīga to Russia.

In the hopeless situation of 1915, when Germany had conquered Courland, the moment was propitious for a generous gesture from Nikolai II. He agreed to grant a request hitherto persistently refused; henceforward the Latvians might serve under their own officers as a separate Latvian unit. They were known by the name of *strēlnieki* or riflemen, in Russian *strelki*. These volunteer battalions, later regiments, were thrown into battle at the worst places at the front. Their fighting made a great impression on the Russians (and Germans). Latvians demonstrated a priori their loyalty and support for the Russian state, in the hope that the Russian authorities would show them appreciation. Russia, however, did not promise reforms, not to mention autonomy. Nevertheless the men considered themselves to be fighting for Latvia.[4]

Because of the incompetence and betrayal by Russia's high command and the provisional government, the sentiment in Latvia turned against the Russians. Their blood had been shed in vain. Tens of thousands of Latvians had died, been wounded, or became prisoners of war.

The German Kaiser had great plans in store for Latvia (to settle over a million refugees in Courland), and the same was true of Lenin's Bolsheviks (Latvia was to be a bridgehead for world revolution) and of Russia's White armies (Latvia would return to be a part of monarchical Russia still with no promises of autonomy). The Entente, the Allies, had their own plans (independent Baltic countries would be the *cordon sanitaire*, a safety zone and advance guard, which would separate Soviet Russia from the West).

By the Treaty of Brest-Litovsk Soviet Russia abandoned Latvia to Germany and after the armistice the Allies allowed the Germans to remain there.

Both Woodrow Wilson and V. I. Lenin proclaimed the principle of national self-determination in 1917–1918, and the Baltic peoples took it seriously. The possibility of Baltic countries becoming independent lasted for only a short time – less than 18 months – from the autumn of 1917 until the spring of 1919.[5] The idea of complete separation from Russia was an issue that did not emerge in Latvia until the turn of the years 1917/1918. Until that time the establishment of autonomy within the framework of a federated democratic Russia was the maximum goal of almost all Latvian and Estonian political leaders.[6]

In the autumn of 1918, with the collapse of the Kaiser's Germany, Baltic Germans, who hated seeing their traditional ruling position in Latvia and Estonia disappear, established their own army or national guard, *Baltische Landeswehr*. A broadly based provisional Latvian government headed by Ulmanis declared the country independent in Rīga on November 18th, but the city was under the control of that government for only a short time. Elections could not be organized in a time of war and occupation. Nation building had to start from scratch. The government had many enemies, and the support of its own people and even its soldiers was questionable. The most chaotic period in Latvian history began.

The Bolsheviks took advantage of the power vacuum and attacked Latvia in December with a force of ten thousand soldiers, Latvian strelki among them. Latvia's war for independence had begun. The Reds conquered Rīga and moved on to the west until more than three fourths of the country was under their control. They were able to promise more than Ulmanis – above all, land to the landless. Ulmanis had to be careful of what he said because he was temporarily dependent on German support.

The German Iron Division and the Freikorps volunteers joined the Landeswehr. The German General Rüdiger von der Goltz promised his demoralized men farms in Latvia when it was "liberated," i.e. annexed to the German Empire.

The German plans for the Baltic lands differed little from Hitler's plans twenty years later. Several political forces in Germany, all the way from conservatives and liberals to social democrats, were approximately in agreement that the Baltics should be Germanized and colonized; the area would be better off under Germany than under Russia. There were also plans to settle Russian Germans in the Baltic countries and empty them of Jews.[7]

The Latvians began to conquer their own country from the north along with the Estonians and from the west at first with the Germans. The Germans took Rīga from the Reds and executed some 4,500 Latvians during the following weeks; that may well be called a war crime. Before that the Red terror had claimed thousands of victims in Latvia.

Following that, the Germans turned against the Latvian-Estonian troops in Livonia. On Midsummer Day in 1919 the larger German army suffered a defeat in the Battle of Cēsis (Wenden) and began to retreat. The Western powers did not want the total defeat of the Germans in the Baltics. Through their mediation, an armistice was arranged, which the Germans used only as a pause for breath in order to continue the war under better circumstances.

Now the Russian Volunteer Western Army was born, which was commanded by the Russian monarchist, Pavel Bermondt. To the Russian aristocrats Latvia was only a rebellious province, governed by the lower orders. Bermondt named himself Prince Avalov and promoted himself first to colonel and then to general. The actual commander was von der Goltz. The costs of the army were paid by Germany, and most of the soldiers in this "Russian" army were Germans – the same Germans that had constituted the von der Goltz troops. The Germans and the Russians had found each other again; the configuration was to repeat itself later at the expense of the Latvians.

The publicly announced objective of this army was St. Petersburg, but what was most important to Bermondt-Avalov, who hated the Latvians, was the capture of Rīga. The soldiers were promised land in Latvia, which was to become a dukedom. Bermondt tried to turn the course of history backward and re-establish the Russian Czarist regime from Rīga.

Plundering, burning, and murdering, his army of many tens of thousands marched toward the capital city of Latvia. The very followers of Bermondt called themselves "bandits." They got as far as the Daugava River and bombarded Rīga. The Latvians were gripped by a spirit of national unity not seen before nor to be seen again for generations.

The bold counterattack of the outnumbered Latvians, which British and French warships supported in spite of their official neutrality, brought them victory in Rīga on November 11, 1919. Bermondt-Avalov was driven out of Latvia. During this phase, Latvia was for a time officially at war with Germany, too.[8]

East Latvia, Latgale, was still under control of the Red Army. After a month of hard winter fighting, the Latvians, with support of the Polish army and the Baltic German Landeswehr, were victorious. The whole country had been liberated. Disturbances continued on the border, but in August of 1920, peace was concluded with Moscow. Thus Soviet Russia was the first country to recognize Latvia's independence *de jure*. According to the peace treaty, Soviet Russia recognized "the independence and sovereignty of the Latvian State" and renounced forever "all sovereign rights which had belonged to Russia over the Latvian people and territory."

Only at the end of January in 1921, almost two and a half years after becoming independent did Latvia receive *de jure* recognition from foreign powers.[9] In July of that year Latvia was accepted as a member of the League of Nations. The USA did not recognize Latvia until July of 1922. The Western powers did not want to provoke the Russians, nor on the other hand did they believe that new, small states were stable and capable of surviving and acting responsibly toward their neighbors and minorities. And once the Bolsheviks were vanquished and the Russian empire reborn, would it be right that the shores of the Baltic had been wrung from her?

For the first time, Latvia and Estonia received the status of independent states. The third new Baltic republic, Lithuania, had been a large country, a monarchy, during the late Middle Ages but not a nation from then until 1918.

During the Latvian war for independence, the army of barefoot men which started from scratch grew to a fighting force of 76,000 soldiers whom the nation honored. They were not forced to fight, but volunteered. Over 3,000 Latvian soldiers and officers died, and 4,400 were wounded. Many more civilians died than soldiers: in addition to murders and executions, diseases and hunger killed people. In addition, 35,000 Latvians died in World War I fighting against the Germans in Russian units and another 28,000 at least in the Russian civil war mainly on the side of Lenin against the Whites: a total of at least 63,000 – a huge sacrifice for a small nation, and, one may add, a mainly futile sacrifice. When refugees and forcibly displaced people are added to the figures, Latvia lost almost 700,000 residents, most of whom were of working age. The population of the country shrank by 37 percent. Thousands of children remained unborn. In the 1930's in Latvia there were a hundred women to every 86 men, the largest difference ever statistically recorded anywhere.[10]

For some six years (1915–1920), battlefronts had ground their way over Latvia. The destruction was worse there than in any other European country involved in World War I. Only Belgium can be compared to Latvia in material losses, and only Serbia in human losses.[11] About half of Latvia's municipalities were battlegrounds. Every fourth building was destroyed wholly or partially. Ten thousand farms were ruined and almost 30 percent of tilled land was left fallow. Manufacturing disappeared almost completely, and the number of inhabitants in Rīga fell by half.

Victory for Europe

The victory of the Latvians and Estonians meant not only the birth of a free and democratic Latvian state, it may be considered a positive achievement of international significance. At least for a time it made the intrusions of great powers into the Baltic fruitless. The Red Army was driven back across the eastern border; German and Russian monarchists' efforts to renew the rule of empires were thwarted.

Latvia adopted a democratic constitution almost unique in Europe, guaranteeing citizens the full range of rights and freedoms. All residents were entitled to citizenship, regardless of ethnicity.

Minority rights and liberties were granted in a most generous manner – they were among the most comprehensive in the world. Minorities had cultural autonomy and their own schools which were funded by the Latvian government. Women had the right to vote and run for office earlier than in many other European countries. Social legislation was the most modern and progressive in Europe.

After the Russian Civil War and the establishment of Latvia's independence plus the subsequent agrarian reform, aristocratic Russian exiles and Baltic Germans waged an intense anti-Latvian propaganda campaign in Western Europe. One of the damning proofs they submitted was the Latvian flag, almost completely red, "just like the Bolshevik banner," as the British MP's were informed in 1921 by an expert on Latvia. Never mind that the communists' flag is bright red and the flag of Latvia maroon. A prolific polemicist on the subject was the British-born *New York Times* chief reporter Walter Duranty, who first worked in Rīga and then moved on to Russia.[12]

A monarchist victory would have meant the rule of the large landowners and the continuation of misery in the rural areas. Almost 70 percent of Latvia's population lived in those areas, and in turn, 60 percent of these people there were landless, so that land ownership was the key question. The situation was potentially explosive. Ulmanis redeemed his pledge, and independent Latvia took up land reform as its first task, a reform that was the most radical in all of eastern Europe. The barons' lands – most of the land of some 1,300 big estates – were confiscated and divided among 140,000 families.

Latvia became an agricultural country (68 percent of its work force worked in agriculture, forestry, and fishing in 1935, but this sector produced only 35 percent of the national wealth).[13] The economy was typified by many small farms.[14] This change of ownership alleviated the tensions in society and cut the ground from under extreme left- and right-wing support. Agriculture became the foundation of Latvia's export and its economy.[15]

The confiscation of manors and castles without compensation heightened the tension in relationships with the Baltic Germans, in whom anger already smoldered from 1905 and 1919. Many Germans who left the country later swore allegiance to Adolf Hitler. They blamed the Latvian social democrats and the Jews for the wrongs they had suffered. The Baltic Germans have always written more favorably of the Estonians than of the Latvians. Estonia's officers and politicians leaned in Germany's direction by the end of the 1930's. The Baltic Germans saw the Estonians as racially superior to the Latvians by the followers of Hitler.[16]

The previously mentioned Imants Lancmanis complains that very little has been written in Latvia about the tragedy that Latvia inflicted on the Baltic

Germans in 1920. "Half of Latvia was parceled out, lovely lands, beautiful manors," he says. "Land reform is a sacred cow."[17]

Some young historians claim that disappearance of large-scale manufacturing in the cities combined with the transformation of rural laborers into small landowners meant almost "complete loss of the upward and outward mobility" in a society that is necessary for the functioning of a dynamic, modern market economy and liberal democracy. And that the new national elite came to be dominated by civil servants and politicians.[18]

They seem not to realize that manufacture and commerce did revive; Latvia was self-sufficient not only in food but also in most consumer goods. A thriving, educated Latvian middle class developed – and many were children or grandchildren of farmers. Isn't that mobility?[19]

At first Latvia hoped to develop into a transit bridge, but the isolation of the Soviet Union and the chilling of relationships with her thwarted those hopes.

Minorities, the most significant being the Russians and Germans, were a problem. They were granted liberal minority rights, but for the most part, they were not loyal to the Latvian state, nor did they generally support independence. Latvia accepted as citizens all those who desired citizenship and had lived in the country at the start of the Great War, regardless of nationality or religion. Thus in 1925, a full 96.5 percent of the population were already citizens. In the early years in the Parliament, *Saeima*, one could freely speak both Russian and German.

It is interesting to observe that some have also begun to belittle the second struggle for independence in a way that is calculated to weaken the people's self-esteem. I am referring to the establishment of the Popular Front in 1988, the so-called singing revolution, and the 1991 "barricades period" in Rīga when the residents peacefully, by sheer numbers, protected the parliament and other key functions from the Soviet troops. "Only" some half-dozen people died. Some now call it a carnival and a picnic, and explain in addition that it was initiated by the KGB or was directed by it and used to its advantage. Old KGB officers have lately tried to take credit for the fact that Latvia became independent without bloodshed.[20]

6

Why did the Latvians not resist the Soviet army's taking over their country in 1940?
Did the people carry out an anti-bourgeois, anti-fascist revolution, after which Latvia joined the Soviet Union legally, by means of elections?

The people who cast the votes decide nothing. The people who count the votes decide everything.

Stalin

The questions in the above title are often heard and fundamental, and the answers to them have legal consequences even today. The neo-Stalinist interpretation (thus *The Economist's* correspondent Edward Lucas) of history is as follows: "The events of 1940 were in accord with the then prevailing conception of international law."[1]

Viktor Kalyuzhny, the Russian ambassador to Latvia, said in February 2006: "Russia has never conquered Latvia; we have always been its liberators."[2] We Finns may be of a different opinion about liberation, having experienced the Winter War of 1939–1940.[3] Could it be that the diplomat does not know Soviet history? Surely not that – he merely wants to forget the Kremlin principle to cast brutal operations and interventions as initiatives of the countries involved or as requests for help from them.[4] So it was with Finland in 1939, so it was with Latvia in 1940. So it was with Czechoslovakia in 1968 and so it was with Afghanistan in 1979.

The ambassador further declared: "Russia is not legally responsible for the actions of the Soviet Union." She does not consider herself responsible for Stalin's crimes even though she proclaims herself the legal continuation of the

Soviet state. Former President Boris Yeltsin settled the question: when on a visit to Latvia also in 2006 he said that the Soviet Union, not Russia, had occupied Latvia.

First, of course, one must investigate what kind of Latvia Soviet troops entered in 1939–1940 and under what conditions, and secondly: what kind of Latvia joined the Soviet Union and under what circumstances.

Having become independent in 1918, Latvia was for more than 15 years a liberal parliamentary democracy, with the ability to guarantee the welfare of its people and to administer minority rights which were considered exemplary. The centrist Farmers' Union leader Kārlis Ulmanis (1877–1942), who had tirelessly fought for Latvian independence, cut short democratic development. He was energetic and ambitious, and had an obsessive desire for power. As one historian writes, Ulmanis completely dominates the history of Latvia, as both a leader and a legend.[5]

On May 15, 1934, Ulmanis, who was then prime minister for the fifth time, carried out a bloodless coup with the aid of the Army and the Home Guard. There was no opposition to it – neither strikes nor demonstrations. Ulmanis became *Vadonis* (Leader), and concentrated all internal and external political power in his own hands. Political parties were prohibited, the parliament *Saeima* was dissolved, and the press was gagged. Ulmanis' regime was the most authoritarian in the Baltic republics.

The cause of the coup is still argued, as well as whether Ulmanis was a "good" or "bad" ruler.[6] The regime itself was not unusual in the Europe of the time, where democracies were becoming rare. Since Latvia was doing comparatively well, the international economic depression cannot be considered the main cause of Ulmanis' coup.

The coup was directed at both the right and the left. The Communist party had already been banned, and the communists expelled from parliament, along with the radical right, the anti-German and anti-Jewish Thundercross organization (*Pērkoņkrusts*). The Social Democratic party also had a militant paramilitary wing. Ulmanis' greatest concern was undoubtedly that the extreme right was sure to win a victory in the coming election,

The constitution, which Ulmanis suspended, was very, perhaps overly, democratic and gave all the power to the parliament. Afterwards it has been said that the people had been "in the grip of an anti-democratic hysteria," and were tired of political quarrels, of corruption, and of the fragmentation in politics. (In the previous *Saeima* 24 parties and groups had been represented, and there had been 103 electoral lists.) However, voter participation had been particularly high – 80 percent in the election before the coup, which is rare nowadays in democracies.

Ulmanis also appointed himself president in 1936.[7] He promised a new constitution, but it never arrived. Schools were built, the land grew richer, and culture flourished. Ulmanis believed that the best hope for a future national existence was to raise the standard of living and of culture to a high level.

Although the coup seemed at first to have broad support and although Ulmanis developed the country, the people were not unanimously behind him. According to published reports, some 55–65 percent of the people would have supported him at the beginning of 1940.[8] Although the conservative politician and editor Arveds Bergs supported him at first, his later assertion soon became a byword, "Even a good dictatorship is worse than a bad democracy."

Ulmanis had studied in the United States and could be described as an anglophile. Contrary to what has been claimed, he was not an admirer of National Socialism. Mussolini's corporate state capitalist system, on the other hand, appealed to him.

To deal with his opponents, Ulmanis maintained for a short time a prison camp in Liepāja, where for a while there were at most 800 political prisoners, no more than in the democratic Finland of those days. Whether his was a relatively mild dictatorship or an authoritarian government, no one was tortured or executed during the Ulmanis era.[9]

Pravda, choosing to forget the nightmare of the Soviet Gulag, wrote in 2006 that the Latvians have "carried out acts of almost indescribable cruelty in their concentration and extermination camps [during WWII]. Indeed, the Latvians began building concentration camps long before Hitler arrived on the scene – the Fascist dictator Kārlis Ulmanis began building one in 1934."[10]

The watchwords during the Ulmanis era were unity, nationalism, and patriotism.[11] Ulmanis himself set the example, advised and spurred Latvians on, and spoke to them just as if they were a greater and a special people. It has been conjectured that Ulmanis' grandiloquent nationalism and the boost to national self-esteem perhaps helped Latvians to persevere during the horrible trials of the decades to follow.[12]

Ulmanis' objective was a "Latvia for the Latvians" and ethnic Latvians dominated in the economy, the politics, and the military. National minorities, however, were not actually persecuted. Ulmanis did not approve of anti-Semitism, but he did undertake measures to lessen the influence of Jews, Germans, and Russians in manufacture and trade.[13] (There is more on relationship with Jews in the next chapter.)

Picture 10. Among others, the Baltic countries and Poland were divided between the Soviet Union and Gemany by their secret agreements of 1939. The signatures of Stalin and Joachim von Ribbentrop appear on the map. From the collection of the Latvian Museum of the Occupation.

The Soviet Union and the Germans pressured the Baltic countries into non-aggression pacts, but otherwise these countries were left completely to themselves during the 1930's, without any allies. Nothing came of efforts advocating cooperation of the border states in general or of Baltic cooperation in particular. Lithuania and Poland were hostile to each other. Finnish politicians did not want to tie Finland's security to that of the Baltic lands. Latvia and Estonia concluded mutual agreements in 1923, among them a military pact which obligated both of them to consult each other in foreign policy and "undertake to afford each other assistance should either suffer an unprovoked attack." The agreement remained without any practical meaning. When the pact was renewed in 1934, Lithuania joined in its political features. This *Baltic Entente* was never a serious factor in providing stability and security; it was a hindrance rather than a help.

In their day, the Baltic countries counted on the support of the League of Nations and the Western Powers, but they were bitterly disappointed. They did not succeed in obtaining security guarantees from the great powers. Like

Finland's, their policy of neutrality was based on the conflict of interests between Germany and the Soviet Union. At the end of the 1930's, Latvian foreign policy turned more pro-German than pro-Soviet.[14]

"Protected" by the Soviet Union

In March 1939, the Soviet Union announced unilaterally that it was taking the Baltic countries "under its protection" and guaranteeing their independence – whether they wanted that protection or not. Stalin considered it his right to decide which political changes in them were dangerous (for him). The West urged the Baltic countries to accept Stalin's offer. It was not until the autumn of 1939 that serious efforts at negotiation and cooperation between the Baltic countries developed, but by then it was too late. They did not have joint military maneuvers, for example.

It can perhaps be understood that Stalin wanted to assure a protective zone for Russia. But how can one explain the fact that the Russians kept on occupying the Baltic lands 49 years after Nazi Germany had been completely crushed?

Analysts have been critical of Baltic politics, and so have many Balts themselves. After the fact it is easy to say that leaders have made mistakes. But it is difficult to determine where the errors begin, if errors have been made. However, the turning point was the fall of 1939: after that no alternative views are really possible.

The strength of the Latvian army was 20,000 men, and there were weapons and equipment for a reserve of some 130,000 men. The backbone of the defense forces was four infantry divisions. In heavy artillery there were only 24 cannon and ammunition for them to last only one day. Militarily all the Baltic countries together were slightly stronger – at least on paper – than Finland, which mobilized 337,000 soldiers for the Winter War of 1939.[15] Latvia's situation was less advantageous. Finland was a bigger country and harder to invade, and Latvia, unlike Finland, had to be prepared for a war on two fronts.

Although soldiers and home guard units occupied a prominent place in society, one could not call Latvia a particularly military state. In 1938–1939 the defense expenses were 24 percent of the budget, and internal security 7 percent. The figures were similar and even higher in Finland.[16]

In the Soviet army and security forces there were over 1.6 million men in 1938. It had 4,500 planes and some 4,000 tanks. The navy was strong. In 1939, the Politburo decreed that the strength of the peacetime army should be 4,163,000 men, and that goal was already achieved in the summer of 1940.[17]

All of Latvia's war plans were defensive. Moscow, however, reckoned her among potential attackers, and considered her an enemy for almost the entire time between the two world wars and prepared for military action against her.

The leadership of Latvia felt that the country was especially vulnerable in the east, but they did not trust Germany, the other historical enemy, either, or ask her for help, except for last-minute overtures in a desperate situation. The Latvian leadership promised repeatedly that Latvia would fight if attacked.

In August 1939, to everyone's surprise, Germany and the Soviet Union signed a non-aggression (the Molotov-Ribbentrop) pact, a secret clause of which divided Eastern Europe into spheres of influence. Among others, Finland, Estonia, and Latvia were consigned to the Soviet sphere. Hitler would have divided Latvia in half, but Stalin unconditionally wanted the harbors of Ventspils and Liepāja, and got all of Latvia.[18]

World War II was about to begin. The parties to the agreement attacked Poland and divided it. Latvia immediately proclaimed her neutrality in the war at the beginning of September 1939 and mobilized three age groups. A general mobilization was not carried out so as not to provoke Russia.

Now it was time for Finland and the Baltics to pay the bill drawn up on the tables of the two great powers. Estonia's foreign minister was summoned to Moscow at the end of September. The result of the trip was a mutual aid agreement and a secret agreement on military bases in Estonia. Estonia had already decided in advance to surrender.

Latvia received a summons immediately after Estonia. And for all practical purposes, their dice were cast. Both countries were under severe pressure during the negotiations: the Soviet Union concentrated powerful troops on their borders. At the end of September and the beginning of October, there were nearly a half million men supported by heavy equipment ready to attack these countries. In the event that Estonia and Latvia should resist, Marshall Kliment Voroshilov issued an order to attack which contained precise routes to follow and objectives to take.[19] In the Baltic armies there were altogether about 73,000 men.

In the negotiations with Latvia, Stalin made no secret of the fact that Latvia would be attacked if it did not yield. He also revealed what had been secretly agreed. "I tell you frankly, a division of spheres of interest has already taken place. As far as Germany is concerned, we could occupy you."

The Latvian government gave the foreign minister the authority to sign a ten-year agreement in Moscow.[20] Lithuania was the next to yield.

Young Latvian officers would have been ready to fight, but the Latvian leadership considered that resistance would cost the country too dearly: war would destroy most of the people. Poland's example was disheartening: in September 1939, Poland's defense had collapsed in a few weeks. Finland's example did not yet exist: Finland defended herself against the Red Army for 105 days in 1939–1940 and preserved her independence.

Ulmanis' censorship prevented the release of information and free discussion of the event. He alone made the decisions. According to Ulmanis, a "friendly army" was coming into Latvia to establish bases there.

Stalin made a small concession – "only" 25,000 Red Army ground and air force soldiers would come to Latvia "for the time the war went on." The agreement did not mention that in addition a naval force of 5,000 men would be sent to Latvian ports. Further auxiliary forces of different kinds also entered the country. Even not counting the Navy, the Red Army contingents stationed in Latvia exceeded the Latvian army both in numbers and armaments. [21]

According to histories written during the Soviet era, the negotiations were carried on "in a friendly atmosphere;" the agreement "gave both participants fully equal rights," and it was not supposed to "affect the sovereign rights" of the parties. In addition, "the working people of the Baltics had long demanded" such agreements, and they arose as "the result of such pressure," but "reactionary governments flagrantly violated them." [22]

To many it was already clear that an occupation of the Baltic States was being prepared for. Some historians, however, conjecture that Finland's resistance and the Winter War forced Moscow to postpone the occupation to the following summer. During the Winter War there were certain plans in Latvia to attack the Soviet military bases, and also Finland put feelers out: would Latvia be ready to fight? [23]

Ulmanis presented everything that happened as a victory for Latvia: peace had been preserved; relationships with the eastern neighbor were good; the agreements had to be fulfilled conscientiously and provocations were to be avoided. Cooperation among the Baltic countries revived somewhat, and Moscow became very suspicious: "plots" were being hatched behind her back.

Thus the Winter War upset the plans, but in April 1940 preparations for the occupation of the Baltic States began anew. In June, when the world's attention was fixed on Paris, which Hitler had just conquered, the Soviet Union occupied the Baltic lands. Mighty armed forces were concentrated on the borders and no effort was made to conceal their presence. In all there were in readiness, counting the troops already on bases in the Baltic countries, 450,000 Soviet soldiers, 8,000 artillery pieces and mortars, over 3,000 tanks and armored cars, and 2,600 aircraft. [24] The Soviet Union could not afford another fiasco like the one in Finland.

Picture 11. In the summer of 1940 the Communist paper Cīņa published a drawing of a two-faced Latvian sharpening a dagger while sitting opposite a kindly Molotov at a conference table.

Picture 12. "Vote for the Latvian Working People's Block!" In the election organized by the Soviet occupiers in the summer of 1940, the Worker's list was the only one allowed and voting was practically mandatory.
Diena 05.10.2002.

With the *divide et impera* tactics she had already employed the previous autumn, the Soviet Union began to pick off the Baltic countries. In the fall she began with Estonia, where the connection with Finland was broken off; now she shifted her attention to Lithuania, so that the land connection with Germany would be cut. Lithuania was handed an ultimatum in Moscow: she was immediately to form a government friendly to the Soviet Union and to admit into the country the "necessary number of soldiers." Lithuania yielded.

Now Latvia had a common, threatened border with the Soviets (including the weakly defended seashore) of more than 1,500 kilometers, in addition to which she had Soviet bases within the country. The Latvian government and the military leadership unanimously judged the situation to be hopeless. The army would have been ready to fight, but no mobilization was declared.

On the 16th of June, a day after Lithuania, Latvia received her ultimatum, which was to be answered by the evening.[25] According to it, "Latvia not only had failed to break off the military alliance with Estonia, an alliance which was anti-Soviet, but had actually broadened it to include Lithuania and was also trying to draw Finland into it."[26] Latvia was to form a new government and the "necessary number" of Soviet forces was immediately and without interference to be admitted into the most important centers in Latvia.

The accusations were false, but explanations were of no avail. Latvia yielded and powerful armored units already entered Rīga on the following day. Some 100,000 Soviet troops entered the land.[27]

Due to the occupation, Moscow can be viewed as having violated international obligations, among them the agreements made with Latvia – the peace agreement (1920) and the non-aggression pact (1932).

However, not everyone objected to the arrival of the tanks. Many workers and leftists, who had suffered during the Ulmanis era, were pleased at first – they thought the change was to their advantage. Many Jews regarded it in the same way; they believed that only the Red Army could save them from Hitler's claws.[28]

Ulmanis said that everything had happened for the best, both for the state and the people; the Red Army arrived with the knowledge and approval of the government; the Soviet Union was a friendly country. The soldiers were to be received in a friendly manner. "I'll stay at my post, you stay in yours," was the president's message to the people in a radio speech. He did not even sanction anyone's flight.[29]

The Latvian government and the military leadership forbade every action which might provoke the Soviet troops. Officers who refused to obey were punished and dismissed from the service.[30]

The conquest of Latvia was for all intents and purposes bloodless. Deputy Foreign Minister Andrei Vyshinski arrived immediately in Rīga to organize things. As chief prosecutor, he had staged political show trials in the Soviet Union in 1937–1938, where one defendant after another had "confessed" to absurd crimes; now his task was to stage a "democratic and legal transition to socialism." Later this role of his was not mentioned at all in Soviet Latvian history books.[31]

Ulmanis' government resigned, and the Soviet embassy chose, according to Moscow guidelines,[32] loyal and trustworthy ministers from among "democratic" Latvians. Biology professor Augusts Kirchenšteins became the prime minister of the "People's government." The Finnish ambassador assessed him very negatively in his confidential report.[33]

Communists did not get prominent places at first, but the influence of the party, which willingly obeyed the Soviet embassy, grew by degrees, and further "cadres" were sent from the Soviet Union. President Ulmanis remained in office for a few weeks, but he had to sign the edicts of the occupiers.

A Farcical Election

In mid-July, the occupiers hastily arranged for a parliamentary election – the time given for preparations was ten days – under the supervision of the Red Army. It may have sounded promising: an election after all those years under Ulmanis! Vyshinski assured everyone that the election would be honest, and various political forces made serious preparations for them. But the election laws and the constitution of 1922 were blithely violated, and the outcome was determined in advance.

In the end, the occupiers permitted only the "Working Peoples" (Communist and non-partisan) bloc to be listed on the ballot; others were rejected for trumped-up reasons and their candidates were arrested. The Working Peoples candidates did not mention the fact that the objective was to destroy Latvian independence. Everyone had to vote. The official results: the percentage of those voting was 94.7 and the Working Peoples candidates took 97.6 percent of the votes.

The results of the election are generally said to be flagrantly falsified, but some historians say that even the correct figures were very high. There was no opposition and there were no alternatives, the voting was practically compulsory, and the platform of the working people's bloc concealed the real objectives; it was deliberately written to be vague and to have popular appeal.[34]

In its first session the new parliament, without a voting, declared "in accordance with the hopes of the free working people" Latvia to be a workers and farmers' socialistic soviet republic in which the Communist party held power. It also petitioned for admission to the Soviet Union.[35]

Neither subject had been discussed during the election campaign. Latvia's constitution had been violated again, for according to it, such a great change in the system of government and in the international status of the country had to be decided in a referendum.[36]

Within a few weeks, land, large buildings, banks, and factories were confiscated without compensation and nationalized. Before the election a specific promise had been given that property would not be touched nor would there be forced collectivization, but that farmers could voluntarily join cooperatives. The traditional life of the rural areas was thrown into chaos. Bank deposits and valuables in safe deposit boxes were frozen and confiscated. Latvian currency was declared void overnight, pauperizing the population. The theft of private property began immediately. The main streets and the districts of Rīga were named after Stalin, Lenin, and Kirov – men of note in a foreign country.[37]

Ulmanis was deported to the Soviet Union.[38] Censorship became more stringent. The home guard was banned and disarmed. The ranks of the officers were purged, the soldiers were ordered to swear a new oath, and the Latvian divisions, the new "people's army," were joined to the Red Army. Latvia was taken into the Soviet Union as a republic on August 5, 1940. Large numbers of people were already under arrest, and in 1941 the number of prisoners and those deported to the east rose to tens of thousands.

All this occurred without resistance, either symbolic or actual, even without protest, except for a few Latvian diplomats who remained abroad. Ulmanis gave a certain legitimacy to the destruction of the state by remaining in office and signing the decrees of the new government. He himself did not flee or allow anyone to establish a government in exile. In the end, he even handed the "scepter" to his successor. In a sense, Ulmanis was a hostage. Wanting to avoid bloodshed and save lives, he cooperated believing that his compliance would benefit Latvia.

All of this had legal and international political consequences. Moscow could say that everything occurred legally, and that Latvia had voluntarily joined the Soviet Union.[39]

The same men who had fought for Latvia's freedom during the war of liberation now, 20 years later, during the war of liberation. They hoped that by compromise at least the population and a part of the state would be preserved. We cannot know today what they knew and thought, but possibly they pinned their hopes on Germany: according to some historians they may have believed that Germany would attack toward the east and that therefore the presence of

Soviet troops would be short-lived, and it was important to stay alive while waiting for their departure.[40]

Some have viewed Ulmanis' suppositions as a tragic mistake. In the end, Latvia, which "chose peace," lost a much larger part of its population than Finland, which "chose war." Of Finland's population (about 4 million), 94,000, almost all of them soldiers, not civilians, died in World War II. The situations in the two countries during 1939-1940, cannot, however, be compared directly. As well, the Red Army was better equipped and more experienced than before. Others conclude that resistance would have amounted to national suicide for the Latvians.

"Brotherly Help"

In its ultimatum to the Baltic countries, Moscow was claiming falsely that she had to take action because of these countries' secret military collaboration with Finland, which was directed against the Soviet Union.[41] A later explanation for local consumption was that the occupation protected the Balts from aggressors. The mantra in Soviet history was that the Red Army "helped to free the working class from the yoke of capitalist exploitation and from the gang of manor lords;" there was a "revolutionary situation" in Latvia and elsewhere in the Baltics, the people were rising up against their oppressive governments, and the Red Army moved in to prevent bloodshed; there were spontaneous and simultaneous revolutions and the Baltic peoples decided voluntarily to join the Soviet Union.

Many Russians and even some Westerners still believe these myths. This question has recently been studied in Estonia. Over half of Estonia's Russians still believe that Estonia joined the Soviet Union voluntarily; about one third says that there was an occupation. The rest do not know.

That scenario has little to do with facts. How could a revolutionary situation have manifested itself and who were the revolutionaries? The underground Communist party in Latvia was small – it had about 500 members, many of them in prison – and Moscow did not trust it.[42] Stalin had imprisoned and murdered the most loyal Latvian communists in the USSR in the 1930's. There were no disturbances and no organized opposition in Latvia, and all weapons were in the hands of the Ulmanis government, the army, and the Home Guard. The new rulers were so uncertain about the outcome of the election that they did not dare organize an honest one.

Reports of Western diplomats document a low level of social conflict in the years before the summer of 1940. In January 1940, the Latvian minister of agriculture, with the aid of regional agronomists, took an extensive survey of the state of mind of the rural population, and nothing in the results indicates any revolutionary sentiment, at least not in the rural areas.[43]

In fact, *none* of the classical indicators of a "revolutionary situation" were at high levels or were even rising between 1934 and 1940 in Latvia:

- Unemployment
- Starvation wages
- Farmers driven off their lands
- Workers forced to work unreasonably long hours
- Strikes
- Hunger, malnutrition
- Demonstrations and political violence
- Arrests, police brutality, hard sentences
- Number of political prisoners
- Refugees, migration, deportation
- A large Communist party.[44]

Thus any "revolution" in Latvia was accomplished by Russian tanks.

It is revealing that initially, Soviet historians did not say anything about a "people's socialistic revolution" in the Baltic countries in 1940–1941; they claimed that Soviet troops were brought into these countries as a security measure against Nazi Germany. They also wrote about the "restoration of Soviet rule in 1940," which was a "historically inevitable and progressive" development. In schools Latvian history was taught linked with Soviet history, and in 1951 the Chair of Latvian History was eliminated at Latvia State University. The more time elapsed from the events, the more firmly entrenched the concept of a "Socialist Revolution" became.[45]

From later "Chekist" memoirs, it becomes apparent that the occupation of Latvia had long been in the plans, and that the annexation of the Baltic countries to the Soviet Union was "one of the NKVD's most successful foreign operations before the war." The Latvian Communist party even protested this statement to Moscow – it was in contradiction to the "truth" that in 1940, everything had happened through the free will of the Latvian working people.[46]

Was Ulmanis Guilty?

Was July 1940 (Latvia's being declared socialistic) a consequence of May 1934 (Ulmanis' *coup d'état*), as some have stated?[47]

Ulmanis' autocracy divided the nation, caused dissatisfaction and prevented free discussion of alternatives. Latvia accepted its occupiers meekly, and for various reasons, it was easy to persuade or even to pressure Ulmanis.[48] He did not have the full support of the people and the politicians. A democratic state would perhaps have had it easier to find support from abroad (but in Europe of 1940, who would have been able to help?) Would it perhaps have been possible to establish a government in exile, say in Britain?

Ulmanis could not be sure that all of the Latvian army would fight. Every fourth resident was not Latvian, and many non-Latvians were in the army, too. All in all, Finland's kind of "spirit of the Winter War" was perhaps not possible in a country like Latvia, with its authoritarian government. The people did not trust the leaders nor did the leaders fully trust the people.

In the opinion of present-day historians, Ulmanis' decision to remain in nominal power after the occupation in 1940 was a nearsighted policy. "Perhaps he hoped to save something, but now we see that in his name everything he himself had built up was destroyed."[49]

One can argue that Ulmanis' coup was a contributory cause of the subsequent tragedy. But the events of the time in Europe indicate that the aggressors chose their victims not because of their political system but from geopolitical interests. Democracy would not have saved Latvia. European events were governed by dictators who practiced secret diplomacy and power politics. The fact that Czechoslovakia was a parliamentary democracy in the Western sense did not save her in 1938. She was sacrificed in the name of world peace – nor did she try to resist. Neither did the League of Nations raise a finger. Not a single country came to the aid of Finland when the Soviet Union attacked her small neighbor in 1939.

Latvia's fate was decided in Berlin and Moscow. Some historians are of the opinion that the doom of the Baltic countries was predetermined; it would not have mattered what these small states did or did not do. Others, in contrast, maintain that they had done too little to help themselves: as independent states with an efficient defense system they could have played a role in Northeastern Europe and their fate could have been somewhat different.[50]

7

Did Latvians murder their Jews in 1941?
How anti-Semitic is and was Latvia?

Two significant national minorities – first German[1] and then Jewish – disappeared as victims of Latvian history and Great-Power politics during the few years from 1939–1941. In addition to being a tragedy for these national groups, it was for Latvia a deep wound which changed its society forever and slowed its later development. The memory and the trauma of these events haunt the Latvians, and it has poisoned the relations between Latvians and others, particularly Jews, to this very day.

First of all, it is true that an almost complete Holocaust occurred on Latvian soil. More Jews were killed in Lithuania, but the extermination of Jews in Latvia was the most thorough in Europe.[2]

Why? And who was responsible?

In discussions with individual Latvians (and individual Finns, Russians, and Americans…) one can encounter old stereotypes and mistaken conceptions of Jews. For example, many seem to believe seriously that in the Cheka and its successors, the GPU and the NKVD, a disproportionate number of Jews served (incidentally, in the early days a noticeably large number of Latvians worked in the Cheka), and that the Jews had a significant role in the Soviet occupations of the Baltics in 1940 and 1944 and the cruelties associated with them.

There once were many Jews in the NKVD top echelons, but they were purged in the late 1930's.[3] Some 50 percent of the members of the tiny Latvian underground Communist party had been Jews, and the Soviet occupying power did indeed assign some Jews to prominent duties in Latvia, but ethnic Russians and Latvians constituted the vast majority of the repressive institutions' personnel.[4] In the deportations organized by the Soviets in 1941, there were proportionately more Jews among the victims than any other ethnic group: some two thousand or a little more than 12 percent of all deportees, although Jews made up only 4.8 percent or 93,479 people of Latvia's population according to the 1935 census. Of the deported Jews, over half died in Russia.[5] Moreover the Soviet occupiers disbanded Jewish organizations as "fascist (!) and counter-revolutionary."

Should not the Latvian collaborators, who oppressed their own people, earn the severest criticism? As I relate in the Acknowledgements, there are also politicians in present-day Latvia who cynically warn the Jews not to "repeat their old mistakes."[6]

Germany and Russia were the centers of modern anti-Semitism, and from there the idea spread to Latvia. Latvia was not and is not, however, a society permeated by anti-Semitism.[7] Professor Edward Anders (originally Eduards Alperovičs), who lives in the USA, lost his father and many of his Jewish relatives in war time Liepāja in 1941 and was almost shot himself. He makes what to him is an important distinction: "There was no anti-Semitism. But there were anti-Semites." Latvia in the 1930's was "about as anti-Semitic as Switzerland, France, the USA, and Canada; but less so than Germany and several Eastern European countries."

Anders warns of black and white thinking and reminds us of the many shades of grey. At the extreme ends, some Latvians participated in the murdering initiated by the Germans, but some also saved Jews at the risk of their own lives. There are 103 Latvians on the list of "Righteous Gentiles."[8]

I think it is both wrong and problematic to call nations or groups of people anti-Semitic. Nations are composed of individuals, and all such generalizations are false. At most one can make *statistical* statements.

The phenomenon is difficult to evaluate, and people present facile opinions about it. What does it mean that Sweden's Jewish organization reported being "concerned about the spread of anti-Semitism" in Sweden after the results of a new opinion poll were published in 2006? What is to be said of Russia, where at present violent neo-Nazis are active, as well as several publishing houses specializing in rabid anti-Semitic literature, while at the same time Moscow criticizes other European countries of anti-Semitism? Observers are shocked to see how violent anti-Semitism and xenophobia have recently been spreading on Russian net forums.[9]

In Czarist Russia, Jews were generally excluded from society and persecuted. Latvia was one of the few places in the empire where there were no pogroms. With Latvian independence in 1918, Jews living in its territory received full citizenship rights for the first time – much earlier than in Finland, by the way. They also had cultural autonomy and their own schools, where teaching took place in Hebrew and Yiddish at government expense. Some 1,200 Jewish soldiers took part on the side of Latvia in the 1918–1920 war for independence; 37 of them died and many were awarded high military orders for valor and courage.[10]

Free Latvia never had anti-Semitism as an official policy – the situation was quite the contrary. Although Jews were not allowed in the police or in the government service, they were greatly overrepresented in trade, industry, law and medicine. A number of Jewish and German businesses were nationalized by Ulmanis to lessen overrepresentation, but with compensation in hard cash. Ulmanis did not discriminate against *Jewish* businesses but against *private* enterprise; Jews and Germans did suffer proportionally more from this "state capitalism," since they had more businesses.[11]

Jewish culture flourished, and there were in Rīga alone 37 synagogues and houses of prayer. Jews were politically active: their representation in the Latvian parliament was about in proportion to that in the population. No anti-Semitic laws were passed, even under the authoritarian regime of 1934–1940, and Kārlis Ulmanis banned Pērkoņkrusts (Thundercross) and their anti-Semitic tracts.[12] The Jews could not compete with the Germans as the most disliked minority in Latvia.[13]

At the end of the 1930's, the Latvian Jews followed closely and with concern the developments in Germany. Until the very end, refugees from Germany, Austria and German-occupied Czechoslovakia arrived in Latvia with Latvian visas; proportionally, Latvia gave temporary refuge to more Jews than England. Moving to safety farther away, however, was almost impossible. When Germany attacked in June 1941, the Soviet Union closed its borders with Soviet Latvia and turned back many Latvian Jews, as well as some 2,000 foreign Jews who had sought refuge in Latvia.[14] Still, before the Nazis arrived, ten percent of Latvia's Jews had succeeded in fleeing and two percent had been deported to the east by the Russians. The rest were trapped by the German occupation.[15]

There was no thought of going east in large numbers: the older Jews remembered Russian anti-Semitism all too well, and besides, in 1918 the German army had behaved relatively well toward the Baltic Jews while the Czarist government had ordered the removal of all Jews from Courland. The Courland Jews, especially, had for centuries had a pro-German tradition.[16]

The German forces conquered Rīga on July 1, 1941 and a week later they were in control of all of Latvia. Many places experienced an interregnum, when the Red Army had fled and before the Germans established their rule. This interregnum was quite short; in many places it lasted a few hours or at most one day.

During this brief period, deliberate or spontaneous expressions of violence involving loss of human life were very rare, and even according to the worst possible calculations, the overall number of victims of politically motivated murders committed in the entire territory of Latvia did not exceed a few dozen. There was indeed some settling of accounts with collaborators (ethnic Latvians as well as Russians and Jews), individual humiliation, beatings and looting, but not "pogroms," and certainly not mass executions.[17] Under German control martial law was established and a curfew was imposed. Members of the Latvian resistance were ordered to turn in their weapons – after the first few days anyone who had a weapon without a German permit was threatened with the death penalty. The inhabitants were not in the grip of rage at the Jews, and the "worst" of the officials, who feared revenge, had fled with the Russians, says Juris Pavlovičs, who has studied the interregnum.

Despite many rumors and claims, no one has ever been able to identify the time and place where any interregnum murders of Jews as such occurred and what people were involved, writes Andrew Ezergailis. Edward Anders, a Jew who lived in Latvia in 1941 and has studied those times, agrees.

Many Latvians watched what occurred during the German occupation with indifference, horror or helplessness. The vast majority of the population respected the rule of law. In Latvia, as in most places in Europe, participation in crimes against humanity was reserved for marginal elements.[18]

Nevertheless a general conception lives on that the Latvians began to kill their Jewish neighbors on their own and that many eager volunteer executioners reported to the Germans when they arrived. Discussion of the extermination of Jews is also plagued by basic confusions, such as the claim that it was Latvian Waffen-SS soldiers who were guilty of it. (See Chapter 8.)

As a residual effect of the Soviet era, the Latvians have a vague and spotty notion of history such as of the Second World War, for example (the same is true of the Russians).[19] It has been said that the Latvians are so accustomed to always seeing themselves as the victims of history that they cannot grasp or approve a view of themselves as henchmen.[20] There may be some truth in this, but in spite of, or perhaps because of it, we must ask what actually happened in 1941.

Liberators Turned into Butchers

Having experienced the "year of horror," the Soviet occupation of 1940–1941, many Latvians now saw the Russians and communism, instead of the Germans, as their chief enemy. At the start of the German occupation, they welcomed the Germans as liberators.

A Finnish officer who traveled around Latvia in 1942 reported to Marshal Mannerheim that the Germans were welcomed with joy at first, but that the feeling soon changed. The cause was the Germans themselves and their "stupid and misguided" policies.[21] The German general von Heunert complained to the governor of Finnish Lapland in the spring of 1942 that the Baltic peoples first greeted the Germans as liberators, but that only four weeks after their arrival, the Latvians "had begun plotting and intriguing against the Germans."

The three Baltic countries and part of Belarus became *Ostland*, a protectorate of Greater Germany, with administration of the area in Rīga. The National Socialist regime had decided that even a limited autonomy would never be considered for the Latvians, nor would an army of their own. The Germans viewed Latvia as a former Soviet territory and governed it in the same way as the rest of the occupied Soviet Union.

This attitude did not change substantially during the war. All the plans were directed to the same end. The Baltic countries would become an integral part of Germany: Latvia would be Germanized and colonized, racially acceptable individuals assimilated and the rest of the people moved to the East or liquidated. The goal was to settle privileged Germans – also Volga Germans – in Courland after the war. Belarusians would be brought in as workers. Local languages were to be forbidden. Only by becoming German could a Latvian rise to an important position – just as in the 19th century. Baltic Germans had become familiar with such plans during World War I; they now returned to Rīga and were appointed to high offices.

Heinrich Himmler believed that Latvia and Estonia could be totally Germanized in twenty years. Latvia's wartime economy was subordinated to Germany's: the aim was to plunder all of Latvia's resources and use the population as a work force in the war industry and as cannon fodder in the war.[22]

It should be noted that there was no longer a Latvian state or Latvian governing authority during the war which could have had an effect on such matters.[23] Also, the Hague Convention clearly describes the establishment of law and order as the duty of the occupying force. Thus it is strange to read in *The Nation* of "Latvia's disturbingly tolerant view of its own Nazi past" and that the "people do not recognize Latvia's war guilt."[24]

As indicated above, in 2005 *The Nation* also wrote that the Holocaust in Latvia was made possible *only* by enthusiastic local collaboration (my italics). The Germans, then, would have left the Jews in peace? On the contrary, initially the shootings were all done by Germans and only days, weeks, or months later did they entrust part of the job to Latvians. These killers and their accomplices were only a small part of the Latvian nation.

The Germans organized and controlled all the collaboration in Latvia; any Latvian initiatives in this area were rejected. Germany armed certain groups in Latvia, and kept them totally under her command. The occupation government placed General Oskars Dankers in the most important civilian position given to a Latvian, as a member of the so-called confidence council. The Latvians' nominal "self-administration," *Landeseigene Verwaltung*, was a powerless support agency. It was created in 1942 to carry out the commands of the German civilian and military officials. It has been proven that in Europe, the less there was of an independent power to make decisions in the occupied countries or among the allies of Germany, the more complete was the extermination of the Jews.[25]

The Germans planned this extermination carefully and in advance. The goal was to destroy all Baltic Jews, but not, however, under the eyes of the world. In Central Europe, the extermination was carried out on a mass scale, but secretly, in concentration camps; in the East the places of execution and mass graves were the forests. The Germans were thinking of their later reputation. It was important to have assistants in their dirty work, to distance themselves from the blame and lay it on the shoulders of others.

They incited attacks on Jews and hoped for spontaneous pogroms, but those were not forthcoming.[26]

The mass killings in Latvia were anything but spontaneous local outbreaks of violence – it took a long time to organize them. Some executions were photographed and filmed, preferably in such a way that executioners shown in them were not Germans, at least not Germans in uniform. Since then the photographs and accounts have been material for Holocaust researchers: East Europeans have not been able to testify on their own behalf.

Heinrich Himmler's "right hand man," SS-General Reinhard Heydrich, issued an order on June 6, 1941, before the attack on the Soviet Union began, according to which "temporary local defense units" were to be established and connected conspicuously to the "cleansing" operations. A little later he advised the leaders of the murder commands to conceal the killings and make it appear that the "natives" were doing it. The plan was to induce "self-cleansing" by the local peoples. To make it appear that Germans were not responsible, they ordered the "self-defense" men in Latvia to wear an armband in Latvian red-white-red colors on their civilian attire.[27]

In July Hitler himself gave the order "to do nothing that might obstruct the final solution [killing of Jews in the occupied areas], but to prepare for it only in secret."[28]

Everything was ordered, organized and directed by the Germans. As Professor Aivars Stranga writes in a recent study of the German occupation, there was no "Germanless Holocaust." The extermination of the Jews was an official decision by the German state in Berlin; it was to be a well-organized large-scale operation. Adolf Hitler lied about it to the world and to his people. He spoke of the annihilation of the East European Jews for the first time on the 22nd of July 1941, when his visitor was a Croatian marshal, and in this connection he mentioned the vengeful Balts in a few phrases, which are fundamental to the later myth.[29] (See the Prologue.)

It is strange that although Hitler's statements are not otherwise valued as truthful, some people trust his words on just this matter. The Nazis succeeded in giving the impression that civilians killed the Jews on their own initiative, and even today many researchers seek an explanation for the Holocaust in East Europe.

The Canadian historian Modris Eksteins (born in Latvia during the war) is, as mentioned in my Prologue, of the opinion that hatred and anti-Semitism were deeply ingrained in Latvian and East-European souls. He writes that zealots killed Jews before German rule was firmly established and German killing squads arrived. According to him, massacres began immediately. "Latvians aimed to satisfy their own impulses."[30] A reader almost gets the impression that the Germans were horrified and tried to control the "disorganized" murder.

The first and later much-cited book dealing with the destruction of Latvian Jews appeared in 1947. Max Kaufmann's *Die Vernichtung der Juden Lettlands* relates, among other things, that the Latvians rejoiced in killing, participated in the brutality and murdered many people before the Germans arrived in 1941. Bernard Press's *Judenmord in Lettland 1941–1945* for its part includes many dramatic photographs, which are said to be from Latvia, but as a matter of fact were taken in other European countries. Press also writes that according to the statements of witnesses, the killing began before the Germans arrived and that the Latvians acted as torturers in prisons.[31]

The mother of Saul Bellow, the American writer, was a Jew, originally from Rīga. Bellow said in an interview a few years before his death: "Perhaps murder is a privilege," an opportunity many are glad to seize and "a secret feeling of any human being." He related what he had heard about Latvians and Jews – that civilians took part in the killing of the latter. "People enjoyed these murder picnics."

In 1996, the American professor Daniel Goldhagen published a best seller, *Hitler's Willing Executioners*, which prompted much discussion and criticism. In it he presents the age-old German murderous anti-Semitism as the cause of the Holocaust. Goldhagen admits that the non-German peoples who assisted

Germans in murdering Jews have not been sufficiently studied to date. Nevertheless he writes later on:

> The most important national groups who aided the Germans in slaughtering Jews were the Ukrainians, Latvians and Lithuanians, about whom two things can be said. They came from cultures that were profoundly anti-Semitic, and the knowledge that we have, little as it is, of the men who actually aided the Germans suggests that many of them were animated by vehement hatred of Jews.[32]

The well-known Holocaust scholar Deborah Lipstadt writes about ethnic groups which "collaborated in the annihilation of the Jews;" and from this unsubstantiated generalization she derives another – that even today Eastern Europe is still "increasingly beset by nationalism."[33]

The strangest book of all on the subject is the one by Benjamin Wilkomirski, who presented himself as a Latvian Jew. In *Bruchstücke* (1995), the author "recalls" his oppression and sufferings as a child in Latvia and in a German concentration camp. The work was translated into twelve languages and won respected literary awards in the U. S., Britain, and France before it was revealed as a falsification and a fabrication from start to finish.[34]

In his book *Perpetrators, Victims, Bystanders* the US historian Raul Hilberg underlines the important role of the Baltic peoples in the implementation of National-Socialist power and racial policies. On the basis of some examples he maintains that Latvian battalions were involved in the persecution and murder of Jews in Latvia, Belarus, Ukraine and Poland. Hilberg interprets the notion of "voluntarism" very loosely, broadly placing in the category of volunteer everyone who in some way served or worked for Germans.

A new German book on the subject (Angrick and Klein, *Die "Endlösung" in Riga*, 2006) declares in its introduction that "it was immediately [after the occupation] evident that anti-Semitism and violent nationalism were no import by entering German troops but that a broad segment of Latvian society had built up its hatreds earlier."[35] There was no distinction between the anti-Semitism and rage of the Nazis and that of Latvians. Angrick and Klein speak of the Latvians' traditional anti-Semitism that made them willing to "attack their neighbors." On the other hand the writers seem to understand and even to prove that Germans fanned anti-Semitism and tried to organize pogroms, but then again they write that "sadistic Latvian nationalists" acted at once, without orders, in rage and revenge. There was an "uncontrollable eruption of violence and destruction."

Victims and Perpetrators

In the beginning, 1941–1942, the so-called police battalions in Latvia were made up mainly of volunteers, insofar as one can speak of volunteering in occupied countries. They were formed after the mass murders of the Latvian Jews and served in anti-partisan warfare behind the front, often a "dirty war," and guarded the Warsaw ghetto, for example. Later they served at the front. The *Schutzmannschaften*, volunteer assistant police, were another matter. They mainly carried out normal police functions but were also ordered by Germans to arrest Jews, escort them to an execution site, and guard or shoot them.[36]

Friedrich Jeckeln, the supreme commander of the Police and SS in Ostland, is reported to have said in 1946 at a post-war trial in Rīga that the killing began before the arrival of the Germans, that the Latvians were better, more hardened executioners than the Germans, and that therefore Jews were brought to Latvia from other places in Europe. The words were put into his mouth after the fact; historian Rudīte Vīksne has gone through the trial papers and found nothing of the sort in them. Also Pēteris Krupnikovs, the (Jewish) translator at the trial, has declared that Jeckeln said nothing of the sort.[37]

Along with the first German troops, *Einsatzgruppe A* arrived, first under the command of *SS-Brigadeführer* (Major General) Walter Stahlecker and then of *SS-Obergruppenführer* (Lieutenant General) Jeckeln. The responsibility of this special force was the liquidation of the Baltic Jews. It became the bloodiest of the mobile Eastern Front killing units. All German occupation authorities were involved in this systematic extermination operation – the *Wehrmacht*, the naval forces, various types of police, both military and civilian, and the civil administration of the occupied areas.[38]

The arrest and execution of the Jews began in all of Latvia as soon as the Germans arrived. In less than half a year some 60,000 were murdered and the killing continued until the end in 1944. Zemgale or South Latvia was declared *Judenfrei* in August 1941. At first the Rīga Jews were confined to a ghetto. In the fall of 1941 the mass shootings began, similar to those in Ukraine and Belarus.[39] There were no extermination camps as yet.

The mobile killing unit, Arājs Commando, was recruited immediately after the arrival of the Germans in July 1941 and was headed by a 31-year-old former leftist officer, Viktors Arājs. The unit was made up of volunteers, and was the only one of its kind in occupied Europe. In 1941 at the time of the mass killings, it had 300 Latvian members, a figure that rose to 1,200 by 1943.

Contrary to what has been thought, very few in the Commando's ranks were members of the extreme right Thundercross or of student fraternities. Rudīte Vīksne, who has investigated the backgrounds of all known Commando members, relates that typically they were poorly paid young laborers with an incomplete secondary education or former policemen or soldiers, coming from "socially and morally marginalized groups" and driven by selfish motives, not by a lust for revenge or a hatred of Jews (cf. Goldhagen's judgement above!).[40] Only one of them mentioned later in court that his motive was hatred of Jews. Every ablebodied man had to work or serve somewhere, and some believed that they would be getting off easy in this unit and would also be paid well.

The recruiters wanted to enlist the kind of men who had lost their relatives during the Soviet occupation. To inflame vengefulness, the Germans forced Jews to dig up the graves of the executed and presented them to the inhabitants, as one of several attrocities commited by "Jewish Bolsheviks". A propaganda blitz began on the radio even before the occupation, and later the press published venomous articles the purpose of which was the dehumanization of Jews. The Nazis cynically exploited people's thirst for revenge and tried to redirect the anger of Latvians about Soviet violence in their country at the Jews.

Arājs Commando executed Jews and burned synagogues. The first to be executed were the Jews in small towns, then those in Rīga. His unit is calculated to have killed some 26,000 people in Latvia (including 2,000 communists and 2,000 Roma and mentally ill). In all, the Commando was involved in operations which took the lives of 60,000 people in Latvia. After that, a unit of 200 men participated in "mop-up" and counter-guerrilla actions in the Minsk and Warsaw areas and around Leningrad. There is not even a rough estimate of the total number of their victims.[41]

Viktors Arājs landed in Western Germany at the end of the war. He was arrested 30 years later and received a life sentence for his part in the shooting of 13,000 Jews in the Rumbula Woods near Rīga in December 1941. He died in prison in 1988. Ironically, he just happened to have an alibi for that bloodbath. The actual executioners at Rumbula were 12 men of a special SD unit that Jeckeln had brought with him from Ukraine. The reason for this arrangement was that the Jews who had been brought from the ghetto were bringing with them hidden precious jewels and gold which were to be confiscated at the place of execution.[42]

"Get Self-Cleansing Going!"

Ostland's *Reichskommissar* Hinrich Lohse was of the opinion that Jews capable of working should be put to forced labor, which was to benefit Germany. The SS-SD, claiming higher orders that could be discussed only orally, prevailed, however. Stahlecker reported in October that 31,868 people had been murdered in Latvia, mainly Jews. Berlin was dissatisfied; this was thought to be too slow.[43]

Stahlecker wrote at that time that it was important "to establish as unshakable and provable facts for the future that it was the liberated population itself which took the most severe measures, on its own initiative, against the Bolshevik and Jewish enemy, without any German instruction being evident."[44] He went on: "It was the task of the Security Police to set these self-cleansing movements going and direct them into the right channels in order to achieve the aim of this cleansing as rapidly as possible."

Stahlecker affirmed that his opinion from the beginning had been that pogroms alone would not solve Ostland's "Jewish problem." He complained that the killing by local civilians was not progressing as had been hoped, mentioning the Arājs action of 4 July as the only exception.

> It proved to be considerably more difficult [than in Kovno, Lithuania] to set in motion similar cleansing *Aktionen* and pogroms in Latvia. …
> In Rīga it proved possible, by means of appropriate suggestions to the Latvian Auxiliary Police, to get an anti-Jewish pogrom going [on July 4, 1941], in the course of which all the synagogues were destroyed and approximately 400 Jews killed. As the population on the whole quieted down very quickly in Rīga, it was not possible to arrange further pogroms.[45]

Stahlecker did set down this revealing statement: "The goal of the cleansing operation … *in accordance with the fundamental orders* [my emphasis], was the most comprehensive elimination of the Jews possible."

Daugavpils was Latvia's second most important Jewish center – one fourth of the inhabitants of this large city were Jews. The leader of the German killing unit complained in his report at the beginning of July 1941: "The Latvians, including the leading active ones, have so far behaved passively towards the Jews, and did not dare to rise against them. … Latvians have hesitated in organizing and mobilizing themselves against the Jews."[46]

In November Himmler ordered the extermination of the remaining Latvian Jews. He had moved Jeckeln and his staff to Latvia because they had "distinguished themselves" in the Ukrainian massacres including Babi Yar. The Rīga ghetto was emptied. On the 30th of November and on the 8th of December, some 26,000 Rīga Jews were shot and buried in mass graves in the Rumbula Woods.[47] It took only 12 German SD men to carry out the killing. It is true that the task of guarding and leading the victims from the ghetto to Rumbula employed some 1500 men – Arājs Commando and part of the Rīga municipal police were ordered to participate. In the Biķernieki Woods Reichsjuden were shot; they had been brought from elsewhere in Europe. Now there were 6,000 Latvian Jews left, who were moved to camps as labor.

The German SS and Police chief of the Liepāja area reported that during three days' "action" in mid-December, some 3,000 Jews had been shot and buried in a large grave and that the extermination had been completed in Ventspils and other communities. "This applies chiefly to the women and children." Courland was now declared *Judenfrei* – and later in the same month, so was all of Latvia. (Which was not quite true, even by the Nazis' own count.)

Earlier, the mayor of Liepāja reported "great distress" in the city about the killing of the Jews. Soon after the Liepāja massacre the local *SS- und Polizeiführer* reported:

> The execution of Jews carried out during the report is still the topic of conversation of the local population. The fate of the Jews is widely deplored, and thus far few voices have been heard in favor of the elimination of the Jews.[48]

In six months, over 90 percent of the Jews that had stayed in Latvia when Germany attacked had been murdered. Trainloads of Central European Jews were also sent to Latvia, for forced labor and extermination – 24,600, of whom the majority died. Several thousand of them were sent to the Stutthof concentration camp in 1943.[49]

According to the calculations of Andrew Ezergailis, some 85,000 Latvian civilians were murdered in Latvia during the war. The Nuremberg proceedings led to the same number. At the end of the war, just one percent of the 70,000 Jews who were caught in the trap survived. The rest were dead, taken to camps elsewhere, or had succeeded in hiding or escaping. Over half of Latvia's Roma were killed.

It is easy to refute the charge that Latvian war criminals have not been punished. Proportionally, whatever their guilt, more Latvians have been punished for Nazi crimes than Germans.[50] After the war the Soviet Union mercilessly hunted down those suspected of collaboration with the Nazis, kept after them for years, even decades, and executed many of them. It is true, however, that the most expert in their ranks could find employment with the KGB.[51] Clearing up the mass murders of Jews was not a first priority with the Soviets, as I will explain in the next chapter.

Besides the thousands of Latvians who fought on Germany's side winding up in prison camps automatically during the Soviet era, hundreds accused of war-time crimes were sentenced from 1944 on, many to death, the others to 15–25 years in prison or forced labor camps where many died. Among them were suspected guards, executioners, and thieves of the victims' property. Often one informer or witness – and not even an eyewitness at that – was enough to condemn a person.[52] No effort was made to find evidence of specific crimes. Service in Nazi military or police forces was reason enough for conviction. Arrest automatically meant a guilty verdict. The search for truth later on was made difficult by the coerced confessions which the Soviet system employed.[53]

During the years 1944–1967, the Soviet authorities captured 356 former Arājs Commando members. They were all sentenced. Some thirty received the death penalty and 150 were sent to prison camps for 25 years, the most common sentence.[54]

Numerical comparisons are revealing. The Western Powers began by arresting 182,000 people in occupied Germany on suspicion of participating in war crimes or belonging to criminal organizations. In the main trial of the International War Crimes Tribunal at Nuremberg, 12 of the leaders were sentenced to death by hanging in 1946.[55] In the subsequent trials held by the Americans, also in Nuremberg, twenty-four persons received death sentences, of which almost half were commuted to life imprisonment. Twenty were sentenced to life imprisonment and 98 were given prison sentences of varying lengths. The Americans are known to have executed 318 people in the jails of their occupied zone, and according to various sources, the Western allies executed a total of 486 Germans. In these trials both war crimes (which do not apply in the case of Latvia) and crimes against humanity were the issue.

A radical cleansing of Germany seemed impossible even before the outbreak of the Cold War, after which it was considered politically unwise. The Allies had to bind Germany to the defense of the West, and that reinforced the tendency to consider mercy as justice. In practice, all those who had been charged with war crimes were freed during the 1950's. In addition, German courts were given the right to try German citizens, but of the 103,823 Nazis under investigation or prosecution in West Germany only 6,432 were

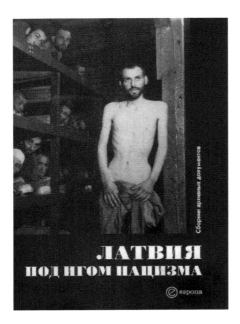

Picture 13. On the cover of a new Russian book, "Latvia pod igom natsizma" (Latvia Under the Nazi Yoke) there is a picture of the Buchenwald Concentration camp showing Elie Wiesel among the prisoners in the background. Neither has anything to do with Latvia or the contents of the book.

Picture 14. The Salaspils concentration camp was located near Rīga and is now a memorial. Its nature is the subject of heated debate between Latvian and Russian historians and the media of the two countries. Sketch Kārlis Bušs, Museum of the Occupation of Latvia collection.

punished in any way. The West German constitution, approved in 1949, prohibited the death penalty.[56]

A greater percentage of Latvians than Germans were given harsh sentences. Nevertheless Efraim Zuroff of the Wiesenthal Center, whom Latvian
historians have publicly named "the Inquisitor," continually demands further
arrests and sentences in Latvia.[57] Zuroff claims that not a single person
involved in the Holocaust has been brought to trial in Latvia. Now he is
offering sizable sums of money as rewards for those whose information leads
to finding Nazi criminals in Latvia.

Many of the guilty and the suspect have been prosecuted long ago and
many have died. The Latvian government has promised to collaborate with
international groups investigating Nazi crimes and to find those who still may
be free in Latvia. Zuroff has been unable to show that any are still living there.
At the end of the 1990's, an aged Latvian emigrant, Konrāds Kalējs, was found
in Britain. He had belonged to the Arājs Commando and had served in
1942–43 as the commander of the perimeter guard at the concentration camp
established by the Germans at Salaspils. Kalējs died before the extradition (to
Latvia) process was completed. No accurate account of his deeds has been
obtained, but the world press commonly wrote of his having taken part in the
"murder of 30,000 Jews."[58]

The Riddle of Salaspils

Salaspils near Rīga, a camp built by deported German Jews in 1941–1942,[59] is a
story in itself. According to the Soviet myth, which the Russian press still fosters, Salaspils was "the Baltic areas biggest extermination camp" where at least
a hundred thousand or even "hundreds of thousands"[60] of prisoners were
murdered, most of them Jews. It is further claimed that thousands of children
were murdered, or died of other causes there, and that medical experiments
were conducted on the inmates.[61]

Salaspils was not, however, a death camp, although it is known that some
1,000 Jews died either there or after being moved elsewhere. According to
Latvian researchers, 1,000–2,000 people died in this camp, which is, of course
a large number, but very different from one hundred thousand. A new German
book claims that in addition to hundreds of German Jews, 2,000–3,000 prisoners died.[62] "Specifically at Salaspils the number of dead probably did not
reach one thousand," writes historian Ezergailis.[63]

Some of the victims were children brought from Belarus who died in the
camp hospital during a smallpox epidemic. Altogether 632 bodies of children
have been found. There is no evidence concerning the medical experiments.

Most of the deaths were from illness, work, cold, inhumane treatment, and punishment. Some 400 prisoners were shot or hanged.[64]

If the Soviet claim regarding at least 53,700 victims at Salaspils were true, at least 20 bodies would have had to be buried in every square meter of its cemetery. But truth does not seem to matter in this case. The Soviet Union accused all East Europeans – excluding the Russians, of course – of racial or war crimes, and it wanted to find extermination camps in every country which had belonged to the German sphere. Many tourists and even Latvians still believe the fabrications in books, camp displays, and information plaques from the Soviet era in Latvia.

The 1970 Soviet-Latvian encyclopedia states that 53,700 people were murdered at the camp, but in the next printing in 1986, that is during Mikhail Gorbachev's *glasnost* (openness) period, the number had risen to 100,000, of whom 7,000 would have been children. In 2004 the Russian Foreign Ministry claimed that 101,000 "Soviet citizens" had been murdered at Salaspils.

From 1941 to 1944, all told there were about 12,000 prisoners at Salaspils;[65] of them, as already stated, at most 2,000 or one-sixth died. At least 83 percent lived to be released or transferred to Stutthoff and other camps in Germany. Let us compare these numbers with those of the Soviet Vyatlag "labor correctional facility," where, along with others, thousands of Latvians were held. After one year in the camp, 36 percent had survived; after five years, fewer than 5 percent were alive. The total death rate at Vyatlag was 4.8 times greater than that of the infamous German Buchenwald concentration camp. In the Soviet Norillag camp 564 Latvian officers were imprisoned; of them fewer than 80, or some 14 percent returned home alive. These are matters that representatives of Russia do not wish to discuss.[66] But the Soviet regime turned Salaspils into a memorial complex which became an obligatory part of tourist visits and where guides embellished their explanations with a generous sprinkling of exaggeration. Salaspils is chronicled, among other matters, in the new Latvian *History of Latvia. 20th Century*. Russia and Latvia's Russian media conducted a furious campaign against this "untruthful" book when in 2005 the Latvian President presented it to Vladimir Putin. Russia's foreign ministry issued public statements, according to which the book is "a mixture of facts, unverified information, and outright falsehoods." The statements also described Salaspils as "Latvia's Auschwitz."

Apparently the main specific objection to the book in the Russian media has been the inclusion, on one page of the book, of a translation of the official German name of the Salaspils camp ("Expanded Police Prison and Work Rehabilitation Camp"). This was corrected in the next edition to "concentration camp." Besides the Germans, the Soviets coined their own term – to them it was a death camp. The most accurate term would be "concentration camp" or a "hard labor and transit camp".

In the summer of 2006 the Russian embassy in Rīga began to distribute a book entitled *Latvija pod igom natsizma* (Latvia in the Yoke of Nazism), put out by Evropa, a publisher specializing in political writings. The book is advertised as containing documents from Soviet times which were found in the Russian archives. No compiler's name is mentioned in the book, and the writer of the preface is also anonymous. According to this preface, in Latvia, in contrast with the rest of Europe, "influential political forces disseminate the Nazi spirit systematically and effectively, with the direct or indirect support of the ruling circles."

According to this book, 100,000 prisoners were killed in Salaspils, and a total of 200,000 European Jews ("hyper-hyperbole" according to historian Ezergailis) were killed in Latvia. In addition the book relates that 35,000 "Soviet children" were murdered, from whose arteries blood was sucked out to give blood transfusions to sick or wounded German officers. This "information" comes from the old KGB disinformation booklet *Daugavas Vanagi – Who Are They?* It apparently did not occur to the writers that the claim is impossible solely on the grounds of racial hygiene – one could not transfer the blood of inferior races into German veins.

The cover of the book has a picture of wretched prisoners in a concentration camp. No source is mentioned, but one familiar with the matter can easily discern that the picture was taken during the liberation of the Buchenwald concentration camp in April 1945, and that one of the prisoners in the background is Elie Wiesel, later a Nobel peace prize laureate. Neither the camp nor Wiesel has anything to do with Latvia – nor with the contents of the book. From the documents in the book it becomes clear that the "truth" about Latvian Nazism had in a sense already been written when the Soviet Union reoccupied Latvia at the end of the war, and that this "information" continues to serve the purpose of at least some Russian historians.[67] By branding the entire Latvian population as fascists, the Russians tried to justify themselves and others having had to resort to a large-scale deportation of Latvians and the mass immigration of Russians and other Soviets into Latvia.

In exploring the question of guilt, it is well to remember the Katyn forest massacre in the spring of 1940. There and in at least two other places the NKVD, the Soviet Union's secret police, executed some 26,000 captured Polish reserve officers and policemen, along with civilians.[68] I guess that no one today inquires about the nationality of those who did the shooting; it is enough to know that the Soviet Union was responsible for the crime. With good reason it has been asked: Aren't questions about the nationality of the executioners and an emphasis on their national traits akin to racism? At least the Latvians seeking the guilty have been advised not to blame the atrocities of the Soviet era on the Russians, but on the Soviet Union.

We have to remember that if everyone is guilty, in the end no one is guilty.

Murder never falls under the statute of limitations, and of course everyone involved in it bears a part of the guilt. It is futile to plead the old Nazi defense at Nuremberg: "We were only obeying orders." As the historians write in the introduction of a new book on crimes against humanity in Estonia 1940–1945: "It is not fair to hold the entire nation responsible for deeds by some of its members, but likewise it is unfair, if criminals try to hide behind the role of victim."[69]

In my opinion, it is important to emphasize that not only the one who pulls the trigger is guilty, but also those who plan the murders, arrest the victims, stand them up at the edge of the pit, hand the weapons to the executioners, and give the command to fire.

8

Why did tens of thousands of Latvian volunteers
fight in the SS troops, and why are SS veterans still
allowed to march on the streets of Rīga
instead of being brought to justice?

This question relates to the theme of the previous chapter, Holocaust, or has
been linked to it, whether rightly or wrongly.

Both Hitler and Stalin established Latvian divisions during the Second
World War. In the summer of 1941, Hitler categorically decreed that only
Germans could bear arms in the East. However, already in 1941–1942 Estonian,
Latvian and Lithuanian police battalions – at first voluntary – were estab-
lished. The flood of volunteers soon dried up.

These volunteers and draftees soon became disillusioned: they were scattered along the entire length of the Eastern front, far from their homelands,
and used for various tasks, as their German overseers saw fit. Those who had
enlisted for a limited time found themselves stuck for the duration of the
war.

After the disastrous fall of Stalingrad in February 1943, the situation was so
desperate that Hitler permitted and also ordered the Chief of the SS, Heinrich
Himmler, to form a "Volunteer Latvian Legion." Himmler, in an attempt to
build up his power, had been systematically increasing the number of troops
under his command. He succeeded in getting the Latvian and other foreign
units under his wing by subordinating them to his elite Waffen-SS. When far
too few Latvians volunteered, compulsion was resorted to: from March 1943
Latvian young men were conscripted into the *Lettische SS-Freiwilligen
Legion*.[1]

Latvia and Estonia were the only European countries where Hitler resorted
to mobilization. Disagreements between the Lithuanians and Germans led to

a different decision in Lithuania – only police battalions were established, not a legion; in addition some 75,000 Lithuanians were sent to work in German war production, and some Lithuanian officers were sent to concentration camps.

Latvian general Oskars Dankers, who according to some historians was a German agent, in effect decided the issue in Latvia: he saw to it that the young people submit to the mobilization. In the end even many Latvian children were sent to German auxiliary forces.

Historians accuse Dankers and former finance minister Alfreds Valdmanis of being the most important collaborators during the Nazi rule. Some even write that such men are partly guilty for the critical demographic situation in Latvia as compared to Lithuania.[2] Others say, that Valdmanis at least tried very hard to get political and economic concessions for Latvians – to no avail.[3]

The formation of the Legion was contrary to international law: the Hague Regulations Respecting Laws and Customs of War on Land (1907) proscribe conscription of citizens from an occupied territory.[4] The prohibition was circumvented nominally by affiliating the Latvians with the Waffen-SS instead of taking them into the *Wehrmacht*, and by calling them volunteers. And in any case, Hitler had quietly renounced the Geneva and Hague Conventions when the German army began its push to the East.

Men from 19 to 24 years of age were summoned to report for induction or face punishment according to military law. (Later the military obligation was extended to the ages of 16–45.) It was an *Einberufungsbefehl*, an order to join a "voluntary legion." According to it, they were "thereby subject to the armed forces of Germany and its commands." A normal punishment for draft dodgers was 15 years forced labor.[5]

In reality the alternatives were to join the Legion, to be scattered among the *Wehrmacht's* auxiliary units, do labor service, or go to jail. Some 20–30 percent evaded the draft by various means – they hid, wounded themselves, took powerful medications, got papers from physicians certifying illness or managed to get exemptions due to employment in the war industry.

The core of the Latvian Legion was two divisions: the 15th and the 19th. Some 15 percent of the men were volunteers, the rest draftees. The police battalions were retroactively classified as part of the Legion. Some of them were incorporated into the two core divisions. Under the Luftwaffe there was also a small Air Force legion.

The Legion was thrown into heavy fighting against advancing Soviet troops; Latvians fought to avert an approaching catastrophe.[6] Among Waffen-SS troops the Latvians were, in proportion to population, the fifth largest national group. In all of Germany's military formations, there were some

115,000–165,000 Latvians serving – historians have not agreed on a precise number. Of them, 60,000–70,000 died in the fighting or in postwar prison camps. In the Red Army, nearly 100,000 Latvians served, of whom perhaps half died.[7]

SS Unit in Name Only

Many have wrong ideas on the subject, whether with or without ulterior motives. Latvian politicians themselves have begun to speak of SS-men and of war criminals in the same breath, and are often unable to explain to foreigners the essence of the subject. Perhaps they themselves do not know.

The Latvian Legion was an SS unit in name only. Latvian soldiers *did not and could not* belong to the German SS organization, nor has any international organ ever associated the Legion's divisions with war crimes or crimes against humanity. They did not take part in guarding concentration camps or ghettos; they fought exclusively at the front, and only against the Red Army, not against the Western allies. American prisoners-of-war, who happened to land in a German camp guarded by Latvian soldiers, report that Latvians treated them very well and called them friends.[8] Captains and crews of many Latvian ships placed their vessels in British and American service during the war. Most of the ships were lost to U-boat action.

In all, 600,000 foreigners served under the Waffen-SS, more than the Germans themselves. The Latvian Legion, however, was very different from the German Waffen-SS divisions. The Latvians did not have the same training, status, privileges, command organization, equipment, and emblems as the German SS men. They wore the Latvian emblem on their sleeves. Other differences were:

- there was no requirement of "Germanic blood"
- they did not undergo a check for Aryan pedigree six generations back
- there was no ideological training
- they practiced religion and had army chaplains
- they swore a different oath
- they had smaller food rations
- their weapons generally were inferior

Latvians could not be accepted as genuine Waffen-SS members, for they were neither German citizens nor "Aryans." A clear differentiation was made between Germans and other Germanic peoples, and an even clearer one between Germanic and other peoples.

As the British military historian John Keegan points out in his book, *Waffen-SS: The Asphalt Soldiers*, the official names of the SS divisions tell of Nazi racism. In the Order of Battle of the Waffen-SS on the one hand there were *SS-Divisionen* and *SS-Freiwilligen-divisionen* made up of German volunteers and non-German "racial brothers" (for example, the 5th Viking to which the Finns belonged), and on the other hand of *Waffen Divisionen der SS*, comprising mostly East Europeans. The latter included the Estonian 20th and the two Latvian divisions – the 15th and the 19th.[9]

For the Germans, national legions generally were only weak auxiliary forces, and most of these were not given any artillery.[10] Keegan writes: "Most of the European SS was riff-raff with the exception of the Latvian and Estonian divisions, which were fighting in the defense of their homelands. The rest were contemptible or pathetic and did nothing to further the German war effort."[11]

In World War II no one, not even the great powers, could afford to choose their allies on ideological considerations. In spite of massive propaganda, neither the ideological nor the military aims of Germany appealed to the Latvian soldiers; they fought not *for* Hitler or for his "new Europe," but *against* Stalin. They were above all patriots, fighting to keep the newly advancing Red Army out of Latvia, and they were hoping that the victorious powers would help to renew the independence of Latvia after the war. Now of course it is easy to say that this was merely an illusion and that they were naïve, as is often written abroad in a sarcastic and skeptical tone.[12]

The Germans formed the Legion only after the collapse of the Eastern front and after "total war" had been proclaimed in 1943. It was clear to the Latvians that they were being used for the good of the Germans, but they hoped that if they helped Germans in the time of their need, they would be rewarded by concessions, possibly all the way to Latvian independence. The Germans were happy to lead the Latvians astray, giving them to understand that the they were fighting for their freedom, but they never revealing any specific plans for Latvia. As SS-Gruppenführer Gottlob Berger is said to have remarked cynically: "For every foreign-born soldier who dies, no German mother weeps."

The Marshal of Finland, Mannerheim, thought that the German policies in the Baltic countries were "incomprehensible in their short-sightedness." In his memoirs he wrote that not even autonomy was promised, although these nations welcomed the Germans as liberators in 1941 and were ready to fight the Soviets. The Finns, as well as Mannerheim himself, often suggested changes to make in the occupied Baltic countries, but although the German military listened, the suggestions were ignored as being against the party line fixed in Berlin.[13]

The legionnaires might be compared to the *strēlnieki*, Latvian riflemen who were permitted to form their own units by Czarist Russia. They too did not want to die for Russia, but for Latvia. On both occasions, 1915 and 1943, the "masters" misled the Latvians. The Red Army's Latvian soldiers were also betrayed.

Here we come to the core of the Latvian tragedy. Jānis Krēsliņš, Sr., a historian who has examined the Latvian myths, writes:

> The sad truth is that the Latvian riflemen serving under different colors during the First World War in Latvia and in its aftermath in Russia, and the very great number of Latvian soldiers both in the German and Soviet armies during the Second World War, mostly forcibly drafted, were not fighting for the independence of Latvia, no matter what they thought in their hearts, but were cannon fodder in the armies of the Great Powers. And they were encouraged to fight by politicians and were led in battles by officers who had received no promises from the leaders of the Great Powers in whose armies they had to serve that they would support the restoration of the sovereignty of Latvia, its political independence. Furthermore, it is profoundly tragic that both the Red and Hitlerite leaders found a certain number of Latvians who needlessly stained their hands with blood in participating in the criminal undertakings hostile to their own people, including providing assistance to the occupying powers in carrying out the mass deportations.[14]

It must be added that there were also some officers and a secret organization called the Latvian Central Council (LCP) that fearlessly refused to cooperate with either one of Latvia's occupiers – Germans or Russians. The LCP, led by Professor Konstantins Čakste, son of a former president of Latvia, was a non-violent resistance organization. It called for an independent and democratic Latvia and free elections. Čakste died in a German concentration camp. LCP hoped for the support of Western allies but was only used by their intelligence services, not helped by them.

No Nazis

The legionnaires were not supporters of Nazi ideology nor was there any attempt made to convert them to it. As they were constantly reminded of their inferior race and status, they had no reason to become ideological Nazis.

"With regard to a world view and in a party political sense, we had nothing in common with fascism," officer and author Arturs Silgailis has written.[15] As mentioned, Latvians swore a different oath to Hitler than the other SS soldiers – "In God's name" – vowing to fight only "against bolshevism" and no more.[16]

The end for which the legionnaires strove was to fight against all occupiers. If need be, many were ready to turn their weapons against the Germans, which of course was wishful thinking.[17] In sentencing several Latvian resistance officers to execution in 1944, a German military court proclaimed that the circumstances of "the year 1919" must not return – a reference to the time when the Latvians had their own army which fought against the Germans.[18]

Relationships at the front were not always good. According to reports by the men, the talk among the troops was quite anti-German, for they were viewed as Latvia's historical enemy. And this happened in an occupied country, where "incorrect" speech was dangerous. The Russians were feared, the Germans were hated.

Dr. Stephen Weiss, a lecturer at the War Studies Department at King's College, London, knew, or thought he knew it all better when the Reuters news agency interviewed him on the Latvian soldiers' memorial day in March 2006. He dismissed claims that the Latvian soldiers were patriots. "I can't get over how little we've learned in 60 years. Many might claim patriotism, but ideology drove them," Dr. Weiss said.[19] I dare say that this is a totally ignorant statement.

After the war, the UNRRA accepted explanations by Latvian refugee officials and diplomats that the legionnaires were not of a mind with Hitler but ordinary Latvians of whom the majority were neither SS nor volunteers but were recruited or coerced to participate. UNRRA told the Allied troops occupying Germany to free any interned legionnaires.

It is well documented that the German Waffen-SS committed atrocities. The Nuremberg War Crimes Trials declared the SS, the SD, and the Gestapo criminal organizations. Almost all elements of the SS were considered to be criminal, "except conscripts who had committed no crimes," that is, Waffen-SS divisions composed of Balts. Thus many former Latvian legionnaires were used to guard the prison and the Nuremberg Palace of Justice for a couple of years beginning with spring 1947.[20]

The U. S. intelligence service investigated the legionnaires and cleared them of charges. Ignoring Moscow's objections, the U. S. Immigration and Naturalization Service did not refuse the immigration of Latvian legionnaires. American Displaced Persons Commissioner Harry Rosenfield announced in September 1950: "The Baltic Waffen SS Units (Baltic Legions) are to be considered as separate and distinct in purpose, ideology, activities, and qualifications for membership from the German SS, and therefore the Commission holds them not to be a movement hostile to the Government of the United States under section 13 of the Displaced Persons Act, as amended."[21]

At the end of the war, it was to the advantage of both Germany and Russia to call the legionnaires volunteers. The Germans wanted to forget having decreed illegal military service, and the Russians wanted to exaggerate the number and strength of the fascists in order to highlight their victory and the "liberation" of Latvia.

The truth about the legionnaires was known already during the war by the intelligence services of many countries – also of Germany and Russia. Although the Germans stated that they fought well (over three thousand of them received the Iron Cross), at no time until the end of the war did they really trust the Latvian soldiers and officers.[22]

The leadership of the NKVD reported in Moscow in 1943 that the legionnaires were nominally volunteers, but "as a matter of fact, the whole age group had been forcibly mobilized," and that there had been cases of men who hid or fled. Soviet military intelligence asserted that the Latvians' winding up in the German units could "hardly have happened voluntarily."[23] Likewise the U.S. intelligence service, the OSS, reported a large group of fugitives living in the woods and stated that the "volunteers" as a matter of fact had no choice.

A British political intelligence survey on Latvia in July 1943 remarked that all Latvians were oriented against Germans and Russians and that while there were many "quislings" in Latvia, especially among the lower bureaucracy and in the officer corps, on the whole Latvians were nationalists.[24]

The fact that the Legion fought only on the eastern, not the western front is one of the reasons the Soviets hated the legionnaires so much that they executed Latvian prisoners, even men who defected from the Legion and surrendered to the Russians.[25] The legionnaires did not give up their fight after the war, either: many of the leaders and members of the national partisans or forest brethren, who fought the Soviets until 1956, were Legion veterans.

On a visit to Finland, President Vladimir Putin laid a wreath on the grave of Marshall Mannerheim, Russia's old archenemy, whose troops attacked the Soviet Union beside the Germans in 1941. At the same time, Russia finds it impossible to approve the choices the Latvians were forced to make during the war.

Some scholars still speak of the Latvians as volunteers, without taking into account the pressure applied.[26] The heat aroused abroad by the Latvian veterans reflects a double standard: no one accuses the Finnish Waffen-SS veterans of anything. Yet a 1,400-man battalion of Finns, attached to the Waffen-SS Division Viking, was made up of true volunteers. It fought alongside the Germans all the way to the Caucasus at the time when Finland and Germany were *Waffenbrüder* (brothers-in-arms). From the ranks of these veterans came, among others, two defense ministers in Finland's post-war governments.

Also, hardly anyone wonders that Rīga's tallest and most visible memorial nowadays is the one erected by the Red Army to honor its victory. Russian war veterans decked out in their uniforms and medals of honor and carrying their flags, men and women who glorify Stalin and the Soviet Union, gather at it every May 9th – the most important day of their year – to celebrate, drink vodka and sing without interference, for freedom of speech prevails in Latvia, and the Latvians are tolerant.

Guilt by Association

The Latvian Legion as such could not have had anything directly to do with the destruction of the Jews, for the Legion was formed a year and a half after the Jews' mass murder in Latvia, as is evident in the preceding chapter. But some of its men who had previously served in other uniformed units undeniably had blood on their hands. The fact that Germany assigned individuals and whole units from police battalions to the Legion, eventually even including some 300 Arājs Commando SD men (and Arājs himself), is, however, no reason to brand all 57 000 legionnaires war criminals.[27] Doing so is a typical example of "guilt by association."

Judging from a cable it sent to the commander of British troops in Berlin in 1946, he British Foreign Office understood this. The FO stated that no citizens of Baltic countries can be extradited to the Soviet Union as war criminals and traitors, if the only accusation against them is that they fought the Red Army. Every case had to be decided individually.[28]

However, the Swedish book *Om detta må ni berätta* (*Tell Ye Your Children*) that was presented in different languages to European school children in 2000 makes exactly that mistake – of accusing the legionnaires of being participants in the Holocaust.[29] The book was part of the Swedish government's campaign "Living History" to inform Swedes and the rest of Europe about the horrors of the Holocaust.

The 19th division of the Legion fought with distinction in the Courland pocket to the end of the war; the 15th division was transferred to Germany to re-equip. The archives of the 15th division were found in 2000 in Berlin during work on a construction project. All the division's operations and activities from April 1944 to April 1945 are recorded in those archives. From these documents it becomes clear that the soldiers did not participate in any actions against the civilian population, but only in battles.[30]

Soviet propaganda constantly kept alive suspicions about and accusations against the Latvians, especially against those living in the West. Moscow initiated, for example, the publication *Daugavas Vanagi – Who Are They?*, which was printed in several languages in 1962–1963. In this propaganda pamphlet, dozens of Latvian exile leaders are branded as war criminals; it is clear that the booklet was primarily intended as a tool against them, and it may be that the perpetrators themselves were eventually surprised at the results. The historian Andrew Ezergailis estimates that only some ten percent of the book's information is correct. According to him, the book is an example of one of the most successful post-war disinformation operations by the KGB. The writer, Pauls Ducmanis, who served both Germans and Soviets, is according to him, "a unique chameleon in the history of Latvia." Ducmanis was the author of anti-Semitic and anti-communist propaganda published during the German occupation.

Not only did the Daugavas Vanagi pamphlet have an effect on public opinion and even on the official attitude in the US toward the Latvian exile community, but surprisingly enough, on scholarly research in the West as well. Based in part on it, even extradition processes and court cases have been initiated against a number of refugees whom Ducmanis had accused of specific war crimes. All this effort, however, has not resulted in any convictions.[31]

The main weapon in the KGB disinformation campaign was collective accusations directed against whole ethnic groups of émigrés, who were indiscriminately stamped with the mark of Cain, says Frank Gordon, a Latvian Jew living in Israel. "Holocaust survivors, overseas Jews, and influential Canadian and American Jewish organizations were for years sent English-language brochures fabricated in Moscow, Kiev, Vilnius, and Rīga," he writes. "The gist of these brochures, which was picked up by various media in the US and Canada, was as follows: Those Ukrainians, Latvians, and Lithuanians, they're all Jew-baiters. Those savage Slavs and Balts fled from their homelands with the poor Jews' jewels and gold."[32] Instead of stating something like "many" or "some" Latvians collaborated with the Nazis in killing Jews, it was stated or insinuated that these deeds were done by "the Latvians." An example is the book *Wanted! The Search for Nazis in America*, by Howard Blum.[33] Judging from its contents, Blum most likely took his information on the Latvian exile community almost exclusively from the *Daugavas Vanagi* book and other Soviet pamphlets published in Rīga. Blum's dramatic book, which reads like a suspense novel, has no sources or footnotes.

As stated above, not a single Latvian legionnaire has ever been tried in any court for crimes committed in the context of the Legion's activities.[34] The Soviet Union, for its part, convicted people on the grounds of formal membership in organizations they had belonged to and not for their crimes, and the heaviest punishments were for those who had fought as soldiers. At least 2,652 former legionnaires were tried by Soviet Latvian courts after 1946.[35]

The Jewish Holocaust, on the other hand, was ignored rather than investigated in the Soviet Union, and it was not mentioned in history textbooks and monuments to victims. Jews were not allowed to compete for public sympathy with the Communists as coequal victims, resistance fighters and victors, as the Swedish historian Klas-Göran Karlsson writes. "Also in post-Communist Russia, there has been a certain reluctance to acknowledge the victimization of the Jews during the war. ... The Communist victims and victors in Soviet textbooks have been replaced by Russian patriots, but the millions of Jewish victims are still passed over in silence."[36] The Russian archives were (and still are) closed to foreign researchers who were interested in knowing on what grounds Moscow accused certain refugees of crimes.[37]

The claim that criminals were not punished in Latvia has been answered in Chapter 7. In this small country more of them were sentenced than were Nazi criminals in West Germany after the war – and to harsher punishments. Soviet power saw to that. The United States was not greatly interested in hunting for German war criminals, nor did it send German soldiers to camps. The U. S. occupation officials went to much more trouble in preventing communists from slipping in among refugees and soldiers.[38]

In Latvia the executions began even before they did in Nuremberg, that is, in February of 1946, when seven high-ranking Germans were publicly hanged in Rīga. As if the crimes committed in Latvia were not great enough in themselves, the number of their victims was wildly exaggerated in the sentencing statement.[40] After the war, Soviet scholars presented this kind of an "accurate" tally: during the German occupation in Latvia 923,445 people died!

It was the former Latvian legionnaires in Latvia who experienced an especially hard fate in Soviet "filtration" (screening) and prison camps. Stalin considered them to be Soviet citizens who had committed treason. Fleeing abroad did not always help; Sweden, for example, still turned these men over to the Soviet Union in 1946.[39] Nevertheless, there remained in Sweden several hundred former legionnaires who from time to time have been publicly accused of being war criminals.

Thousands of former legionnaires were punished and discriminated against in Soviet Latvia. It was only a few years after Stalin's death, in the fall of 1955, that amnesty was granted to them, and they began to return home from the Gulag.

The Going Gets Hot in Rīga

Every year when the veterans of the Latvian Legion gather for commemorative events in Rīga or at the Lestene military cemetery, feelings run high in Latvia and elsewhere. The observance occurs on March 16, which is the anniversary of the Velikaya River battle (1943) where both divisions fought side by side.[41] As a result of international protests, this day has not been an official memorial day in Latvia for a few years now. There are already more journalists, camera crews, and demonstrators of different sorts on the spot for the observance than there are veterans, whose ranks are constantly growing thinner.

Recently Russia has proposed resolutions to the UN Human Rights Commission and the Council of Europe, among others, "to resist the rebirth of Nazi ideology." In December 2005, Russia proposed to the UN General Assembly a resolution "condemning the recent manifestations of racism and xenophobia," a resolution which was directed primarily against "Latvian and Estonian fascism." Russia was "quite concerned" and "simply could not understand" why the EU countries did not support the proposal. The Russian multiportal *KM.ru* commented poisonously: "Among those refraining were Georgia, Ukraine, and Moldova. Awaiting another present from Uncle Sam, these states' antidemocratic governments have in fact taken a stand supporting the rehabilitation of fascism."[42]

The well-known investigative journalist Anna Politkovskaya was murdered in Moscow in October 2006. The murder sent shock waves through Europe, and Finland, the presiding country of the EU, promised to discuss human rights and democracy, among other things, with President Putin, who was to attend a meeting in Finland. The Russian ambassador to the European Union said that it would be best if the EU would discuss the state of democracy and human rights in its *own* member countries. As examples he mentioned Latvia and Estonia, their Russian minorities, and the attitude toward their SS veterans.[43]

The media abroad keep writing about "the march of old Nazis in Rīga." Among others, the BBC and the Swedish, German, and Russian foreign ministries criticize the Latvians. Ironically enough, the Russians and the Germans, whose nations started the war, show the veterans the least understanding.

Picture 15. "March 16, Say NO to fascism!" Russian-language leaflets like this are distributed in March before the veterans' memorial day, when the veterans of the Latvian Legion remember their fallen comrades.
Latvijas Avīze 25.02.2006.

"Ethnocentrism and xenophobia are increasing, and the ideologies of anti-Semitism are spreading," the Russian foreign ministry said of Latvia in March 2006, without elaborating.[44]

In February 2004 the Russian foreign ministry published a memorandum "Latvia's SS Legion's participation in war crimes beginning in 1941 [when the Legion did not yet exist] and efforts at a revision [in Latvia] of the Nuremberg tribunal's sentences." According to the memorandum, in Latvia some 313,798 civilians were killed, a figure which has long since been shown to be wrong.[45]

In several Russian cities, anti-Latvian demonstrations have recently been organized, and Latvian tourists' automobiles have been smashed. There have been various boycott campaigns against Latvian goods in Russia. People have been threatened at athletic events, and tourists and journalists who come to the games have been abused. The Latvian embassy in Moscow has repeatedly had to ask officials for protection. Just the same, its windows have been broken and its walls defaced.

In reality, the SS-men's march is a procession of civilian men and women walking from the church to the Freedom Monument with flowers in their hands. No uniforms, flags, or Nazi emblems are visible. The legionnaires' cemetery is far from Rīga, and the only statue there is the sculpture of a mother figure. (Russian special forces blew up memorials in four other Latvian military cemeteries on one December night in 1990.)

Russia has protested the gathering at the cemetery and has called the Cabinet ministers who have visited the place fascists. Nevertheless it is in my opinion the basic right of every nation to recover its own deceased from a battlefield, to bury them in sanctified ground, and to remember them. Unlike at the Yasukuni Shrine in Japan, no known war criminals are among those buried in Lestene.

In 1998, observance of the Latvian soldier's memorial day, March 16, began. The event has since ceased to be an official national holiday, as mentioned above, and representatives of the Latvian leadership no longer participate in its observance. Latvian leaders wish that all fallen soldiers would be remembered on Army day (Lāčplēšu diena), the 11th of November, because on the March date, mostly extremist groups gather, along with the foreign media. According to the government, the March day is used for provocation, in an effort to gain publicity and to discredit Latvia.

In March 2006, officials warned of disorder and even of the danger of terrorism, whereupon the leadership of Latvia could think of no other remedy than to seal off the traditional gathering place, the Freedom Monument in Rīga, together with its surrounding area. On the night before the Memorial Day, a high metal fence appeared around the square under the pretext of beginning repair work. The action astonished and enraged the older citizens, with whom the President wound up in an unpleasant dispute near the Freedom Monument.

On the following day, the local Russian newspaper *Vesti Segodna* spread a banner headline across its front page with the old anti-fascist slogan: *Nye proshli!* ("They did not get through.")

The Latvian veterans had already moved the more important memorial observances out of Rīga. The foreign media nevertheless reported the event year after year, always using a variation of the same phrase, "the Nazi march." There is little hope of explaining the matter to foreigners. Typical is the Norwegian *Aftenposten's* description of the event in April 1998 (the Russian *Izvestija* published the same article later). It tells of how "500 SS-legionnaires organized a demonstration in Rīga." Involved was "a part of the former Latvian army which had fought on the side of the Nazis." Present were also "present holders of power, which sends a very negative signal" to the outside world. "Do the EU and NATO need such a member country?" During the event, "the destruction of the Jews, which in Latvia was especially pitiless, was not mentioned at all." According to the paper, no one can believe the Latvians' claim that they supposedly fought for independence.[46]

Every March, the world is flooded with negative news about Latvia. Journalist Aija Cālīte has researched what the *BBC* has said of the March memorial day. "I read everything the BBC wrote in the years from 1998–2005," she tells us. "The writers may have changed, but the texts are so similar that one can assume they are simply copied from the previous year's archives." The legionnaires were "elite Nazi troops," who fought against the Allies. They were "supporters of the Nazi ideology," and "young radical nationalist Latvians" were continuing their activities. There was also a "counter-force," the Latvian-Russian community which, "in order to save the honor of the country," organizes "anti-fascist demonstrations." The mass murder of the Jews is added to the mix, and the concoction is complete.[47]

In 2006 Ms. Cālīte tried to discuss "Latvian Fascism" with a thirty-year-old Associated Press journalist, who had traveled to Latvia from the US. However, he cut the conversation short by saying: "The Latvian legionaries shot the Jews, and that's all there's to it! I do not have anything else to say to you."[48]

The Irish Times had a piece written before the 2006 memorial day by their former Moscow correspondent saying that Latvia is "slow to face up to unsavory aspects of its past;" there is "an ambivalent attitude to the Nazi past" among Latvians. There continue to be attempts to "cover up the activities of Latvian collaborators during the Nazi occupation." The idea that the Waffen-SS was simply fighting for the country's independence "does not stand up to scrutiny." And finally: "While a number of Communists have been brought to trial for crimes, no Latvian involved in the Holocaust has been convicted."[49]

Although there were no plans to organize any further memorial events in Rīga than a religious service in the church, in February 2006 a group of organizations sent to all members of the EU parliament by means of the Latvian parliament's computers an e-mail message in which they requested that the parliament "prevent the rebirth of fascism and the SS men's celebrating in Latvia."[50] At the same time a europarliamentarian from Latvia sent two letters to her colleagues in which she warned against Latvian neo-Nazism. A Czech member of the EU parliament sent all his colleagues a letter in which he proposed passing a resolution condemning "Rīga's traditional Nazi demonstration." According to him, there was "evidence" that the Baltic Waffen-SS soldiers had taken part in "Hitler's Germany's wars of aggression and in the mass destruction of the Jews."

When in 2005 the Council of Europe was deliberating whether to condemn the crimes of communism, Russia's delegation informed the council that

Picture 16. "Someone has the fields all mixed up." "No to fascism!" In 2005 athletic fields became nearly battlefields in games between Latvia and Russia. Ēriks Osis, Latvijas Avīze, July 2005.

as a counterweight they were preparing a proposal to condemn the "idealization of Nazism occurring in the Baltics." "The SS is marching in the Baltics, and everyone is silent about it," said the Russian Communist representative Gennady Zjuganov.

In March 2006, Russian television (RCTV channel, controlled by the Moscow city government) showed a new documentary film, *Natsizm po pribaltijsky*, "Nazism Baltic Style," the main intent of which is to show that fascism once bloomed in Latvia, and that neo-Nazism now prevails in that land. In the background of this assertion the Latvian parliamentary building and the Latvian flag are shown in the film. The documentary was made at the time when the Council of Europe decided to end monitoring human rights in Latvia. Some concluded that the film was Russia's answer to this decision. Latvia protested, claiming the film incited ethnic hatred.

Into an emotional and fast-moving film are inserted flashbacks of Nazi brutality in different countries during World War II and of demonstrations in present-day Latvia – including, of course, the old legionnaires. According to the film, Latvia voluntarily joined the Soviet Union, 80 percent of the people opposed Ulmanis, and deportation was resorted to in 1941 to avoid civil war. We are reminded that in Nuremberg the SS was branded a criminal organization, and a Latvian Legion division is said to have taken part in crimes against civilians in Russia in 1943–1944. (If such evidence is to be found in Russian archives, it has never been published.)

The film compares the murder of the Jews in Latvia to the Turkish genocide of Armenians in 1915. Many of the episodes in the film have nothing to do with Latvia, as the director of the Rīga Jewish museum testifies. Thus the film reminds us of the previously mentioned Soviet propaganda book on *Daugavas Vanagi*, where the pictures were also tendentiously chosen, to put it mildly, and of the Russian book *Latvija pod igom natsizma* mentioned in the previous chapter. According to the vice-director of the Latvian war museum, what is involved is "political pornography."[51]

One Russian-Latvian teacher declared publicly that in the teaching of history in her school, not a single history text printed in Latvia is used. Instead, Latvian history is taught from "original sources and by viewing such films as *Natsizm po pribaltijsky*."[52]

It is interesting (and a little worrying) to see that the new British documentary film on Latvia, *In Hitler's Footsteps*, directed by Richard Bradford, seems to be as slanderous and as far from the truth as the Russian film – if not more so. This film, too, uses pictures of Nazi concentration camps that have nothing to do with Latvia. I believe that the "facts" of the film must emanate from Russia, and the total lack of comprehension of the history of Eastern Europe makes the end result a terrible mess. Looking at it I felt, for the first time while writing this book, that somebody should be sued for spreading irresponsible hate propaganda.[53]

The "SS men" are a fundamental factor in creating Latvia's reputation. Many would prefer to remain silent about them; they hope that the problem will go away. They say that the world will never come to understand the Latvians, so that it is better to keep a low profile and accept the accusations in silence. Some seem to think: to hell with world opinion, they are our heroes, anyway.[54]

I think that neither approach is right. The only solution will be open discussion, continuing serious research on the subject, and informing foreign audiences tirelessly. To me the tragedy of Latvian soldiers is a triple tragedy: at the end of the war they felt let down by the West, the East branded them criminals and punished them; and now both the East and West are attacking them together.

9

Did the Soviet Union occupy Latvia?
Were the Latvians victims of genocide?

Where there is a person, there is a problem – no person, no problem.

STALIN

In addition to the view that Latvia was legally and voluntarily united with the Soviet Union (Chapter 6) still held by some, it is also claimed that Latvia was not occupied, but was part of the Soviet Union, on a par with all the other Soviet republics, and that its inhabitants were as well (or as badly) off as the Russians of Russia.[1] Whatever had happened, was an "internal affair" – "accepted" by the West, as American and British "passivity" proves.

This is an important issue, and not merely one of semantics and terminology. If the term "occupation" is accepted, many of the acts committed in Latvia by the Soviet authorities were clearly illegal under various international laws and conventions. This would give Latvians the right to request compensation.

First I would like to state that for me it is completely clear that Latvia was occupied three times: by the Soviet Union in 1940–1941, by Germany in 1941–1944/45, and by the Soviet Union in 1944/45–1991.

The occupation has been officially denied by Moscow for 65 years.[2] Even today not everybody in Latvia understands or recognizes it for what it was, a situation which is, in the eyes of some scholars, a threat to future development. Social historian Leo Dribins writes that the split in historical points of view is a serious matter, for in Latvian society, two diametrically opposite views prevail regarding Latvia's recent history. For one faction, Latvia's post-war era was difficult: it meant another occupation by the Soviet Union and another loss of independence, while for immigrants arriving from the East, settling in Latvia meant a better life after poverty, humiliation, and years of war.[3]

Moscow did not, as a matter of fact, consider Soviet Latvia a republic comparable to the others, but as an occupied area in which they were to behave as occupiers should. Latvia was a military outpost; the greatest privileges and the "good life" did not belong to Latvian party leaders but to Russian commanders of the Baltic military district and to the KGB elite.[4] Military and security forces were directly subordinated to Moscow, and both perceived Latvia as an occupied, hostile territory. They had a negative attitude towards Latvians and dealt with them accordingly.[5]

Listening to Latvians of older generations, the eyewitnesses of the events of 1940, one gets the impression that for the great majority what happened was occupation. Those born later may have a different perception. Political scientist Rasma Kārkliņš writes that Latvians nowadays often view World War II as beginning in 1941, forgetting that everything began with the agreement between Hitler and Stalin in 1939. "I read recently of a questionnaire regarding Latvian attitudes towards the occupation of 1940. Almost half of the respondents thought there had been no occupation. In my opinion that view reflects the effect of the Soviet schools, but certainly it is also a question of not thinking the matter through – many think that since there was no resistance when the Soviet army arrived, there was also no occupation."[6]

That historical point is understood even less in Russia. The British historian and writer Anthony Beevor said in an interview in a French paper: "Putin's version of history is to appropriate Stalin's Great Patriotic War with all its myths and all its victims, and the Russian militarists to whom the 70-year Soviet regime gave birth resist the publication and exploration of unpleasant facts."[7]

At a press conference during the celebration of Victory Day in Moscow in May 2005, President Putin said that in speaking continually of the "occupation" and demanding Abrene back, the Balts only got themselves "a dead jackass's ears," and went on to give a lecture on history: Under the Brest-Litovsk treaty in 1918 Russia had to turn over some of its territories (the Baltics) to Germany. "In 1939, there was another collusion between Russia and Germany, and Germany returned them to us, and these territories joined the Soviet Union." Consequently, "in 1941 we could not possibly have occupied them, inasmuch as they were already a part of the USSR. ... Whether this was good or bad, such was history. It was a secret deal, the small states being a currency of exchange."[8]

Whatever one's opinion of this statement may be, this juggling of historical dates by a head of state is almost incomprehensible. The Soviet Union occupied the Baltic countries in *1940*, at which time they were also joined to it, and in 1941, *Germany* occupied them.

Also, Putin ignores Latvian independence (1918) and implies that for decades Latvia was German property. Moreover, Brest-Litovsk was superseded by the 1920 peace treaty between Latvia and Soviet Russia.

Faithfully following the plot laid out in Soviet school texts, Putin said that this issue was not a question of an occupation, but a benevolent attempt to prevent bloodshed when "a revolutionary situation had developed." He made a joke of the matter by adding: "I did not do very well at university, because I drank a lot of beer, but I remember some things; we had good teachers."

As historian Irēne Šneidere writes, "for its part, the Russian Federation, the successor state to the Soviet Union, still refuses to admit not only the fact of occupation itself, but also the fact that the Soviet regime committed crimes against humanity, which, as is generally known, are not subject to a statute of limitations." Šneidere also observes that the Soviet Union has attributed its own crimes to others and vilified those who dared to speak of these crimes, calling them "traitors to the Fatherland" or "Nazi collaborators."[9]

Ultimatum and Submission

First it must be said that international law does not consider agreements between unequal parties to be valid, when one party dictates them from its position of power – even less so if the weaker party is the object of military pressure and if the negotiation offer falls under the heading of an "ultimatum."[10] Such was the occurrence in the case of Latvia, as was explained in Chapter 6. Or, more than ultimatum, it was an announcement that the Red Army was coming in, whatever the Latvian government did. Latvia had nine hours to give the answer that she agreed to the Soviet's terms. Chapter 6 also indicates that the annexation to the Soviet Union flagrantly violated the laws and the constitution of Latvia.

It can be said that by sending its troops into Latvia in 1940 the Soviet Union broke many treaties it had signed, treaties that forbade war, blockade and aggression. We have to remember also that the two countries had signed a peace agreement in 1920 and a non-aggression treaty in 1932.[11]

Things were complicated by Ulmanis' unfortunate speech on June 17, 1940. As indicated above, he did not mention the ultimatum and told the nation that a "friendly" military force was entering the country and should not be opposed; he seemed almost to welcome the Red Army. Is it right that Latvians must silently suffer for decades for of the unfortunate wording of their leader's speech and his subsequent actions (signing the new decrees, laws etc.)? Was he in fact guilty of treason? We could state that he did not express the will of the

Picture 17. In June of 1940 the New York Times published a one column news report about the occupations of Latvia and Estonia. Museum of the Occupation of Latvia collections.

majority of the people and that he was not a democratically elected leader; this again would give the Soviets a chance to say that they helped depose a dictator (replacing him, of course, with a much harsher dictatorship).[12]

The official Soviet Union and Russia have always held the opinion that the annexation of the Baltic States was not an illegal action. According to their explanation, "before the founding of the United Nations, there was no international norm forbidding a nation to use pressure or threaten with the use of force."[13] According to the Russian foreign ministry, the annexation of the Baltic countries was in accord with the international law of the time and "all formalities were taken into account."[14]

Nikolai Kabanov, a Russian member of the Latvian parliament, says: "Occupation means a state of war, but Latvia was not in a state of war with the Soviet Union in June 1940." We might add: there was no state of war between Germany and Denmark, either, and still we know that Denmark was occupied. In fact, Hitler did not declare war on the USSR on June 22, 1941.

Russian Ambassador to Latvia Viktor Kalyuzhny says that Russia never did bring an occupation government onto Latvian territory (true, they did not *import* it – they picked local collaborators), but that Latvia itself joined the Soviet Union. He has said that Latvian historians "fantasize about an occupation" and blame the Russians due to ignorance. He is prepared to approve the term "iron curtain," but not the word "occupation." The ambassador recommends the establishment of a Russian-Latvian research group to study the matter.[15]

For decades the Soviet Union did not admit publicly making the secret agreement regarding spheres of interest with the Germans, which gave them the "right" of occupation. At the Nuremberg war crimes trial, the accused Germans tried to present a copy of it, but the chief Russian prosecutor, with the help of the judge, did his best to prevent its admission. The Soviet Union feared that its own war crimes and crimes against humanity would come to light at Nuremberg. Most troublesome was the fact that the intelligence and secret police agency, the NKVD, had worked closely with just those Nazi organizations that were proven criminal at Nuremberg. One could not speak of that.

Soon after the start of the Nuremberg trial, the USA, the Soviet Union, Great Britain, and France made a secret agreement that the 1939 pact as well as the question of the Soviet Baltic republics would be omitted from the proceedings. Additional problems arouse regarding the mass murder of Polish prisoners at Katyn in 1940, the handling of which the Soviets demanded, against the advice of the West. The Soviets falsely charged the Germans with this bloodbath, and many in the West believed them. It is true that at the same time the Germans were carrying out their own somewhat smaller mass murder in western Poland, which they had conquered.[16]

When the secret protocols were published in the West, Moscow claimed they were forgeries. The Russians asserted that the original of the secret portion of the Molotov-Ribbentrop pact could not be found in the Soviet archives. The same claim was made as late as 1989 when an Estonian representative in the Soviet parliament demanded it, along with a discussion of the legality of the Baltic occupation. At the same time, a Latvian deputy of the parliament, Mavriks Vulfsons, aired the issue; he had talked with a German diplomat who had witnessed the signing of the secret protocols.

During Christmas of the same year, the Soviet People's Congress (parliament) made a "political and legal judgment" accepting the non-aggression pact but not its secret addendum on the partition of Europe, which was not "in accord with Leninist foreign policy principles" and was an offense to the sovereignty of several third-party states. The deputies condemned "Stalin's ultimatum politics" and viewed the secret agreement illegal and invalid. Since it had not been presented to the Soviet parliament in 1939, it did not "in any way reflect the will of the Soviet people who do not bear any responsibility for this plot."[17] The Soviet parliament never linked the secret protocols to the annexation of the Baltic countries. This was because its mandate concerned only the year 1939.

In the autumn of 1992 it was revealed that the original of the secret agreement had been found in the Communist Party's Politburo archives. Russia did not go so far, however, as to admit to having occupied the Baltic States and to ask pardon for it, as the Baltic governments expect.

Continuity or a New State?

Was Latvia occupied by the Soviets?[18] The question is not only one of terminology, as I have stated. When the independence movement declared Latvia independent again by the resolutions of 1990 and 1991, the starting point was that this Latvia was a legal continuation of the first republic (a democratic one, not Ulmanis' Latvia) and not a new state. In the interim the country had merely been occupied. Thus the people who had been brought into the country during the occupation did not automatically have the right to citizenship. Those who had been living in Latvia before the summer of 1940 and their descendants would become citizens without further ado.

Estonia and Lithuania have also retained this principle of "state continuity." Russia instead considers that in 1991, three new nations were formed in the Baltics.[19]

Also, Latvia had concluded a peace treaty with Soviet Russia in 1920, an agreement by which Moscow promised to honor Latvia's independence and inviolability forever. Latvia was larger then; Russia annexed Abrene in 1944. This is a sensitive matter; the Russians suspect that the Latvians will make territorial demands.

Many western countries also view Latvia's regaining independence as a continuation of the "old Latvia." They have not made separate resolutions recognizing its independence, but have merely announced that the *de jure* recognition granted in the 1920's has never been withdrawn – only diplomatic relationships had been cut – and is again in force.

When Latvia was accepted as a member of the UN in 1991, the Security Council declared that "the independence of the Baltic countries was *regained* [my italics] through peaceful means."[20] The Soviet Union, one of the permanent members of the Council, did not then protest this interpretation of continuity. Latvia emphasized that it was not a successor to the former Soviet state. Moscow alluded to this declaration when it recognized Latvian independence.

It was only a couple of years later, when the debate over the Russian troops in the Baltic States and the Latvian and Estonian citizenship laws came to a head, that Russia came up with the argument that agreements between Latvia and the USSR were legal, that Latvia had joined the Soviet Union voluntarily, that there had been no occupation, and that a new country had now been formed that had nothing to do with the "old" Latvia. Russia insists that all those residing in the country in 1991 should therefore have been granted citizenship on equal terms.

In fact there had been, of course, no "agreements," and the Russians had also broken the promises they had made when their troops entered Latvia. An illegitimate parliament established by a rigged, single-slate election had passed a resolution (by asking whether anyone objected!) proclaiming Latvia a Soviet republic, and then by an equally fraudulent resolution asked for admission to the USSR.

The U. S. has never acknowledged that Latvia and the other Baltic States were a part of the Soviet Union either *de jure* or *de facto*. This political principle was formulated by Under Secretary of State Sumner Welles as early as July 1940.[21] This, however, was a formality only. The West, not wanting to offend Moscow, its important ally, practiced *realpolitik* from 1941 on and accepted Soviet occupation as a "lesser evil." Western allies adopted ambivalent policies toward the Baltic States: *de facto* recognition of the occupation and Soviet hegemony on one hand, and *de jure* non-recognition of the annexation. on the other[22]

The Soviet Union joined the Western Allies – the USA and Britain – in September 1941 in formulating the Atlantic Charter. This charter, like the United Nations proclamation of 1942, stated principles of self-determination, including "the right of all peoples to choose the form of government under which they live" and expressed a wish "to see sovereign rights and self-government restored to those who have been forcibly deprived of them." In addition, it rejected territorial changes made against a nation's will. Moscow, however, was permitted a reservation regarding the inviolability of borders: she would approve only the 1941 borders, and in that year, the Baltic States already had been included in the Soviet Union.[23] To help explain to the West why Latvia had to be annexed, Russian diplomats branded Latvians "Nazis" and pro-German.[24]

President F.D. Roosevelt said in March 1942, that he would have nothing against Russia occupying the Baltic States again. For domestic political reasons he did not want to declare this publicly.[25] His view became known to Stalin, at the latest, at the Teheran summit in November–December 1943, where the post-war fate of the Baltic States was a major but unofficial subject of controversy. The Allies announced ostentatiously that they had decided to "eliminate tyranny and slavery, oppression and intolerance," while the foreign ministers of the USA and Britain recognized in practice the incorporation of the Baltic States into the USSR. Roosevelt said privately to Stalin that he understood the latter's territorial demands in the Baltics. After that the Baltic countries were not discussed further in the conferences of the great powers.[26]

The Yalta summit in 1945 has been denounced as a sell-out, because Roosevelt "yielded" a number of Eastern and Central European countries to Stalin's sphere of influence. Stalin, however, already had them. We must take into consideration that the Red Army at the time had occupied all of Eastern Europe, so that the West was in a weak position. It would have been impossible for the Allied armies to liberate the Baltic countries. Faced with that reality Roosevelt and Churchill gave up on them and tried to get some concessions elsewhere – and for a while thought they had.

In his 49-page account of the Yalta Conference in *The Second World War,* Winston Churchill does not say one word about The Baltic countries.[27] Almost all the sessions of the conference were devoted to Poland, an extremely important issue. As Churchill writes, "we could never accept any settlement which did not leave Poland free, independent and sovereign."[28]

When Europe was again thus divided into spheres of influence, the Baltics were no longer mentioned separately. According to Stalin, the matter was "an internal Soviet question." The fate of the Baltic countries was no longer an international problem.

In Potsdam in the summer of 1945, the Western powers accepted the western border of the Soviet Union. The Paris peace treaty in 1947 confirmed what had been decided at Yalta. Estonia, Latvia and Lithuania found themselves the only occupied European states whose independence was not restored after World War II.

Notwithstanding Roosevelt's position, the USA has always insisted that it had not approved the forcible annexation of Latvia. This was a nice gesture but did not mean anything in practice (before 1991). The Latvian embassy was allowed to continue functioning over the decades as a recognized legation in Washington. The US Congress approved several proclamations, which condemned the annexation of Latvia to the Soviet Union and demanded freedom for the Baltics.

Britain acknowledged the occupation *de facto.* Its foreign ministry did not approve the credentials of Latvia's refugee envoys nor acknowledge their official notes. It treated them as individuals, not as embassy heads or representatives of a state. (The London Legation nonetheless continued to be able to issue passports.)

Latvia and its history disappeared from the *Encyclopaedia Britannica* in the 1970's; now there was only an entry titled *Latvian Soviet Socialist Republic*, written by a Russian academician. This is the first sentence of the article:

> Latvia was constituted on July 21, 1940, as one of 15 republics of the Soviet Union and was proclaimed a Soviet Socialist Republic on August 5, 1940.

This first sentence already contains factual errors, what is more important, the encyclopedia assumes that Latvia has no history before 1940. The only mention of earlier times in the long article is the following enigmatic, sentence: "Song festivals have been held in Latvia since 1873 and are popular throughout the Soviet Union."[29]

Consistent Occupation

Was Latvia then an occupied country or not? At least Marshal Timoshenko reported to Stalin in 1940 on the situation in the "conquered republics" – a clear reference to occupation. As early as July 1940 Soviet officials arrested some 150 Latvian citizens and residents, deporting seventy of them to Russia. That occurred before the meeting of the new Latvian parliament, that is, before the country was annexed to the Soviet Union, even before she "petitioned" for annexation. The goal was "to cleanse the state apparatus from reactionary elements and enemies of the people." It is almost unheard of for the officials of a neighboring country to arrest citizens of another, nominally independent country, and to transport them out of their own land. Among the victims were most Latvian government ministers. Already before the July 1940 elections, the Soviet State Bank demanded the gold reserves of the Baltic countries' banks from Sweden, the US and Britain for itself.[30]

At the end of August, the Soviet Constitution replaced the Latvian Constitution. By then, 450 people had already been arrested. In the autumn of 1940 the Russian Federation's criminal law went into effect in Latvia, and it also became retroactive. For "treason to the Fatherland [the Soviet Union]" people were sentenced for what they had done, for example, in Latvia's liberation war 20 years earlier. 1,086 officers, half of the officers of the Latvian army, were killed, detained or deported, or disappeared in 1940–1941. Every sixth soldier – 4,665 men of 30,843 – in Latvia was taken prisoner or killed.[31] The Latvian

Communist Party, the only party that was allowed, was made an affiliate of the Soviet Communist Party CPSU(b).

The process of Sovietization embraced all aspects of society. According to Russians, this was not the imposition of Soviet rule but rather its "restoration," which sounds more than a little far-fetched if we consider that Red rule in the Baltic countries in 1918–1919 was very limited in terms of both time and territory. Soviet premier Vyacheslav Molotov declared that his country was "retaking territory" that the western powers had torn from it then.[32]

The term "restoration" was consistent with the Soviet reduction of the Baltics' period of independence to a historical episode only. The Soviets were keen on wiping this "episode" from the minds of the population – for example, memorials to the liberation war were destroyed, books were banned and burned, and schools had to celebrate the anniversaries of the October Revolution, of Stalin's Constitution Day, and the birthday of Lenin instead of national holidays.[33]

In Latvia the word "occupation" was uttered publicly for the first time in June 1988, when the previously mentioned Communist official Vulfsons declared at a forum of creative arts unions that the events of June 1940 were an occupation, not a socialist revolution. At the end of 1990 Latvia's first free political party, the LNNK demanded that Latvia be declared a state under occupation.[34]

A German historian, Erwin Oberländer, who is well versed in Latvian history, has noted that Latvians spoke previously of the "Soviet era," but that from the mid-90's on, of the "occupation." Oberländer understands why the man in the street should speak thus, but in his opinion the latter term does not belong in learned discourse. The question is one of "more than occupation, something even far worse, namely annexation." Occupation is generally the temporary condition of a conquered area during wartime, annexation is long-term, and is "meant to be permanent."

Oberländer says that one could speak of occupation if the Russians had been responsible for everything in Latvia – had decided and done everything without the participation of the Latvians. After Stalin's death, when a slow process of "de-sovietization" began, opportunities to take action opened up even for Latvians.[35]

Was It Genocide?

Did the Latvians fall victim to genocide? According to the United Nations 1948 "Convention on the Prevention and Punishment of the Crime of Genocide" certain "acts committed with intent to destroy, in whole or in part, a national, ethnical, racial or religious group" meet the criteria of genocide. That convention forbids, for example, "measures intended to prevent births in the group," and "forcibly transferring children in the group to another group." Forcible population transfer in an occupied country also qualifies as genocide.[36]

Oberländer says that the Stalin era with its deportations "nearly" gives us cause to speak of genocide; at least it was in itself a crime against humanity; both are crimes which have no statute of limitations.[37] Deportation alone is not, however, ethnic murder, even if many people die during it. "Before one can be condemned for ethnic murder, one must be able to show that he has from the beginning planned the destruction of some ethnic, religious, or racial group."

Latvian historian Kaspars Zellis writes that "genocide against Latvians is a myth." Another myth fostered by Latvians is, according to him, "the year of horror" 1940–1941 (the Soviet occupation), when as a matter of fact, the more horrible year was 1941–42 (during the German occupation). "One must understand and admit that the Russians and Jews also suffered." In Zellis's opinion, it is also dangerous to identify the Soviet regime with the Russians.

On the other hand, the Latvian historian Heinrihs Strods, who is well versed in foreign, also Russian, archives, specifically uses the words "occupation," "colonization," and "genocide."[38] "Not only during the deportation periods in 1941 and 1949, but during the entire occupation, the ethnic murder fell upon the Latvians as a people," he says.[39] Strods writes that today the majority of Russian historians admit that the Baltic States were occupied, but they tend to deny that the sovietization had an ethnic Russian character."[40]

Strods points out the military nature of the process, including the settlement of retired military personnel throughout the country. He also stresses the fact that the Latvian Communist Party was controlled by Moscow's interests and its proxies in the membership, which was overwhelmingly Russian.

Some historians claim that an ethnic cleansing and genocide of Latvians began in the Soviet Union as early as 1937. By November of the next year, according to some Russian historians, the death penalty had been imposed upon at least 16,573 Latvians. However, according to the new *History of Latvia*, killing them cannot be called genocide; Stalin did not intend to kill all 150,000 Latvians in the USSR. Historian Aivars Stranga writes that Stalin's hatred towards Latvians was not ethnic or racist in nature; he wanted only to end the influence of Latvians in the Communist party.[41]

According to a book published in 2002 by the Museum of the Occupation of Latvia, "though not directly, *in effect* these [Soviet] policies and practices threatened the physical and national survival of the Latvians in their homeland." The book observes that the UN Convention on Genocide speaks only of

Picture 18. Every May large numbers of Russian veterans gather to celebrate Stalin and the liberation of Rīga at a victory monument erected by the Soviet state. The highly visible monument is the city's largest.
Uldis Briedis, Diena 14.05.2005.

Picture 19. "This I got for the five years on the battlefields, and this I got for 16 years of suffering in nationalist Latvia".
Gatis Šļūka, Latvijas Avīze 09.05.2006.

various means of *physical* destruction of a group in whole or in part. "It does not deal with the possibility that a ... group can also be destroyed 'as such' by destroying the cultural and social characteristics that distinguish it as a distinct entity from all others. Soviet policies and practices, first by brutality, later by Sovietization and russification, threatened the Latvian nation with both forms of extinction."[42] Other historians speak about "social genocide."[43]

I am not sure whether the term genocide could and should be used in this way. A better term may be cultural imperialism – marginalization of the local language, culture, religion, and customs by energetic colonization. This process was also used in the republics of the Caucasus and Central Asia. Some of them have a Russian population on the same order as Latvia, similarly privileged and arrogant.[44]

The previously mentioned historian, Šneidere, writes that practically all researchers looking into the June 1941 deportation now agree that it was a crime against humanity, and some say that it qualifies as genocide. People were deported without having any charge brought against them, without a trial or a chance to defend themselves. This, according to Šneidere, was in violation of the 1929 Geneva Convention that prohibited "individual or mass forcible transfers, as well as deportations" of persons from occupied territory to the occupying country or to any other country for any reason, and the transfer of colonists to this territory."

The 1907 Hague Convention on Warfare states that "Territory is considered occupied when it is actually placed under the authority of the hostile army" (Article 42).[45] The Convention applies to all cases of occupation, even if the occupation meets with no armed resistance. "The authority of the legitimate power having in fact passed into the hands of the occupant, the latter shall take all the measures in its power to restore, and ensure, as far as possible, public order and safety, while respecting, unless absolutely prevented, the laws in force in the country" (Art. 43). "It is forbidden to compel the inhabitants of occupied territory to swear allegiance to the hostile Power" (Art. 45). And another article (46) that was breached in Soviet Latvia: "Family honour and rights, the lives of persons, and private property, as well as religious convictions and practice, must be respected. Private property cannot be confiscated."

A research group writing of "repression" in Latvia feels that according to the Hague Convention, the national partisans or "forest brethren" of Latvia fall into the category of combatants (armed military personnel). According to the scholars, Soviet officials violated the Convention rules in the unconventional "dirty war" against this enemy.[46]

Let it be stated that an international organization has "recognized" that Latvia was occupied. On January 13, 1983, the EC (presently the EU) parliament almost unanimously approved the decision, which condemned the Soviet Union for having carried out "the occupation of these formerly independent and neutral [Baltic] countries." The annexation to the USSR was declared illegal under international law.[47] In 1960, 1963, and 1987, the Council of Europe parliamentary assembly condemned the illegal annexation and the "military occupation" of the Baltics and affirmed that the majority of governments of the world had not approved it. According to the resolution, the "voluntary union with the Soviet Union is a myth." "As a matter of fact, the [Baltic] countries are colonies of the Soviet Union."

In 1965–1966, the US Senate and the House of Representatives unanimously approved a resolution according to which the Soviet Union had robbed the Baltic peoples by force of their right to self-determination and was continuing to change the ethnic constitution of the population.[48]

A few years ago, the European Court of Human Rights, in dealing with a Russian family's complaint, affirmed that in 1940 Latvia was subjected to occupation by the Soviet Army, and that the independent Latvia of 1991 was not a new state, but the Latvian Republic which had declared its independence in 1918.

In March 2006 The European Court of Human Rights declared with rare clarity in its decision on "Ždanoka v. Latvia" that Latvia was an occupied country and had been joined to the Soviet Union by force.[49] The Court noted that "Latvia, together with the other Baltic States, had lost its independence in 1940 in the aftermath of the partition of central and eastern Europe agreed to by Hitler's Germany and Stalin's Soviet Union by way of the secret protocol to the Molotov-Ribbentrop Pact, an agreement contrary to the generally recognized principles of international law." The Court affirmed that after an ultimatum, the Soviet Army had attacked the country and that Latvia had become a part of the Soviet Union by force. The annexation was directed by the Soviet Union's Communist Party, of which the Latvian Communist Party was a branch. A foreign country's – Russia's – army had remained on Latvian territory until 1994.[50]

So much for Mr. Putin's "jackass's ears" when Balts speak of an occupation.

10

Did the Latvians succumb to Soviet power, cooperate with the Communist authorities, and start their independence movement only after the Lithuanians and Estonians had begun theirs?

*The Latvian is like a mushroom. He grows immediately from
the effect of rain, but the mushroom also strongly absorbs
all noxious poisons and radiation.*

A BALTIC GERMAN HISTORIAN IN 2007

As is clear by now, the Soviet and German occupations were a severe blow to the Latvian people, culture, and economy. It is surprising that the people have survived to this day. It is a sign of their great resilience.

Latvia was vulnerable to colonization, for almost a fourth of her pre-war population had been lost – an even greater proportion than that in Estonia and Lithuania.[1] The British historian Norman Davies writes in his new book: "Soviet protection" has cost the Baltic States up to a quarter of their population. Most western history books don't even mention it: if they do, they employ the blandest of tones."[2]

It has been calculated that a total of 600,000 to 700,000 inhabitants of Latvia suffered violence, persecution, and upheaval during the 1940's and 1950's, and that the total losses were at least 325,000 inhabitants.[3]

In 1935 Latvia had 1.47 million inhabitants of Latvian origin, but there were only 1.38 million of them in 1989 and 1.37 million in 2000.[4] Latvia's total population in 1914 had been about 2.6 million; now it is under 2.3 million. In comparison, Finland's population has risen during this time from 3.1 million to over 5.3 million.

Particularly injurious for Latvia was the fact that its elite – her cultured, prosperous, educated, politically active secular and spiritual leaders – were killed, deported to the East, or fled the Red Army to the West and remained there. Among the refugees in the West there were 627 university faculty members, 564 physicians, 766 engineers, 336 clergymen and 52 writers. A Latvian scholar has estimated that 70 percent of his country's writers, artists, musicians, and actors made it to Western Europe in 1945.[5] They hoped to return home soon; they believed that the West would insist on the restoration of the Baltic States' independence. Very few did return, although they were under heavy pressure to do so.

In all, some 217,000 refugees and other Latvians ended up in German territory or Sweden, that is, 12 percent of the population. 30,000 of them were soldiers. About 120,000 made it to the West and remained there.[6]

The occupation and the sovietizing that occurred during it injured society in many ways. Those who had fled to the West became non-persons, of whom nothing was ever heard in Soviet Latvia, at least not anything truthful. It was dangerous to receive mail from them. Those who were taken to Siberia were "traitors to their country," so that it was difficult to maintain contact with them as well. Lasting gulfs of suspicion opened up. To put it simply: the Latvians who remained in the country now feel that the refugee-emigrants have "had it easy" and do not understand what the Latvians had to endure at home; the refugees consider that Soviet rule corrupted the home Latvians, that they need to be taught what democracy is, and that they are no longer able to speak and write Latvian correctly.

The conflict flared up again recently when the academician Jānis Freimanis wrote that the Latvian emigration was *economic* in nature, that if the Latvians abroad were political refugees, they would have returned to Latvia with its liberation in 1991 (as if it would have been so simple after 47 years!). To him it seemed that they could no longer be called refugees. And further: "The Latvian people survived thanks to those who stayed, not to those who went abroad."

People have replied to Freimanis that most of those who left feared for their lives, and that internment in refugee camps in Germany during and after the war was not easy, much less "economically enticing." But it is often conceded that the nation survived because so many did, despite everything, remain in Latvia.[7]

Poet and scholar Uldis Bērziņš writes that when he was a child, a family friend, a Latvian university teacher, walked along the empty seashore at Jūrmala and impressed on him: "You are to remember that in the West there is truly 'another Latvia,' that parallel to the history of Latvia under Soviet rule the history of the independent republic of Latvia is still continuing there. If it were not so, Moscow would be speaking to us in a totally different tone."[8]

A Wedge in the Middle of the Baltics

Latvia is located between Estonia and Lithuania, and Moscow's actions made it a wedge in the center of the Baltics. More people were deported from Latvia than from the rest of the Baltics, and the occupier sent more Russian soldiers and settlers into Latvia. Already by the spring of 1947 nearly 59,000 demobilized Russian officers and ex-servicemen with their families had been settled in Latvia. Rīga was a preferred location, and there were inducements: above all the possibility of getting a place to live. Decommissioned officers had the right to bypass others in the waiting lists.

Latvia had a strategic military significance for the western border of the Soviet Union. The headquarters of the Baltic military district was established in Rīga and many other military and intelligence installations were located there. Three percent of Latvia's area was taken over for military use; there were in all 850 military sites, more than in the other Baltic countries. Nuclear weapons were kept in Latvia until the 1990's.[9]

Matters pertaining to defense, as well as internal affairs and security installations, came directly under the control of Moscow, and thus were not decided by Latvia. Also large "All-Union" factories, which often belonged to the military sphere, were controlled directly by ministries in Moscow.[10]

In contrast to what Soviet propaganda claimed, most Latvians did not receive the Soviet system with cheers in 1940. The occupation was a shock and a lasting psychological trauma to many. Any initial enthusiasm soon turned into hatred – except among the beneficiaries of the Soviet regime.

William L. Shirer, whose anti-German bias is well known, when writing about Latvia and the other Baltic States in his *The Rise and Fall of the Third Reich*, stated that Stalin, in dealing with small countries, could be as crude and ruthless as Hitler, and even more cynical.[11]

On the 14th of June, 1941, the Soviet Union, which evidently sensed that the war would spread, deported to the east, in one night, without a court order, some 15,500 inhabitants of Latvia as "suspect and socially alien elements" – soldiers, policemen, farmers, home guard members, teachers, students, clergymen, businessmen, officials along with their families – the elite of the country. Among them were 2,300 children under ten years of age.[12] Of those deported, over 5,000 were imprisoned and a full 10,000 sent to exile settlements. They were told that they were exiled for life. Some five thousand or 34 percent of the deported perished in the east or on the journey there, or were executed. The German attack prevented a second scheduled deportation for which the lists had been prepared.

Not all readers were amused when the politician Aleksandr Gilman wrote in the newspaper *Chas* on the deportation memorial day in 2005 of the "June 14th myth" giving people to understand that the matter was only a summer pleasure outing. "Many young people live together in one barrack, fall in love, celebrate, laugh at amusing happenings – it was not exile but an excursion in free and beautiful nature."[13]

During the first occupation by the Russians (1940–1941) a total of 25,000 Latvians were imprisoned, deported, or murdered, and thousands fled.

Toward the end of the war significant civilian and military resistance movements were active in Latvia. Their goal was independence and they resisted both occupying countries. In 1943 the Latvian Central Council (LPC) was established, a western-oriented movement which was mentioned in Chapter 8. The resistance movements had contacts with the outside world, and were of great concern to the occupiers. Both Germany and the Soviet Union imprisoned and executed the movements' leaders. The USA and Britain did, however, receive some intelligence information gathered by the resistance.

The resistance continued for a long time after the war in rural areas. The Latvian "forest brethren's" struggle and the campaign against them took as many lives as had been lost in the Latvian war for independence. According to some estimates there were about 20,000 or two division's worth of "people's partisans" – a very impressive number, if we remember what had happened to young and adult Latvian men in the previous years. Many of the forest brethren were farmers or former soldiers. According to calculations they had up to 80,000 helpers and supporters. The resistance movement wanted a return to the first republic, but not to Ulmanis' regime.

Against the forest brothers ("bandits" to the Soviet regime), the Soviet Union set a large force of fighters, agents, and informers. In confrontations some 6,000 people died on both sides and some 18,000 were wounded. The struggle instilled hope in the Latvians, harassed the occupiers, and somewhat impeded the fulfillment of their plans in the country and small towns, but also led to measures taken for revenge which resulted in suffering for bystanders. Aside from a few agents that were sent over to the resistance, no help from the West ever came. Finally the fate of the Hungarian uprising in 1956 showed the Latvians that it was fruitless to wait for tangible help.

In the spring of 1949, by a top-secret decision, "kulaks and their families, bandit and nationalist families, and supporters of bandits" (in Interior Minister Kruglov's words) were deported to the East. Kruglov estimated in advance that 13,000 families, some 39,000 people, were to be taken from Latvia. They would be deported for "the rest of their lives."

In one night 13,624 families, all told nearly 43,000 people, or 2.3 percent of the entire population of Latvia, were loaded onto trains. The number was larger than in Estonia (20,700) and Lithuania (30,000), where deportation was arranged at exactly the same time. (There had been a large deportation in Lithuania already in 1948). The majority (72.9 percent) of the "enemies of the people" deported from the Baltic republics were women and children. During the last week and a half of March 1949, these republics lost about three percent of their native populations.[14]

Thus the resistance to the collectivization of agriculture in Latvia was crushed and the forest brothers deprived of their support. Since it was particularly the farmers, the best of them, who were victims in this 'farmers' and 'workers' state – they made up over half of the deported – it can be said that the backbone of Latvia had been seriously injured. Over sixty percent of the Latvians had lived and worked in the countryside. Already in the first deportation of 1941, half of the victims had been farmers.

Also, of those deported in 1949, some 5000 died. This time over 10,000 children and young people were taken away from Latvia. Of the deported Baltic children 2,080 had already died by the end of the year 1949. A large part of the deportees were young women of childbearing age, so that deportation had a part in Latvia's demographic catastrophe.

It should also be mentioned that the property of the victims was confiscated. This property was not returned later (in Soviet times) or compensated.

Even after the death of Stalin, those who returned were neither rehabilitated nor granted amnesty, since they had never been tried in court. Certain categories of those who were expatriated were permitted to return only in the 1960's and the 1970's.

"They Are So Intimidated"

After the first deportation, in 1941, most Latvians were livid with anger; they were determined not to succumb. The second deportation, in 1949, was almost too much for them. Administrative exile, the secret deportations without a court order, which were not explained afterwards even to relatives, had the effect of demoralizing the people. They lived in continual suspense, believing that the deportations could be resumed at any moment and that perhaps everyone in the country would wind up in Siberia.[15]

Demography and immigration researcher Pārsla Eglīte comments that the deportation figures do not tell the whole story, nor does the collapse of the birth rate in Latvia. According to her, psychological damage and consequences are perhaps the most important, for they are still felt today. The events of 1949 were the final blow, and it most affected those who were then children and young people.

> It hurts me that up to the present people who were not even deported are so afraid that they speak Russian in stores and on the streets. Why am I asked in a bus if I am getting off in Russian if I can tell from the accent that the inquirer is Latvian? They are so intimidated that even today, 50 years later, they are unable to orient themselves anew.[16]

She reminds us that Latvians are traditionally peaceful and tolerant, and that is exactly why so many immigrants flooded into the country after the war, many more than into Armenia, for example, where Russians have had more difficulty in adjusting.

The Dutch psychologist, Professor Ronald Reuderink says that among the Baltic peoples, Latvians are the most timid. They feel themselves to be a minority, although they are not so numerically (they are, in the cities – J.R.). "Of all the Baltic countries, the cultural atmosphere in Latvia has been damaged the most, since the people's mentality has changed."[17]

Pressure, privilege, and propaganda did not at first produce results in the countryside: Before the 1949 deportation, only ten percent of the Latvian farmers had joined kolkhozes (collective farms). Immediately after the deportation, in one full week, 1,740 new kolkhozes were formed. Already by the year 1951 it was announced that the "voluntary collectivization" was complete: almost all private farms had disappeared from Latvia.[18]

When Stalin died in 1953, of the Latvian Communist party's 42,179 members, 29.2 percent were Latvian. Of the party's central committee officials, 42 percent were nominally Latvian, but not all of them could speak Latvian. The second secretary of the Latvian party was always a Russian sent from Moscow, actually a *viceroy* or *gauleiter*. Rīga's party machinery was almost completely in Russian hands. The Latvian share in the Latvian government was 44 percent. Of the 66 leaders of the largest enterprises, only 8 were Latvians, and of the leaders of the many big *sovhoz* state farms, a mere five were Latvians.[19]

After Stalin's death, it was Lavrenti Beria who determined the party line for a short time. He was of the opinion that mistakes in national policy had been made in the Baltics. Efforts should be made to favor local "cadres" and use the Latvian language more. For the first time in Soviet Latvia there was open discussion of faults – mistakes in cadre politics and the sparse representation of Latvians in leading positions. The leadership of the Latvian KGB became Latvian, and its operation became more flexible. Nikita Khrushchev soon sidelined Beria, but at first the changes made in the summer of 1953 remained in effect.[20]

Especially after party leader Khrushchev had condemned Stalinism in 1956, the leaders of the Latvian Soviet republic tried to stem excessive immigration, the distribution of housing to soldiers, and russification, as well as to promote the use of the Latvian language, and to foster the Latvian cultural heritage. They opposed heavy industrialization and the economic policies dictated by Moscow in general, and demanded that the people's standard of living be raised.[21]

In the summer of 1959, Khrushchev visited Rīga. He received complaints from Latvia's Russians, mainly the leadership of the military district, who told him that the key positions in the party and society were controlled by nationalistic Latvian communists. Arvīds Pelše, the second secretary of the Latvian party, spoke of "bourgeois nationalism." Before Khrushchev's visit he had responded to Latvians' strivings sympathetically. The "thaw" ended years earlier in Latvia than elsewhere in the Soviet Union.

The Latvian party leader "admitted his mistakes," the party was cleansed, and officials were dismissed. Most of the republic's ruling elite was replaced. Cultural life was subjected to tighter control. There was also a return to discipline directed against "bourgeois nationalism" and "revisionism," and a new flood of heavy industry, workers, and soldiers arrived in Latvia. This was described as "help from brotherly republics in the construction of socialism."[22]

It was relatively easy to strike this counterblow since the nationalistically minded communists lacked strong popular support. Their places were taken by Latvians slavishly loyal to Moscow. Eduards Berklāvs, one of the leaders of the reformers, was sent to Russia for eight and a half years of "voluntary internal exile."

Moscow's Latvian lackeys themselves accelerated the russification of the country. They did it to advance their own careers and prosperity. It is said that later, during the national awakening, they became turncoats and "concocted" Russian scapegoats. They, too, began to accuse all those who had never even been party members, even Russians born in Latvia, of being occupiers, rather than determining what was truly responsible – the Communist system. Chauvinistic hatred of Russians became conducive to a new, stylish, and productive political career, and former dissidents are also accused of following the trend. But as the Estonian writer Reet Kudo says: "I don't identify the Soviet dictatorship with the Russian people, but with the ideology, of which censorship and *nomenklatura* are a part."[23]

At the time of Stalin's death, a half million Russians and other Soviet peoples had already been settled in Latvia. At the end of the Soviet era, the number of Russians, Belarusians, and Ukrainians in Latvia had grown to nearly a million, and Latvians were becoming a minority in their own republic. Latvia was the only Soviet state in which the mechanical population growth (immigration) always exceeded natural population growth. The number of Latvians decreased in percentage and in absolute numbers. Although there were already 2.67 million inhabitants in Latvia in 1989, an all-time record, there were nevertheless fewer Latvians than before the war (80,000 fewer).

In early 1971, the Swedish *Dagens Nyheter* and some other Western newspapers published the sensational, secretly-transmitted appeal of seventeen Latvian communists which was addressed to their foreign party comrades. It complained of "Great-Russia chauvinism," of russification, and of the forced assimilation of peoples. It branded as guilty the leadership of the Soviet Union's Communist party for having distorted Marxist-Leninist principles. The letter of protest offered numerous examples of the Latvians' wretched situation in their own republic. The writers were soon discovered, and they found themselves in trouble in Soviet Latvia.

Although violent resistance ended in 1956, a bold spirit of non-violent opposition persisted among Latvian pupils, students, people of culture, and old soldiers, which could bring upon them dangerous reprisals – long prison sentences and confinement in insane asylums.

What Kind of Collaboration?

Historians traditionally distinguish between cooperation in general (collaboration) and traitorous cooperation (collaborationism). In many cases it is nearly impossible to draw a distinct line between the two; each occupied country has specifics of its own. The boundaries between collaboration, cooperation, resistance, slyness, and nationalist sentiment are wavering, and this field is especially confusing in the Baltics, which were the object of many occupations. It is difficult to say positively afterwards who did what and why.

Nowadays it is perhaps too easy to condemn those who belonged to the party. There could be other heroes besides the known dissidents.[24]

During the Soviet era, Latvians are said to have been divided into three groups. In the first were the collaborators, and the second comprised a "gray area" of accommodators who, without any great interest in things, did as they were told. The third group was made up of dissidents and those in the resistance movement, to which some 5–10 percent of the people belonged at one time or another.

People had various reasons for belonging to the party. Some were ideological: they were communists by conviction. Or they could be opportunistic: they saw a possibility to improve their social status, build a career, secure an education, and ensure better opportunities for their children. Then there were the realists: they had no illusions, but they found their place in the system. They perhaps wanted to take leadership positions so as not to have Russian bureaucrats and communists come in.

For example, the popular ideological secretary of the Latvian Communist party, Anatolijs Gorbunovs, who was also respected by Moscow. For his part Gorbunovs helped to guide the country carefully and wisely to independence at the end of the 1980's. He could perhaps have risen to the presidency of independent Latvia, but he did not want to become a candidate because he understood that he was nevertheless too controversial a person and had embittered critics. The same can be said of the poet Jānis Peters.

In 1980 there were some 158,000 members in the Latvian Communist party (95,400 in Estonia and 165,800 in Lithuania), and in the final phases of the Soviet era, January 1989, there were 184,182 members and candidates. In the Estonian party there were at most 120,000 members, in approximately the same proportion to the country's population. The Latvians were a pronounced minority in the Latvian Communist party. In the final phases 43.2 were Russian by nationality, and 39.8 were Latvian and Russian Latvians.[25]

In January 1991 a mass exodus from the party occurred when the occupiers resorted to violence in Vilnius and Rīga. After that the remainder were considered dyed-in-the-wool communists and in a practical sense, enemies of Latvia. With Latvian independence the Communist party was outlawed. The communists moved to other parties, joined other organizations, or went into business life. Some went to prison.

The events of 1959 were a hard blow to the Latvians and it may have been a lesson to the Estonians and Lithuanians. They understood that one had to advance wisely and cautiously to be spared the fate of Latvia. A conservative junta was in power in Latvia, and in the 1960's Latvia began to lose its leading position in many spheres. Its own people began to see that Latvia's leaders were the least likely to protect the republic's interests and were the most diligent in carrying out Moscow's instructions.

Historian Heinrihs Strods' interpretation is that Latvia's population had yielded to a greater extent to the political pressures of the two occupants, Nazi Germany and Bolshevik Russia, and thus the total proportion of victims of deportations and executions was higher than in Lithuania and Estonia. "The submissive policies of Latvia's Bolsheviks allowed the occupation power to staff the many headquarters of the Baltic Military District with its own people, to foster industrialization and bring in hundreds of thousands of colonists."[26] One might ask, on the other hand, what was the cause and what was the effect.

The Estonians in particular are sometimes heard to conjecture that the Latvians were too soft and too ready to cooperate with Moscow. It is partly from the Estonians that writer Anatol Lieven seems to have taken his characterization of Latvians as an unreliable "nation of collaborators."[27]

On the other hand, Strods considers that the speed with which the Baltic States have outstripped the "old Soviet republics" in their development after 1991 shows that in these West-European types of countries, sovietizing had done relatively little damage, if one ignores the demographic situation. Merging Latvians into a united "Soviet people" was unsuccessful, another historian testifies. This was shown with the speed of spiritual liberation from Soviet ideology in the second half of the 1980's.

Strods calculates that in the 1960's, 772 people belonged to *nomenklatura*, the privileged, well-paid leaders in Soviet Latvia. Of them, 523 worked in the party, 131 in industry, and 118 in education and culture. "At present there is not the slightest indication that even one of the then leading class should somehow regret his sins," Strods writes. According to him, they continue to sit in their secure positions, rather than ask the people to forgive their "atrocities."

Lithuania especially is regarded as having done well during the Soviet era – it somehow succeeded in rejecting heavy industrialization and the settling of masses of workers in its area. Its former Communist leaders are respected in Lithuania as defenders of the people's cause and the initiators of independence. The popular former party leader, Algirdas Brazauskas has been chosen president, and just recently he was social democratic prime minister of Lithuania. A former communist leader of Estonia, Arnold Rüütel, also made a comeback as president.

A New National Awakening

The Baltic countries belonged to the Soviet Union for a relatively short time and also received influences from the West. The Estonians, Lithuanians, and Latvians were the first to dare use Mikhail Gorbachev's reform policies to further their own ends. The independence movement began at approximately the same time in all three Baltic republics. One might say it was permitted to begin. Moscow conjectured that it would be easier to experiment with social reforms on a small scale in these republics.[28]

One of the first signs of the change was an international conference in Jūrmala in 1986. There the representative of the U.S. president said that the USA still did not recognize and would not recognize Latvia's incorporation into the USSR. The people were able to follow his speech on Latvian television.

Changes in the Soviet Union may well be said to have started the Rīga demonstrations in the summer and fall of 1986, which demanded – still in the

Picture 20. Some 120,000 Latvians – among them most of the country's intellectual elite – wound up in refugee camps in Western Germany after the war, with the Soviet Union exerting pressure for their return. There was a especially lively cultural and educational activity in their camps. – A group meeting at the Esslingen camp. One document reads: "Our American friends. We fight like Lincoln against slavery."
Private records of Jānis Aperans.

framework of *perestroika* – of the central leadership the protection of nature and further control over the environment after Chernobyl. As early as July 1986, a human rights organization, Helsinki-86, was established in Latvia. It organized the first demonstrations of public opposition.

Large protest rallies were seen in Rīga in the summer of 1987. Of the demonstration on June 14, 1987, it has been said that it was "the first stone thrown by an occupied nation against the wall of the Soviet empire." The militia tried to disperse the next meeting in August by force and made hundreds of arrests. The information media were silent concerning them. The officials reacted in the same way to the celebration of the old independence day in November.

The leaders of the Helsinki group were first arrested and then pressured to move to the West. According to officials, they were "*provocateurs* who carried out the tasks assigned to them by Western intelligence agencies and sowed hatred among nations."

In 1987, a movement for the protection of nature and the environment began in Estonia, and the same kind of movement succeeded in preventing some large construction projects in Latvia. In the summer of 1988, a demonstration against the construction of the Rīga underground transit system (involving a massive influx of immigrant workers) was allowed to organize in peace.[29]

In the summer of 1988, the dam of demands broke at a congress of the Estonian Creative League, and the Lithuanian and Latvian writers' and artists' associations joined in the demands; at the Latvian meeting it was stated publicly for the first time that the country was occupied in 1940. Latvian writers were also permitted to remember publicly the victims of deportation.

The avalanche began. If Latvians, like their neighbors, were able to push hard for independence when the opportunity arose, it was because they were buoyed up by a strong and vibrant cultural identity that consciously distinguished itself from that of the Russian occupier. Culture – traditional songs and dances, poetry, theatre – remained very strong and provided a rallying point for national consciousness which in some Warsaw Pact countries was supplied by the church.

The Estonians organized a "Popular Front for the support of perestroika" (Rahvarinne), and the Latvians followed their example in the fall of 1988. The name of the Latvian organization was the *Latvijas Tautas Fronte* (LTF), and some 300,000 became members. In Lithuania the front was known as *Sajudis*, and went farther in its demands than its neighbors. Such organizations were the seeds of free political parties.

In 1988 the LNNK (the Latvian National Independence Movement) was also established, from which the first non-communist party developed. In the election of 1990 – the first true elections in Latvia after the war – the Popular Front won a clear majority in the Latvian Supreme Soviet or parliament as well as in the Latvian faction of the parliament of the Soviet Union. In May the Latvian parliament issued a "declaration of independence," that is, voted to begin the political process of removing Soviet rule and restoring full independence to Latvia.[30]

As a counterpart, some of the local Russians, especially the military, established the "Interfront" and "preservation committees," which with the obvious help of Moscow campaigned against the independence of the Baltic countries, even resorting to violence. The severest of Moscow's pressure, economic blockade, and punishment tactics were directed at Lithuania, which was the first to begin the transitional phase to independence. Her neighbors followed her example cautiously, having learned from the Soviet Union's reaction.

Even Latvia did not escape fatalities in January of 1991; Estonia got off easier. Some 80,000 volunteers from different parts of Latvia came to the barricades in Rīga to defend the parliament building and other key points with bare hands if need be. Despite violent incidents, the people remained calm and determined. In the spring of 1991 an overwhelming majority voted for independence in a referendum.

At no stage was there any significant help from the West: the Western states wanted Gorbachev's democratic project to succeed and feared that the possible break-up of the Soviet Union would lead to violent conflicts in its border areas. In his previously mentioned book, Anatol Lieven notes that when the Baltic independence movement gained momentum in the 1980's, Russian propaganda also intensified, once more accusing the Balts of complicity in the Holocaust. Moscow knew very well that many in the West were ready to lend an ear to such information.

It was a "singing revolution." The Latvians and the other Baltic peoples were proud to have carried out (an almost) bloodless revolution with only spiritual weapons. In their opinion, others can learn from that.

The Estonians and Lithuanians can thus be considered a kind of vanguard in the Baltics and the entire Soviet Union. The Latvians did not lag far behind, and most of the activities were timed to be simultaneous. The Baltic countries stood together, and their actions were a model of cooperation. One could add: "Still at the time…" In the end, all three Baltic countries declared their independence on the same days in August 1991. Just as in 1918, they were able to take advantage quickly of the opportunity opened up for them.

The Estonians also acted more quickly in 1991. The Latvians announced their restoration of independence on the 21st of August, and the acknowledgements from abroad began to come immediately, the first on the 22nd from Estonia, Iceland, and Lithuania.

The Baltics became a pawn in the Soviet Union's internal power struggle, which might even have benefited them. Boris Yeltsin took a stand in support of their aspirations. As the democratically elected president of the Russian federation, he also signed the acknowledgement of the Baltic States' independence in August, even before the western countries did, and urged the president of the Soviet Union to follow his example. The Soviet Union had to acknowledge the *fait accompli*, and in early September 1991 it too recognized the independence of the Baltics.

Yeltsin lived to regret his action later, for Russia's coexistence with these Baltic neighbors did not turn out to be easy. In Russia there is hatred for the Latvians as well as the other Baltic peoples for having ungratefully "dismembered" the Soviet Union. As President Putin said in 2005: "the greatest geopolitical tragedy of the 20th century was the breakup of the Soviet Union."[31]

The Seeds of Destruction

Thus the seed of the Soviet defeat was already in the victory of 1945: the Soviet Union was never able to subjugate and absorb the Baltic peoples. People from the other parts of the Soviet Union visited the Baltics and were amazed at the "western" life style. The ideal of freedom spread throughout the nation, which collapsed 46 years after the war's end.

Although it may be an exaggeration to blame or thank the Balts alone for the collapse of the Soviet Union, their contribution to the freeing of many states from the Soviet Union was significant, writes Pekka Visuri, a Finnish Ph. D. and colonel, whose specialty is strategy. In his opinion, Yeltsin's stand in support of the Baltics at the beginning of 1991, and the fact that he suppressed the so-called Yanayev junta were decisive.[32]

I'll add here: now when Ronald Reagan is posthumously being made into a great president and "the Latvians' best friend,"[33] it may easily be forgotten that without the Balts and Gorbachev (and the East Germans in 1989), "Reagan's great achievement," the huge change in Europe, would not have been possible.

"I am hurt by the claims that independence was just dropped into the laps of the Latvia, Estonia, and Lithuania because everything was decided and happened elsewhere, and that we ourselves really deserve no credit for it at all," says diplomat and politician Sandra Kalniete. "Unlike what happened in Russia and the eleven other Soviet republics, what occurred here was a true people's revolution, the objective of which was not only the destruction of a totalitarian regime and the return to a democratic and just state, but also separation from the Soviet Union and the achievement of independence."[34]

It occurred very late to people in Washington that there was any possibility of independence for the Baltic nations. More people than will now admit it smirked as each year in July, Captive Nations Week was celebrated, calling for the overthrow of Communism. It has been written, maybe a little unfairly, that this event was just a way for right-wing politicians to show their constituency that they cared about people in Eastern Europe without actually doing anything.[35]

Just as during the first time (1918), the outside world, as well as many Balts, reacted with surprise, disbelief and perhaps dismay to the achievement of independence in 1991. In both instances some western leaders did not in fact want Russia to break up and warned the Balts about "rocking the boat." As a matter of fact, the Russians and the American leaders often understand one another, as great powers always do. When they agree on matters, the small have to adjust. The Soviet Union/Russia has received many kinds of support from the West for their political renovation, and trade relations are flourishing.

So, to me Mihail Gorbachev is one of the heroes of the turning point, but George Bush Sr. supported Gorbachev to the end, no matter what he did or left undone. They stuck to one another like a faithful married couple, and lost touch with others around them. Michael Beschloss and Strobe Talbott testify in their book, *At the Highest Levels*, that largely because of this relationship, they both lost power.[36]

11

Has Latvia always belonged to Russia and benefited from it? Is it a strategically indispensable area for Russia?

I have never before performed in Russia.

A German singer on stage during an international song festival in Jūrmala, Latvia, in 2004

When will the Baltic States become free? When Russia becomes free.

Andrei Sakharov in the 1980's

A third motto for this chapter might be: "The Baltic States are in the end pimples on the Russian back and, in their historic role as entry ports to Europe, better off, for themselves and for Russia, as nominally independent entities." Thus wrote the conservative British newspaper *The Daily Telegraph* in the year 2006.[1]

Over 60 years earlier, another influential British newspaper, *The Times*, spoke about the rights of the USSR to the territory of the Baltic States, which, while being strategically important for the Soviet Union, were of no interest to the UK. And in that same year of 1942, Britain's ambassador to Moscow said in an interview that nobody doubted that the Baltic States belonged to the Soviet Union.[2] Britain was opposed here by the US, which in effect vetoed an agreement the UK was ready to conclude. In 1943, however, President Roosevelt said to Stalin that he fully understood that the three Baltic countries "have historically, and also very recently, been a part of Russia."

This was fully in accord with Moscow's position. A little earlier, the Soviet Union's delegates had told Roosevelt's chief negotiators that "they, of course, would want the Baltic States; that Russia now considered them a part of the

USSR; that they had always been historically part of Russia, apart from the fact that they were essential to it for security reasons." Stalin stated at Teheran that the Baltic provinces had no kind of autonomy under the Russian Czars, who were allies of the US and Britain.[3]

An official American task force deliberating the issue immediately after the war put it thus: "While these [Baltic] states wished to establish their right to independence, they themselves realized that they were not viable as states, due to their economic position. The historic ties between Russia and the Baltic States were taken in account. It was also recognized that the USSR would probably be unwilling to discuss any future for the Baltic States except as part of the Soviet Union."[4]

Let us remember, though, that the US had refused to recognize the 1940 annexation.

It was certainly not by chance that President Vladimir Putin said in February 2006 at a press conference in Moscow "We have in Rīga (*u nas v Rige*) a clear majority of Russians, but nevertheless they have no rights."[5] The president simply did not have his history and geography straight. In another press conference a little earlier, he answered a foreign journalist's question sarcastically, as stated earlier: "If the Baltic countries joined the Soviet Union in 1939, how could the Soviet Union occupy them in 1941?" Then he went on to say: "In the 1918 peace treaty of Brest-Litovsk Russia had to "cede certain areas to Germany. In 1939 Germany returned them to us, and these areas joined the Soviet Union." It was a "treaty matter."[6]

Let Vladimir Kovalev, who wrote during the same period, represent the dissenting voice in Russia: "Even then [in the 1970s] it was obvious to many, visually and rationally, that Estonia and the other Baltic States did not belong to the Soviet Union in spirit, not to mention their culture, which, unlike Soviet culture, is clearly influenced by European tradition."[7]

In Russia, the Baltic countries are often viewed as a single block, an area belonging to the old Russian empire, the "loss" of which hurts the Russian soul. Various methods are employed in an effort to restore the former hegemony. At least the Baltics, *Pribaltika*, are more important to Russia than to others. Stalin already thought so in the 1930's (see Chapter 6).

It was Russian foreign minister Andrei Kozyrev, who shocked the Balts in 1994 by coining the new foreign policy concept "near abroad." Russia would have special rights and security policy interests in this zone. Kozyrev proclaimed: "We should not withdraw from those regions which have been the sphere of Russian interest for centuries, and we should not fear these words [military presence]." He classified the Baltic States as a near abroad region and foresaw the option of maintaining troops there to avoid a "security vacuum."[8]

Interest? Hitler had an interest in Poland; Japan had an interest in China; the US certainly has an interest in Saudi Arabia. Does that entitle them to claim these lands?

In the spring of 2006, the author and Nobel Prize winner Alexander Solzhenitsyn accused NATO of a conspiracy against Russia. He said in an interview that although Russia posed no sort of threat at present, NATO was trying to subject her to its control by "encircling" her so that she lost her sovereignty. In his opinion Russia would be damaged especially if NATO's war machine should extend into the Baltics, which had earlier belonged to the USSR. (I am not denying that NATO is a legitimate worry for a Russian – NATO was, after all, founded as an "anti-Russian" military alliance. JR)

Solzhenitsyn, the former dissident, has recently played the role of a Great Russian nationalist and prophet. The man who was brave enough to tell the truth about Stalin's slave camps and who wrote his book in the 1960's with the aid of the Balts while in refuge in their land for a time, now accuses them of betrayal and hatred of Russians. He cannot now acknowledge how deep a scar those camps left on the Baltic and other peoples, who have turned their backs on Moscow and resolved to join NATO.[9] Solzhenitsyn is enraged at a process which led to the breakup of the Soviet Union in a way that left millions of ethnic Russians on the "wrong side" of the border.[10]

The Russian foreign ministry announced in the spring of 2006 that these ethnic Russians living abroad were a "world political resource" and that Russia's strategic objective was to ensure that they become citizens with full rights in the lands where they live, but at the same time, to have them preserve their ethnocultural uniqueness.[11]

The matter might be put differently: according to a new book by Estonian historians, the ethnic minorities are a fifth column in the Baltics.[12] There is strong evidence for this view.

With the breakup of the Soviet Union, some 25–30 million Russians were left living outside the borders of Russia – relative to the population as a whole, there are more of them in Latvia, Estonia, Kazakhstan, and Ukraine than anywhere else.

When the Russian TV system beams direct transmission telecasts of President Putin's question-and-answer sessions in which citizens throughout the large country can participate, one camera crew normally comes to Rīga – that is, to a foreign country. The Russians who live there complain of their conditions and ask the president questions. *Their* president?[13]

It is certainly true that Latvia was a strategically important area to Russia/ the Soviet Union. It was the central Baltic country, the largest in land area and economically the strongest.[14] Latvia's ice-free harbors have always been important to Moscow. They were necessary to both the navy and foreign trade. In the agreement with Hitler on spheres of influence in 1939, Moscow's absolute demand was to get Latvian harbors. Foreign Minister Molotov said in the negotiations with the Balts that same autumn that the Red Navy would no longer let itself be shut up in "the puddle of the Gulf of Finland."[15]

Strategists have generally been sympathetic to the Russian desire to have some kind of Baltic security zone for the protection of St. Petersburg/Leningrad. They also realize that the Baltic Sea and the Baltic harbors are important to Russia.[16] (There is, of course, no obstacle to using these harbors for trade, as is normal between neighboring countries! And does a security zone demand annexation?)

Rīga was also important to the United States and other countries as well, as a post for observing the Soviet Union before the Second World War.[17] In Moscow, Latvia was viewed as an actual or potential enemy. The Soviet Union's war plans of the 1930's started from the assumption that the small independent Baltic countries, unlike Finland, did not have the preconditions for independence.[18] After the Second World War, Moscow made Latvia its most important outpost in the West.

"Unreservedly and Forever"

It is entirely untrue that the Baltic countries "always" belonged to Russia. Russia first seized Vidzeme (Livland, Livonia) from Sweden by military conquest in 1710 and acquired Latgale in the First Partition of Poland in 1772. As was the custom in the 18th century, Russia did not obtain the consent of the Latvian or Polish people. The Duchy of Courland and Lithuania were annexed by Russia in the Third Partition of Poland in 1795. Russian influence in Latvia was slight; in Courland German and Latvian remained the principal languages. Intensive russification began only under Alexander III (1881–1894), and ceased soon afterwards, with the disintegration of Russian rule during 1915-1918 and Latvian independence to follow..

In 1920, Latvia and Soviet Russia signed a peace treaty, as already discussed. According to it, Soviet Russia.

> Unreservedly recognizes the independence and sovereignty of the Latvian state without any objection and voluntarily and forever rescinds all sovereign rights over the Latvian people and territory which belonged to Russia under the previous structure of state.[19]

As stated previously, Russia (the Soviet Union) once again took over the territory and government of Latvia from 1940 to 1941 and from 1945 to 1991.

There is still some dispute in Latvia about whether it would be better to
develop economic ties primarily with Russia and to act as a gateway between
Russia and the West. The effect of Russian transit is not nearly as large as has
been claimed: it brought Latvia about 130 million *lats* in the year 2005, which
is a large sum, but is, however, only 1.5 percent of Latvia's GNP.[20] Russia is
continually building her own harbors and oil and gas pipelines, so that its
dependence on Latvia is decreasing.

After joining the EU and turning to western foreign trade, Latvia's development gained momentum. According to the World Bank, in the Baltic and
other East-European countries with transition economies, the growth in trade
is the world's most rapid. Export has tripled on the average, and import has
multiplied by 2.5 in ten years. Former Soviet states which have joined the EU
have developed at a time when others have stagnated. In recent years the
growth of Latvia's economy has been basically about 7 percent, but there have
been times when it approached 12 percent.

Latvia belongs to the West European cultural sphere, and is more a "central
European" state than Finland, for example. Nevertheless, the Baltic countries
are situated in a difficult and dangerous area. The road to and from the Russian heartland has always gone through them. They are also a part of a zone of
border states which curves around Russia from Europe to the farthest reaches
of Asia. Therefore they have constantly been the object of a power struggle.[21]

The AIA internet commentator Simon Araloff, when asked how he views
the situation of the country, answered: "Read Toynbee and Huntington. The
Baltics, Latvia included, are a typical zone of passage 'of the break of civiliza-
tions.' Besides, they lie in the very centre of Eurasia [Europe – J.R.]. This is
what defines the agency's [AIA's] interest in the region, and in your country, in
particular."[22]

According to Araloff, Latvia should not give up on the aspiration to restore
the centuries-old unity with the West. "The Baltic countries, including Latvia,
absolutely and unequivocally belong to western civilization. And this fact was
not denied even in czarist Russia which kept this special region as a kind of
reserve of western culture within the territory of the empire. So the reunion
with the West was for Latvia an absolutely natural process."

Russia announced that she was "interested" in the security of the Baltics,
and offered them security guarantees in 1997. The offer resurrected memories
of the 1930's and the security guarantees offered to and forced on them by
Stalin. In a speech to the Duma in February 1998, President Boris Yeltsin
issued a stern warning to the Baltic countries against joining NATO. In his

New Year's speech in 1994 Yeltsin threatened that Russia would protect the rights of the Russian minorities in the Baltic countries "at any cost."

The US Congress decided that same year that all the democratic nations of Europe had the right to join NATO regardless of where they are located on the map. It was a relief for the Latvians to get "back into Europe," as an EU member; the transatlantic tie is, however, the most important one to them now.

The Russian professor Yuri Afanasyev wrote in the mid-1990s that "the independence of the Baltic States still remains something external and foreign to Russians. The independence of the Baltics as an accomplished fact does not yet contribute to the recovery of Russia's own identity."[23]

The Economist's correspondent Edward Lucas wrote in 2006 that President Putin has let loose two frightening forces of the Soviet past: the manifestations of totalitarian security concerns and imperialistic strivings which are firmly rooted in the Russian psyche. "To put it politely," he wants Russia to be strong at home as well as abroad. Lucas continues: "To put it bluntly," Putin is trying to re-create an empire, which Russia's people would fear just as much as their neighbors.[24] Let it also be recalled that Putin has described the breakup of the Soviet Union as the greatest geopolitical catastrophe of the 20th century.

Legends and Chronicles

As Norman Davies writes in a recent book: "None of the three Baltic States was Russian by history, culture, religion, or language."[25] Latvians and Estonians have been the majority population in their present borders for thousands of years. However, the inclusion of Latvia in the Russian cultural and economic sphere has from the time of the Czars been based on ancient semi-legendary chronicles, especially those of Novgorod and Pskov, which became popular again in the Soviet era. Age-old contacts are evident in Latvian linguistic borrowings from the Slavic languages, and these contacts are used to justify the incorporation of Latvia into the Russian Empire and the USSR. Thus according to Soviet opinion Latvia was an "integral part of Russia" a long time ago.[26]

An example of this kind of rewriting of history to conform with legends is the annexation of Abrene (the Pytalovo area in her northeast corner). The Russian Federation annexed it in 1944 and moved the Latvian inhabitants away. Now this action is being justified on the basis of medieval chronicles. Recently a historian wrote in a Russian military journal that Slavs have "always" lived in the area and are therefore not 1400's newcomers, as Latvian historians say. The area's place names can, he claimed, be traced back to

Russian words. According to the writer, in Pytalovo, which belonged to the Grand Duchy of Polotsk, the conquerors, the German Catholic crusaders, torture the Russians. In 1920 Russia had to surrender Pytalovo to the Latvians because of the weakened condition the country was in after the war. Russia signed a "humiliating peace treaty" with Latvia, after which this area was "torn loose" from her for twenty years, until the historic wrong was corrected and the area returned.[27]

In the same way, another Russian historian writing in 1982, called the Pskov region "indigenously Russian territory." An article published in 2005 on the *Russian Civilization* website claims this region to be part of the most ancient Russian lands.

Russian writers are silent about the fact that in the region there lived old Baltic and Finno-Ugric tribes which the Slavs conquered and killed or drove out only in the Middle Ages. Pytalovo is mentioned in Russian records for the first time in 1782. The writers do not even know or mention that the "Russian" name Pytalovo comes from the Latvian language (Pietālava from pie Tālavas), and that there are other place names in the area the derivation of which is clearly Baltic. In the last (1935) census before the annexation in 1944, Abrene's population was 55 percent Latvian and 41.6 percent Russian.[28]

Abrene became a taboo subject in the Soviet Union, and school pupils were taught that the area had always belonged to Russia. However, it had been transferred to the control of the archbishopric of Rīga in the 1300's, and it was defined as a part of independent Latvia in the peace treaty of 1920.[29]

In short: the borders in Europe have always been in a state of flux. Thus, if you go back to the right year of the right century, you can prove for almost any nation that they once owned vast tracts of land. Russia cannot turn the clock back and reclaim lands that she once gained by military or dynastic means. The people have spoken and declared independence. Most former Soviet republics *do not want to* rejoin Russia.

According to Soviet history, Latvia's becoming a part of Russia in the 1700's had a "progressive, benevolent effect," freeing Latvians from the yoke of German landlords. In contrast, a very negative picture emerges of the independent Latvian republic, in which the significance of the workers' movement is exaggerated. According to the Russian encyclopedias, the separation from Russia in 1918–1920 caused a collapse of manufacturing and changed Latvia into a land whose economy was dependent upon the imperialistic great powers and where the farmers were also made wretched by bourgeois economic policies.[30]

Of course the arrival of the Soviet economic system is ascribed an even greater "benevolent effect." According to the history books, the friendship among peoples had a long history, and is characterized by the "common struggle." The climax of it all was the "inevitable" social revolution, which was accomplished under the leadership of the Communist party, which "abolished fascist rule" and brought the people's democratic government to power. The reunion with the Soviet Union in 1944–1945 was "the Latvians' own choice."

According to historians of the Soviet era, joining the Soviet Union ensured lasting peace for the Latvian population, encouraged their economic development and "restored the age-old political, economic and cultural links between Latvians and Russians, thus creating the preconditions for further development of the Latvian people … and the cultivation of Latvian culture under the culture of the great Russian people."[31]

I believe no commentary is necessary; in other chapters I have dealt with the "blessings" – the devastation brought on the Latvians during the last 100 years largely by Russia and the Soviet Union.

Pekka Visuri, Finland's best-known expert on strategy, writes in a recent book that there is nothing on which to base the claim that Latvia is strategically indispensable to Russia. According to him, the strategic significance of the Baltic Sea was already lessened by the reunion of the two Germanys. Russia was no longer in the position of having to maintain and supply its forces in East Germany. The Baltic harbors lost their significance. A large, idle navy on the Baltic was expensive to maintain. The military deterrent units, the bombers and missiles, became unnecessary when in 1987 an agreement to remove mid-range missiles from Europe was reached, and the Baltic republics were no longer necessary for air defense.[32]

On the other hand one may ask what the strategic situation in the Baltic Sea area is in the light of plans for an undersea natural gas pipeline to be built from Russia to Germany, the fact that Russia is once more positioning new submarines in the Baltic, and that there are several new important Russian seaports on the east coast of the Baltic.

The Estonian historians Medijainen and Made are of the same opinion as Visuri about the post-cold-war situation on the Baltic. If Russia resorts to intervention, in these writers' opinion it will more likely be economic than military.[33]

Already in 1995, as Latvian officials formulated the first national threat analysis for the country, the guiding principle was that Russia was not interested in the land area of Latvia; controlling the economy would be better, because that enables pressure which brings about political control.[34]

12

Shouldn't Latvia be grateful for factories, houses, schools, roads, and harbors built during the Soviet era? Shouldn't she pay compensation as well?

With so much know how, what ignorance!
With so much affluence, what want!
With so much expectation, what disillusionment!

IVAR IVASK: BALTIC ELEGIES (1986)

Of all the Baltic nations perhaps the Letts have suffered the most, yet their story is typical.

HUBERT BUTLER: THE CHILDREN OF DRANCY

The Speaker of the Russian Duma, Gennady Seleznjov, remarked in 1999: "I do not know where Latvia would be now, in what backwoods of Europe, if the whole of the Soviet Union had not helped Latvia and Estonia develop."[1]

In a recent interview for a Latvian newspaper, the Russian historian Natalia Narotshnika said that it was the Soviet state which transformed the Latvians into an educated and intelligent European people. She remarked that the present Latvian elite received a good education in schools during the time they were under the Soviets. Culture and science flourished, and Latvia became industrialized.[2]

The Russian ambassador Viktor Kalyuzhny accepted an invitation to visit the Museum of the Occupation of Latvia in the spring of 2005, but he cut his visit short and left because the museum "did not show the good the Soviet Union had done for Latvia."

Later the ambassador said that "not everything done during the Soviet era was good," but that should not affect the relationship to those people who "remained here in 1945, sacrificing their health to build a new Latvia." He added that one could really not speak of independent Latvia's achievements since the number of deaths exceeds that of births and the prices rise by as much as 24–40 percent annually.[3]

The Americans have an expression: "with friends like this, who needs enemies?"

Yes, indeed, where would Latvia be now? How much good did Russia and the Soviet Union do for Latvia?

Some British historians of the younger generation such as Niall Ferguson and Lawrence James are striving to show that the British Empire's legacy to the world is mainly positive. Peace prevailed, the *Pax Britannica*. Peoples were able to build their societies in concord. The construction of a contemporary infrastructure began. Schools, universities, hospitals, and transportation networks, as well as political institutions, were a heritage from the empire. The British wished to insure women's rights, a free press, a multiparty system, and an independent judiciary. The Empire was governed with "a light hand" by recruiting and schooling officials from among the local elite.[4]

Thus speak some British scholars. One may criticize them for admiring colonialism and glossing over instances of brutality and abuse. However, even if we look at the Baltic Soviet republics with "Fergusonian eyes," it is difficult to find much good to say about their occupation by the Soviets.

Undoubtedly a major objective of Soviet rule was peace, the message reiterated time and again in the propaganda, and certainly some construction did take place. But Soviet rule also brought fear, violence, and destruction, and even during peacetime the population was being prepared for war ("defense") from early childhood. Both the culture as well as the infrastructure and production supported this objective. True, some officials were recruited from among local people. However there was never any question of independent institutions and education, much less of any preparation for independence, but rather everything was directed towards a tighter bonding and an ideological submission to the central power.

What kind of legacy did Latvia receive? Let us check the statistics.

In the statistics regarding the standard of living in Europe at the end of the 1930's Latvia was 16th and Finland was 13th; Estonia was 19th, or poorer than Latvia.[5] At that time Latvia was a significant exporter of agricultural products and an employer of foreign labor. Unemployment was low. Cultural life and

education flourished, the level of social security was high, and there was practically no impoverished class. In 1938 Latvia was, after Denmark and Holland,
the largest exporter of butter in Europe, and in terms of the ratio of books
published to population she was in the second place in Europe.

A fact that speaks volumes is that Finland is now one of Europe's and the
world's richest countries, and that the wealth of Finland (per capita) is many
times that of Latvia, which separated from the Soviet Union in 1991 and joined
the European Union in 2004 as the poorest of its 25 member states.[6] At the
turn of the century, Latvia's GNP per capita was 2,860 US dollars; Finland's was
24,900 dollars, or almost nine times greater.[7] It has been calculated that even
if the current slow growth should continue in Finland and the other "old"
European countries, it would take the Baltic countries, even with their current
rapid growth, almost a quarter century to reach the same living standard.[8]

The transition from communism to capitalism was painful in Latvia, as in
other ex-communist countries. During the first years of Latvia's regained
independence (1991), the GNP per capita declined almost by a half, and from
1990–2000 it declined by almost 29 percent. According to the WHO, there was
a drastic decline in comparison with the 1980's, when only a few percent of
Latvians were counted as poor.[9] Despite economic growth, on average the
people seem to be living more poorly than during the last days of the Soviet
era, if one compares the cost of lodging, the consumption of food and the GDP
per capita relative to purchasing power.[10] Statistics show that about half of the
residents, especially the elderly, live below the official subsistence minimum.
Since the beginning of the 1990's the mortality of Latvian children of almost
all age groups has been the highest in the EU and the entire industrial world.[11]
Conditions have been improving lately, especially since Latvia joined the EU.

In the 1600's rich and proud Courland kept Gambia and Tobago as her
colonies. When the Latvian provinces were annexed to Russia in the late
1700's, they were among the most developed and industrialized areas in the
entire empire. At the start of the 2000's Latvia was a notch below the devel-
oping country of Trinidad-Tobago in the UN's statistics on human
development.

In 1900, Latvia, with only 1.5 percent of the Russian Empire's total population, provided 5,5 percent of its industrial production: steel, trams, railroad
cars, agricultural machinery, radios, soon also cars, tanks, and airplanes.[12] In
1913, before the Great War, Rīga was a leading industrial city, ranking immediately after Moscow and St. Petersburg. The size of its industrial workforce was
110,000. The annual rate of Latvian industrial growth was the highest in the
world. Thirty-one percent of the population worked in industry and trade.

Latvia's harbors were the most important ones in the Russian empire – 28 percent of Russia's exports passed through them, and 5,300 ships visited Rīga that year.[13]

The first major blow occurred during the Great War when the Russians, fearing a German attack in 1915, dismantled more than 400 factories in Rīga and took them east, along with the machines and workers. Large quantities of other goods were stolen all over Latvia during the forced evacuation. Rīga alone lost some 300,000 inhabitants, and 40,000 Jews were evacuated from Courland. A third of the entire population, including half of all ethnic Latvians, left the country, a proportion higher than anywhere else during WWI, and many did not return.[14]

After the war, the infrastructure was in ruins. Latvia was no longer a major producer and gateway for Russia, herself in the throes of a savage civil war. And of course the border was also closed. One Finnish diplomat wrote: "Riga was a beautiful capital city, abounding in wealth, with the entire region of Moscow as a natural hinterland. After the war it became a kind of poor little Vienna number 2 – a large city, but one blown empty, whose trade and manufacture had died."[15] (He probably wrote this in the 1920's before Rīga again became prosperous.)

Latvia between the wars was primarily an agricultural country which exported flax, grain, butter, bacon, fish, as well as plywood and lumber, but on the other hand it still had industry – it was self-sufficient in consumer goods, assembled cars and trucks and exported electrical, electronic and optical goods such as telephone exchanges, radio sets and the incomparable sub-miniature Minox camera.

The consequences of later tragedies have been told in earlier chapters. Research into Latvian demographic losses has revealed that as a result of the 1941 deportations alone, Latvia's direct loss was almost 600,000 person years. If we count the impact of deportation on the birthrate, the total loss of potential life caused by the deportation constituted 890,000 person-years.[16]

Tens of thousands of Latvian men fell in the ranks of the Red Army in the Second World War, and at its end in 1944 the newly established Soviet Latvia ceded to the Russian Federation the Abrene (Pytalovo) region, inhabitants and all. The annexation supposedly occurred at the "repeated requests of the people and in harmony with their hopes."[17]

Estimates show that even after 1949, deportations, executions, and other forms of repression cost Latvia the loss of over a million "man-years," years which the victims of violence could have given to the development of their native land – supposing, of course, that the Soviet power had allowed it. In

addition to the deported and dead children, large numbers of children naturally were never born. After 1944 the birthrate of Latvians collapsed in comparison with that of other national groups. When elsewhere in Europe after
the war large numbers were born yearly, few were born among Latvians. Even
now the birthrate in Latvia is among the lowest in Europe.[18]

On the other hand, the largest population growth by immigration in the
Soviet Union was in Latvia – twice the rate of a natural increase. The large
Russian-speaking minorities that moved into Latvia accelerated colonization,
sovietization and russification, and undermined the demographic balance. If
the newcomers now complain that they are victims, one thing is certain: the
Latvians were the real victims.

Many immigrants who came into Latvia were of advanced age. The end
result was an increase in social costs, the slowdown of economic development,
and a shortage of labor.[19]

The Baltic republics were the Soviet Union's display windows facing west.
To justify their actions in the eyes of the world, the Soviet Union engendered
and spread the myth that the Latvian Soviet Republic was a "model of
socialism" – economically flourishing and with the highest standard of living
among Soviet republics. There are many abroad and even in Latvia who still
believe this myth, which was created by the manipulation of statistics. Another
myth is that independent Latvia had been an economically retarded state.[20] A
third myth was that the flow of immigrants from the rest of the Soviet Union
was "aid from brother republics."

During the period of the Soviet occupation, traditional agriculture, the
rural environment, and the architecture of the individual homesteads were
destroyed, and a way made for alcoholism and poverty. The property of count-
less families was confiscated and people were sent to do forced labor. The
national, linguistic, and social groupings of the inhabitants were changed.
Massive factories were built, for which energy, raw materials, and workers
were brought in from outside, and of which the products were taken away.
Only the pollutants, the workers and their bosses remained in Latvia.

It was said that Latvians were "lazy," so workers had to be brought in. There
simply were not enough Latvians to service the giant factories. Laziness in
Soviet times was of course impossible ("He who does not work does not eat").
Now the huge, inefficient factories stand empty.

The creation of such a major industry was not driven by economic feasi-
bility but rather by the desire to colonize the country. Ecologically it was
harmful. Besides, the manufacture was partly of military ware to satisfy the
occupying army's needs. By the eighties the little republic accounted for an
utterly disproportionate share of the industrial output of the USSR. (100

percent of all railroad cars and streetcars, for example, were made there, and most of the radios.)

Many of Latvia's most beautiful places have been spoiled by (now decaying) concrete colossi or drowned by waters with the aid of dams. In the 1960's the huge Pļaviņas dam was built on Daugava River, which for Latvians carries its ancient aura of sacredness to this day. The Latvians did manage to prevent the building of a Rīga underground in the 1980's because of concerns about the huge number of immigrant workers needed. Former collective farms and military bases are a sad sight. In the forests there are hundreds of former secret military sites which may be dangerous to people and the environment. Military training was given in schools. Latvian boys were drafted into the Soviet Army and served for years in the far corners of the earth including Afghanistan as well as in the radioactive cleanup of the Chernobyl disaster; they were not allowed to serve in their home republic.

"A puppet, a half-colony of imperialism"

The version Soviet historians have presented is that Latvia had been a "puppet state, a half-colony of imperialism, an agricultural appendage of the West," which had been "torn away from its natural basis and environment – from Russian raw materials and markets." Latvia's land reform of the 1920's was dubbed "anti-revolutionary." Only with the aid of "brother republics" was Latvia modernized and industrialized. Naturally, the Soviet power, by persecuting gifted specialists and the intelligentsia in Latvia, had herself caused the problems she claimed to be correcting. The newcomers were not all experts, of course, but mostly country folk fleeing from the poverty of kolkhozes in the border areas of Russia.

Latvia's individual private farms were done away with and converted to kolkhozes, and the people concentrated in central villages. It was done in the name of "modernization," "ending the exploitation of the agricultural proletariat" and because the former "small farms were inefficient." No mention was made of the fact that upon the takeover in 1940 the Soviet Union itself permitted only the smallest farms and had done away with larger and more productive farms, as well as all those which used outside labor.

The consequence in Latvia was an unprecedented fall in agricultural productivity. For decades, production per hectare as well as the total harvest of grain was lower than during Latvia's first independence. It was not worthwhile to produce more because of the miserable prices set by the state. Most productive land was the small private plots which people could cultivate for themselves. The amount of land under cultivation decreased,[21] and shortages and food lines appeared in the cities. The solution to the crisis, the "emergency agriculture system," led to catastrophe: sometimes the quantity harvested was less than that sown.

Class warfare was brought to the countryside. Daina Bleiere writes that an entire social class, the farmers, were forced to become members of the proletariat. Both the failure of agriculture and the resistance were blamed on one source – the "kulaks" or wealthy private farmers. According to the interpretation during the Soviet era, there were 11,000 of them.[22]

According to Soviet statistics, Latvia produced 96.6 times more radio receivers in 1984 than in 1940. The numbers can be read differently than as a mark of increased productivity:

In the 1930's Latvia was a giant in electronics production. VEF, the state factory, produced radios, cameras, even airplanes. The people had in proportion to population as many phones and radios in use as in Finland. Only 13.5 percent of the work force was employed in manufacturing, but when calculating the value of industrial output with regard to population, Latvia was in eighth place in Europe.[23] In the last year of her independence, 1939, Latvia produced 43,700 radios, while the entire Soviet Union produced only 160,500. How could the production of an "agricultural appendage of imperialism" be more than one fourth of that of the entire Soviet Union? [24]

When Latvia was annexed to the Soviet Union in 1940, the action was explained by the assertion that the "imperialists, capitalists, and the kulaks" had destroyed Latvia's economy – its manufactures and its agriculture. "Latvia's working people and its working educated class had been condemned to unemployment and death by starvation," insisted one of the speakers at the fateful session of the Supreme Soviet in Moscow. "From year to year, Latvia plunges ever more deeply into destitution. Its economy is sinking and its productive strength is being destroyed." The majority of the rural population was said to be sinking into wretchedness. Now help was promised, as well as freedom, prosperity, social security, wealthy kolkhozes, rapid economic growth, and a happy future under the leadership of the great Stalin.[25]

Industrial production increased over the decades only by virtue of the flow of new labor into Soviet Latvia. It was only in the 1980's that production began to increase because of increased productivity per person. The standard of living (the availability of the necessities of life and housing) in Latvia was lower than in Estonia, Lithuania and Belarus. A stunning example is the rationing of food in the 1980's – food rationing in a productive agricultural country that also had been a food exporter!

The Council of Europe called attention in its declaration of 1963 to the fact that from 1940 to 1960 the number of Latvian residents working in industry had grown from 264,000 to 725,000. According to the declaration, this had been achieved by moving workers from elsewhere in the Soviet Union, not only for economic but also for political reasons.[26]

The health of Latvia's people has suffered a catastrophic decline. The life expectancy of its inhabitants, especially of men, is at the level of Russia; they die the youngest in the EU. According to the UNDP, the life expectancy of Latvian men at birth was 61 years in 1995 and 65 years in 2003, meaning that, on average, they die immediately upon reaching the Western countries' retirement age.[27] The causes are drinking, smoking, suicide, violence, illness, accidents, an unhealthy life style and poor diet. Rising medical costs also play a role.

Russia often claims that at least in the areas of culture and education the Soviet Union contributed much to Latvia and that cultural workers lived well. First, we must state that Latvian elementary and secondary education was at an impressively high level during the first republic, and the cultural workers did not starve. Secondly, it is true that the Latvians are still comparatively highly educated – at least on paper – and that those poets and writers who were in harmony with the Soviet system got their works published, living better than now, as well as did top athletes. However, few of them nowadays yearn for a return to the old days.

What about the other side of the picture? Millions of books were destroyed or locked up in special warehouses. The country of Latvia was eliminated from the curricula or was presented as a fascist dictatorship. The Russian language and Marxism-Leninism became required subjects for everyone. The Russian language and culture were glorified; the influence of western culture in Latvia was denied.

National holidays were forbidden, national symbols were transformed, memorial places destroyed, censorship intensified. Culture was trampled upon to the extent that in addition to Christmas, the Midsummer's or Jāņi festivities were forbidden – the age-old Latvian tradition. The words, folk songs, foods, and recipes which reminded one of Midsummer's Day were eradicated.[28]

The aim of the continual battle against "bourgeois nationalism" was to decrease and eventually obliterate the Western orientation of the Baltic peoples and to end their psychological distancing from the "big brother" in the East. The campaign claimed that the Balts had an undesirable inclination toward nationalism, while the Russians are characterized by distinct internationalism.

(But not cosmopolitanism! That was a dirty word used in anti-Jewish campaigns in the Soviet Union.)

The dominant position of culture during the Soviet era is partially a myth. Although books are now relatively much more expensive than in the Soviet era, three times as many books are now published in Latvia as were then, even though political and propaganda brochures, which no one read, were part of the book count. Moreover, of the 814 books published in Latvia in 1984, for example, fewer than half were in Latvian.[29] According to new research, Latvians are eastern Europe's most avid readers. On the average, nearly eight times more books per person are published here in one year than in eastern Europe on the average.

A 1948 group declaration by fifty US and Canadian educators differs from the official Soviet propaganda. The group was led by the dean emeritus of Princeton, Christian Gauss.

"Mass executions and mass deportations have so decimated the ranks of the Baltic intelligentsia that the mere survival of the Baltic cultures has come to depend more than anything else on the several thousand Baltic scholars who succeeded in escaping abroad. ... It is imperative that the cultures of the Baltic peoples which are today being destroyed by a genocidal foreign regime should be kept alive ..."[30]

Regarding cultural oppression in Latvia, one may say, according to Professor Heinrihs Strods, that about 600,000–700,000 people (34 percent of the population) suffered as a result of the occupiers' efforts to restrict the career and educational opportunities of "the socially dangerous elements."[31]

Compensation or Apology?

Latvians themselves don't feel that they ought to be thankful for the Soviet past, or that they have always been on the receiving end. The present government has established a committee of experts to estimate the losses caused by the Soviet occupation in monetary terms. It would be another matter for Latvia to try to demanding reparations from Russia, which has declared herself to be the legal successor to the Soviet Union.

The Lithuanian parliament passed a law in 2000 which obliges the government to begin negotiations with Moscow to get 23 billion euros in reparations for damages caused by the occupation. The Lithuanian government, however, has not yet taken any practical steps to that end, and the demands have already been rejected in advance by Moscow. Latvia's leading politicians surmise that presenting such demands to Russia would be futile. In the opinion of many, an apology would suffice, but according to President Putin, Russia has already apologized in the 1990's. He is probably referring to the Soviet parliament's December 1989 condemnation of the Molotov-Ribbentrop pact and to his own and President Yeltsin's mention of the oppressive actions of Soviet rule – with rather vague turns of phrase and taking no responsibility for what had happened. Clearly, this would not suffice.[32]

It is estimated that the work of the Latvian committee will take four to five years. The basic principle is to compare Latvia to similar countries which have not experienced an occupation – at least not a long one – Finland, Denmark, and Austria. If Latvia demands reparations, Russia's Duma threatens to demand reparations for the Soviet installations built in Latvia over the decades. The Russian weekly *Versia* recently calculated that Latvia was in debt to Russia for some 60 billion of dollars for roads, a health-care system, and for factories built by Russian workers and money.[33]

After a 12-year investigation, Estonia published in 2005 a White Book on the losses to the Estonian nation by occupation regimes in 1940 – 1991. Estonia's current government has, however, announced that it does not intend to demand reparations from Russia.[34]

Russia's governmental representatives announced in no uncertain terms in March 2006 that they will never pay reparations to the Baltic States and that the topic should be "closed" once and for all. At the same time they made them understand that earlier in the same month President Putin had apologized to Hungary and the Czech republic for the Soviet era precisely because they had not demanded reparations.[35]

Vladimir Kovalev recently wrote in the St. Petersburg Times: "Estonia, Latvia and Lithuania have one simple request – to recognize that Josef Stalin committed crimes against their citizens. In other words, they are asking the Kremlin to do exactly what Germany did decades ago in relation to Adolf Hitler." According to him, the Russian political elite has not learned the lesson.

The answer came in the form of the results of a survey, which asked Russian residents if they think their country needs a ruler similar to Stalin. Almost half of all respondents, 42 percent, said yes. But most worrying was that 45 percent of young Russians – aged from 18 to 24 years – were also positive about the tyrant.[36]

The Worse of Two Evils?

I don't know which was worse, communism or Nazism, or if it is possible or necessary to compare them. In any case, a senior historian at the elite Moscow institute which trains Russian diplomats argued in an interview in March 2006 that "communism was more terrible than Nazism and fascism because it destroyed society down to its foundations" and consequently, it represents an evil which must be rejected rather than a system that could in some way be reformed. Andrei Zubov, who teaches history at the Moscow State Institute of International Relations, argued that Russians must face up to that fact and change their views of the Soviet past.[37]

The political commentator Simon Araloff writes: "For Russia the successes of independent Latvia, Lithuania and Estonia … offer the daily proof of the crime perpetrated on the Baltic nations in the 20th century. These successes testify that if there had been no period of occupation, today Latvia would be in an absolutely different economic situation, and would have much greater weight in the European and international community. To understand this – it is enough to look at the economic parameters of Latvia before WWII."

"Having cast off the yoke of communism, within a decade they [Baltic and other Eastern European countries] have been able to overcome if not all, then a large part of the consequences of its fatal influence."[38]

To the theme of "gratitude" also belongs Russian politicians' and diplomats' idea that Russia "gave" the Baltic countries independence in 1991; the Baltics should be grateful for that, and also for Russia's agreeing to withdraw her troops in 1994. From the perspective of international law, such feelings are irrelevant, writes the experienced Swedish diplomat Lars Fredén, who knows both the Baltics and Russia well. And from the perspective of the Baltic peoples such opinions are incomprehensible – even outrageous and politically unseemly.

Fredén insists that "Baltic independence is a right, not a favor. What is a right cannot be given as a gift, by Russia or anybody else. One may rejoice that an aggression has ceased, but should not also have to thank the offender that it has stopped."[39]

He reminds us that Russia is the Soviet Union's legal successor and that the German Federal Republic has spent many years and billions of D-marks to indemnify, and in some cases, reconcile with, nations devastated by Nazism. He is of the opinion that Russia should at last speak openly of its past – to its own people as well. "Russia cannot become a normal European country without admitting the immense crimes that Communism committed against the Russians themselves."

13

Has Latvia been unwilling to establish good relations with neighboring Russia? Does Latvia champion an intransigent, hostile line toward Russia in the European Union, and did she decline a border agreement with Russia? Does she demand that Russia hand over some border areas to her?

There are no small nations. A nation's size is not measured by the number of its people, just as a person's greatness is not measured by his height.

Victor Hugo

From the Latvian perspective, the questions would be put differently. Doesn't the lack of a border agreement benefit Russia? Did she wish to pressure Latvia into changing her internal policy and, by tarnishing Latvia's international image, prevent her acceptance in the European Union and NATO?

As a think-tank close to the Kremlin wrote in 1997: "NATO cannot accept into its ranks countries with unresolved problems with minorities and with their borders."[1] Russia made several attempts to hinder or even stop EU and NATO expansion to the Baltic States. For example, in the spring of 1998 domestic social tension on the streets of Rīga was fuelled by the Russian media and later framed in the context of the non-citizen issue.[2]

In the end, both NATO and the EU considered that the border dispute was not an impediment to Latvia's and Estonia's membership, and accepted both as members in 2004. At that time the EU silenced the Russian resistance by promising, among other things, to "pay more attention to the plight of minorities in the Baltic countries."

One might also ask if the Latvian politicians are blameless – could they not leave the past to historians and concentrate on the future? On the other hand, the traumas and the damages suffered are too enormous to be forgotten despite any pleadings by well-meaning outsiders. And, as we know, it takes two to tango.

The Finnish respected liberal newspaper, *Helsingin Sanomat*, writes in an editorial that Russia's foreign policy seems to be distancing itself from democracy, as its chilly relationships with Georgia, Ukraine, and the Baltic countries indicate.[3]

George Kennan wrote that Soviet leaders, to enhance their regime's legitimacy and domestic political stability, "never hesitated to depict the outside world as more inimical and menacing than it actually was, and to treat it accordingly. In this way they not only encumbered themselves with imagined burdens that had no real existence, but they also provoked real fears and resentments that need otherwise never have existed."[4] This helps to explain Russia's behavior towards Latvia during the 1990's. The more successful Latvia was in implementing EU and NATO integration policies, the more aggressive Russian discourse became.[5]

First, in 1992–1994, Russia sought to use its military as a tool to affect the status of its "compatriots" in Latvia, linking the issue of troop withdrawal to changes in Latvian policy and even threatening military action. Second, Russia raised the issue of Latvia's Russians in various international organizations – UN, EU, NATO, OSCE, and Council of Europe – to pressure Latvia to change its policies and to isolate her diplomatically. According to Russia, Latvia's regime was a form of "apartheid," its minority policy tantamount to "ethnic cleansing," Latvia was witnessing the "rebirth of fascism." Russia also took part as an interested third party in several court cases involving former KGB personnel, partisans, and military officers, challenging Latvia in Latvian and international courts.[6]

No substantial shift in Russia's attitude towards Latvia has occurred after the latter's accession to the EU and NATO. Russia's foreign minister Sergei Lavrov said at the start of 2006 that "it is difficult to view the relationship of Latvia and Russia positively while human rights violations continue in Latvia." Defense minister and vice-prime-minister Sergei Ivanov stated publicly in February 2007 that relationships with Russia have not improved since Latvia and Estonia joined NATO, but have actually worsened, as the two countries have "wound up in a downright absurd fascism and fostering of racial superiority." According to Ivanov, NATO has, in some incomprehensible way, turned a blind eye. He added that the development of democracy in Latvia and Estonia has gone astray.[7]

President Putin's office announced in November 2006 that as long as Vaira Vīķe-Freiberga was president of Latvia, Putin would not go to Latvia. The

Russian embassy in Rīga had said earlier that the small right-wing minority in Latvian society opposes any attempt by Russia to open a dialogue.[8]

Later the ambassador threatened that because of tense relationships, Russia might cut off all export of oil via Latvia. That may have been a mere threat as the action would be injurious to Russia herself, but if it were carried out, it would be a blow to Latvia, whose major source of livelihood is the service sector. A significant part of that is transport. Ninety percent of Latvia's harbors serve Russia's and Belarus' import and export.[9]

Russia is chiefly responsible for these arrangements but, on the other hand, Latvia has missed many an opportunity to end the emotional race with Russia for the status of one of "the greatest victims of World War II." Observers say that the historical facts are undeniable but that it is time to close the "book of pain" and look into the future.[10]

The new concept of Russian foreign policy adopted in 2000 offers good-neighbor relations with the Baltic countries on one "indispensable condition." It is "respect for Russia's interests in those states, including the central question of respect for the rights of the Russian-speaking population."[11]

The Baltic countries are not Russia's most important neighbors, but there is surely some truth in what Sweden's prime minister Carl Bildt said in 1994: Russia's policy towards the Baltic States was a "litmus test" of both Russia's commitment to international norms and her renunciation of imperial ambitions.[12]

Fascists and Dried Salt Fish

For years it has been impossible to arrange meetings at the ministerial level between Latvia and Russia, let alone presidential state visits. In 2005, relations drifted onto a possibly even worse course, among the consequences being the collapse of the border agreement in its last lap.

It is strange that the crisis began when Vīķe-Freiberga announced that she would go to Moscow for the 2005 celebration of the May 9 Victory Day – as the only Baltic leader.[13] Russia had been surprised at the Baltic countries' and Poland's boycott of the observance and scolded them publicly. The Russians were accustomed to expecting honor and thanks from the countries which they "liberated" in 1945.

The *Financial Times* published the letter from the Russian ambassador to London according to which it was "sad to observe how a biased revision of history can sometimes obscure the memory of the liberators of the death camps and of European capital cities." The Great Patriotic War was "a war for the national honour and dignity." And: "Why should we not look together at

Picture 21. The Russians were outraged when Latvia's President said in the spring of 2005 that they gathered to drink vodka, eat dried salt fish, and sing songs accomanied by accordion music in honor of the liberation of Latvia. Eriks Osis, *Latvijas Avīze,* 2005

the thrust of the attempts to reconsider the history and the outcomes of the second world war."[14]

Before her trip, President Vīķe-Freiberga sent an informative note to Europe's heads of state outlining Latvia's history and her own position on the celebration: the 1945 Victory Day did not mean freedom but occupation, and as a matter of fact, the continuation of the war in the Baltic republics. However, she did explain that she was going to Moscow where the world's leaders were meeting and to extend the "hand of friendship" to Russia.

She wrote that the Baltic countries were subjected to "the occupation by another totalitarian empire," that the Soviet Union was guilty of crimes against humanity and that "millions of colonists poured into the land." She condemned Germany and Russia for their secret agreement, in which they had divided the areas in the east, and said that Hitler and Stalin were responsible for an enormous loss of life and the suffering of human beings.

According to the letter, the end of the war in Latvia really – and finally – came in 2004 when the country joined the European Union. Vīķe-Freiberga appealed to leaders of democratic countries to encourage Russia to express regret for its post-war subjugation of Central and Eastern Europe.[15]

The appeal was successful: Latvia received more favorable publicity in the international press than ever before during the time of her independence. A partial cause was that President George W. Bush visited Rīga on his way to the Moscow celebration. Bush also took an outspoken stand on the historical injustices – and a self-critical one, admitting that the Yalta agreement was a mistake on the part of the U.S.[16]

The Latvian president's paper was a red flag to the Russians, in whose calendar Victory Day was the year's most important international event. The crisis had peaked already when Vīķe-Feiberga handed a copy of the *History of Latvia. The 20th Century* hot off the press to Putin at the celebration of the liberation of Auschwitz, the preface to which she had written. The book was published with the support of the state and the U. S. embassy, and had been put together by five Latvian historians.

The Russian-language press in Latvia and Russia immediately began a heated campaign against the book and Vīķe-Feiberga. According to Russia's foreign ministry, the book was an "ideological made-to-order" job marked by "rumors and falsifications." The term "occupation" was a "sacred cow" of the Latvians. According to Moscow the book "gave a special place to painting black the Russian contribution to Latvian history and culture." Latvia was also said to have disgraced the memory of the Auschwitz victims.

The Nationalist-Bolshevik party in Latvia organized a book-burning near the presidential palace in Rīga and shouted anti-fascist slogans. *Pravda* recommended that the president give up her Moscow trip, and the foreign ministry conjectured that she had not even intended to come to Moscow. Vīķe-Freiberga also gibed at the dried-salt-fish-eating, vodka-drinking, and accordion-playing Russian veterans who boasted about "liberating the Baltics."

In one week Russia's foreign minister released five sharp protests, or "commentaries." According to these, "the Latvians sought historical revenge on even the highest levels of government." And: "One can only lament the fact that the leaders of our neighboring country will not honor a day sacred to the whole civilized world."

The Duma and Russian historians also protested the "provocation and the Russophobic hysteria" and condemned Latvia's "territorial demands on Russia." Some commentators wrote that Vīķe-Freiberga should have stayed in the Canadian psychiatric hospital where she had worked earlier. Vyacheslav Molotov's grandson said on television that "the Kremlin's patience is nearing an end," and that "perhaps the time has come to bang one's fist on the table." Exhortations to boycott poured out, and Latvian exports to Russia declined in 2005.

Picture 22. In the spring of 2005, Latvijas Avīze published examples provided by an anti-fascist cartoon competition (caricatura.ru). Among other subjects, Latvia's president was pictured as the guard at a concentration camp and Latvia as a puppet dangling from a swastika.

Preceding the celebration, Russia announced an anti-fascist cartoon competition on the internet. It is not too surprising that "Latvia's fascist president" was a universal target of abuse. The Latvian flag was denigrated by shaping it in many different ways into a red and white swastika banner. The cartoons are displayed on the internet, and some of them were published in the press.[17]

Against the background of preparations for Russia's celebration, Latvia ran into problems with the border agreements. It might very well have been settled in good time, for the text had already been set seven years earlier, but for various reasons Russia did not wish to ratify it. The EU now urged Latvia to take advantage of the opportunity to sign it in Moscow. The European Parliament also urged Russia to do so, since "human rights are better established in Latvia and Estonia than in Russia."

Latvia promised to sign the agreement unconditionally, and decided to refrain from attaching to it an explanatory political declaration for which the point of departure was the 1920 peace agreement between Russia and Latvia, and which also would have mentioned the "unlawful occupation of Latvia" (or "incorporation" if Russia would not approve of the term), and the continuity of the state.

At the last moment before the president's trip, the Latvian government and parliament began to have doubts. The majority held the view that the constitution, which mentions Latvia's historical provinces and boundaries, did require a declaration referring to the year 1920. Or that the constitutional court at least issue a statement on the matter. Would signing of the agreement mean that Latvia's historical territory would be altered – that Latvia would give up for good the Abrene area, which had been annexed to Russia? Were not changes in the border to be decided by a referendum?

A declaration was drawn up, but contrary to what Russia claimed, Latvia (and Estonia) did not propose any specific additions to the border agreement; their declarations were intended mainly for internal use. Moreover the Latvian leadership specifically declared that it had no territorial demands on Russia. Moscow, however, was offended, and announced that it would not sign the agreement. It is indeed true that the text of the Latvian declaration was subject to a wide range of interpretations, creating the impression that some future government might present new demands to Russia – for example financial compensation for the loss of Abrene.

According to Moscow, the 1920 peace treaty is not legally in force, so that Latvia "is apparently preparing territorial demands." It is politically and strategically important to Russia that she keep her present boundaries; she cannot yield the least bit on this question or even permit the existence of such a notion. Her other fear is that the Baltic countries might demand reparations for the occupation.

What particularly sticks in the mind from the Moscow observance of Victory Day was the Kremlin's verbal assault on the Baltic states, amid complete and even complacent silence on the part of the European Union and their NATO allies. President Putin lost his temper in the press conference on that day. According to him, Latvia's and Estonia's policies "involve stupid territorial demands." He called on Latvian politicians "to stop engaging in demagoguery," because for their demands they will get "only a dead jackass's ears."

Answering in the press conference the familiar planted question about "neo-Nazi sentiments in the Baltic states," Putin replied: "I want to prevent these phenomena from spoiling the atmosphere in Europe and Russia's relations with European countries." The EU presidency seemed to play along. "We will fight together, calmly, against the negative phenomena that were mentioned," said Prime Minister Jean-Claude Juncker of Luxemburg.

Divide et Impera

Russia practices a divide-and-rule policy in its relations with the three Baltic countries: on occasion one or two of them are "good" and the third is criticized and pressured; then the formerly bad one, again contented, finds herself to be in favor, and the others in turn are "bad." From the spring of 2007, the "worst one," of course, has been Estonia.

Mihail Lotman, the professor of semiotics at the University of Tallinn, wrote then that a small country is a convenient enemy for Russia. First, Putin mainly chooses to provoke countries whose response is definitely civilized, and second, no one ever seriously believes that Estonia could be a real threat to Russia.[18]

In May 2007, after long dickering and quarreling among the political parties, the Latvian government and parliament could not agree on a declaration to support Estonia in the "soldier monument" crisis with Moscow – probably just because Latvian politicians were afraid that their border agreement might be endangered.[19]

How this situation was orchestrated is an example of the manner in which Moscow drives a wedge into the European Union and succeeds in ruining its united front. Moscow claims that the new members bring "ghosts of the past" to life.

Their very partners in the EU do not always understand the Baltic countries. Even right-wing politicians among the old EU members have said that the attitude of the Baltic countries and Poland toward Russia is too strict and negative. According to commentators, in this case the EU may be listening to Russia more than to its own new member countries.[20]

Undeniably the Baltic countries have hewn to an "anti-Russian" line, but to me it seems only natural that they use every forum to push back against the steady stream of anti-Baltic charges from Moscow. For example, a 2005 proclamation of the Council of Europe condemning the crimes of communism was largely a Baltic initiative. It has been labeled useless and propagandistic. The Baltic countries opposed the granting of visa-free travel to Russians, and also opposed the Baltic Sea natural gas line project. Baltic politicians have succeeded in eliciting strong reactions by comparing two criminal systems of Hitler and Stalin, for Latvia has had experience with both. Germans especially don't understand this comparison – they consider Germany to have been the worst offender of all.

The Western European countries in the EU are tired of the Baltic countries' anti-Russian stand. Also, the Western Europeans wish to have a share of the gas which is expected to flow through the Baltic pipeline.[21]

In 2005 a columnist in the *Helsingin Sanomat* probed the actions of the so-called Russophobic bloc in the EU and the differences of opinion between the old and new member countries. According to him, the calming and constructive contribution of such countries as Germany and Finland was needed in the EU so as to strengthen its relations with Russia. "The surprising failure of the border agreement is more the fault of Estonia than of Russia, although no one says so in public in the name of EU solidarity." The EU must support Estonia and Latvia, but it "cannot support the strivings of individual countries when they begin to disturb the Union's common policy line."[22]

Putin took up the question of Latvia's and Estonia's minorities during his visit to Finland in 2005. He expressed horror at Russian speakers being treated as "non-citizens and foreigners" and asked the help of Finland as the country of the future presidency of the EU. President Tarja Halonen did not promise this type of "help" but instead defended the Baltic countries. She called to mind the view of international organizations that the legislation of Estonia and Latvia has met all the EU requirements, and that it is normal for every state to set certain conditions for granting citizenship. To a question from a Russian journalist, Halonen answered that no one had cause to be arrogant in these matters. "In every country, undesirable things happen."

Latvia and the other Baltic countries still seem to fear that the large countries will again arrange things over their heads, and they especially fear that there will be a rapprochement between Russia and Germany, which had indeed occurred in Putin's time.

"The Molotov-Ribbentrop pact can be resurrected," said Estonia's ambassador Tiit Kolbre in the spring of 2006. "Great powers make decisions without showing interest in how small countries are faring." In his words, the gas pipeline is a question of economics to Germany but one of politics to Moscow. Dmitri Trenin of the Carnegie Center said that Russia practices a take-it-or-leave-it policy. "Either the Baltic countries approve Russia's views and relations will improve, or they will remain as they are."

It is extraordinary that what Russia concedes to Finland she cannot concede to the Baltics. As early as the 1960's, Russia's (Soviet) encyclopedia testified that Finland was not the aggressor in 1939, but the victim of aggression. In the 1990's President Yeltsin asked Finland's pardon for this imperialistic attack of Stalin's, and later on a visit to Finland, Putin laid a wreath on the grave of Marshal Mannerheim, who was considered Russia's arch-enemy for decades.

Latvia Yields

At the start of 2007, almost two years after being driven into a dead end, Latvia's new government yielded to Russia's wishes in the matter of the border: Latvia would sign and ratify the agreement without any declaration. The question was still being debated in Latvia, but the Prime Minister seemed to give priority to trade relationships with Russia. A majority in Parliament gave the government authorization to sign.

Many asked what the hurry was and to what extent it was worth bowing to Russia's demands. The question was also raised as to why Latvia had acted alone and not in conjunction with Estonia, which was in the same situation as Latvia. A referendum was also demanded. Russia appeared well satisfied, but according to some commentators, Moscow in fact hoped that internal dissension in Latvia would prevent the passage of the agreement. On the other hand, Russia needed the agreement in order to have the EU grant her visa-free travel.[23]

Latvia's ambassador to Moscow warned that the settlement of the border dispute would not, of course, resolve other difficulties between the countries, above all the question of the occupation, the disagreement about history, the question of demanding reparations and of settling the questions about researching the fate of victims of terror.[24]

The Abrene area now is totally russified, and if it were joined to Latvia, the Latvians would be in greater danger of becoming a minority in their own country both in a demographic and political sense. In the prime minister's opinion, it was time to acknowledge that Abrene was lost forever. According to him, legality and continuity as a state would be taken into account well enough without any special declaration.[25]

Putin, who had said that he would not come to Latvia as long as Vīķe-Freiberga was the president, received the Latvian prime minister when the latter arrived at the end of March to sign the border agreement. The Latvian president did not get an invitation.

It appears that Russian relations with the state of Latvia had not improved, only those with the government and prime minister of the day had.

Just as this was being written September 2007 the Russian Duma finally decided that the border agreement could be ratified.

In March 2006, *The Baltic Times* interviewed the former foreign minister and soon-to-be president of Estonia, Toomas Hendrik Ilves, then a member of the

European Parliament, and asked him what the future of Estonian-Russian relations would be. Ilves replied:

> As long as Russia fails to come to terms with Estonian independence, or, on a greater scale, with the 'greatest tragedy of the 20th century,' Mr. Putin's characterization of the collapse of the U.S.S.R., I doubt we will see much of a change. This has little to do with Estonia. We see Russia treat Poland, Ukraine, Georgia in exactly the same neurotic way that has more to do with its own inability to deal with its past than anything Estonia has or has not done.[26]

"What exactly are Russia and the Baltic countries at odds about?" asks the Finnish diplomat and political commentator Max Jakobson. "It is no longer about the borders, since that question has been settled. The dispute is about the past. Russia demands that the Baltic countries acknowledge that they willingly and by a large vote joined the Soviet Union, and at the same time accepted the communist system as their own. For the Russians mean, without saying so overtly, that the Baltic countries are still a part of Russia."[27]

14

Have the new leaders of Latvia privatized state property for their own use and are they guilty of massive corruption while the majority of the people live in poverty?

Corruption, irresponsibility, inefficiency – this three-headed monster impedes our development and prosperity.

VAIRA VĪĶE-FREIBERGA 1999

They laugh at us. They suppose such corruption is in our nature. But I would argue that it is merely characteristic of the type of economy which has been thrust upon us.

MARINA LEWYCKA, A SHORT HISTORY OF TRACTORS IN UKRAINIAN, 2005

Yes, but…

First, a little anecdote. A friend of mine once happened to be in a in a women's fashion shop in Rīga, when in walked a woman who began, with a smile on her face, to examine the most expensive creations in the place. After a while, she could no longer restrain herself, but said happily to the sales clerk: "Just think, before I was nobody, and now – I'm the spouse of a member of parliament!"

Corruption is one of the greatest obstacles to the creation of viable democratic regimes and capitalist economies in the post-communist countries, i.e. not only in Latvia. One has to admit that Vaira Vīķe-Freiberga's assertion at the start of this chapter is, regrettably, true to a great extent. A short explanation of a very complicated and controversial matter follows.

There was corruption in the Latvian First Republic, too, but it was not so widespread, says Edward Anders. The present situation is something inherited from the Soviet era; after all, he says, two generations grew up in the atmosphere of cynicism and erosion of morality.

I shall speak with a "greater voice," borrowing Vaira Vīķe-Freiberga's words from a time before she became president. She was the first expatriate Latvian invited to address the Latvian Cultural Foundation's meeting in 1994.

> For forty-five years, everything was decided by a Communist party acting in the name of the Soviet Union, an operation which combined the actions of feudal lords and organized crime. The Soviet Union collapsed, and the party was scattered, but in place of the former state mafia, crime and a private mafia thrive. Legal structures and state institutions have been unable to get the situation under control, and that is no wonder. In Latvia, as in other countries formerly belonging to the Soviet Empire, a deeply rooted avoidance of responsibility on all levels and an incredibly widespread corruption are typical. In addition, there are still, in many high places, passionate advocates of the former system who would rather destabilize than support the new establishment.[1]

In addition, Vīķe-Freiberga complained that "nouveau riche upstarts, abusers of their offices, and bought officials" flaunt their money. "Latvian culture has traditionally been built on such concepts as honesty, keeping one's word, a sense of honor, family values, and pride in one's profession. These traditions have been shaken to their very roots."

When Latvia became independent in 1991, those who were quickest to seize the opportunities and had the most initiative became successful – or in this case, those who were the most ruthless and unscrupulous. Many veterans of the "singing revolution" were disappointed: this was not the kind of Latvia they wanted. Was this what they had fought for?

Here as elsewhere in the Baltic lands, young ultra-liberalistic politicians and economists got into office. Taxes were reduced and a flat tax levied on firms and individuals. State property was quickly sold. Agriculture was privatized and kolkhozes divided back into small private farms. In 1940 small farms could still produce quite efficiently; in 1990 they could not. The movement of money was made freer. Social safeguards were reduced to the bare minimum, the state was to have only a "night watchman's role," and "everyone was to be the shaper of his own fate." Investments were made attractive to enterprises by financial and other aid and by the low wages paid to workers. Trade unions did not hamper business.

There were and continue to be an astonishing number of commercial banks, and one explanation is that they apparently exist in order to launder dirty money. KGB money was also left in the country, and no one seems to know where it is located. In the best position to privatize their property were the directors of Soviet enterprises and the kolkhozes, the KGB leaders, and generally those in leading positions.

"Eat beans and Baltic herring!"

There are those who became wealthy overnight and are still filling their pockets, oftentimes less than legally, but there are many more of those who still just eke out a living.[2] Latvian television, in its food programs, gives retirees information about how to manage on the days before the pension money arrives: cereal without milk, diced herring, bean soup…

There have already been several super-rich ministers. A prime minister many times over, the People's Party's Andris Šķēle got the well-deserved nickname of "Europe's richest prime minister."

The rich get richer and the poor get poorer. Eurostat reports that in 2005 the richest one-fifth of Latvia's population earned 6.7 times what the poorest 20 percent earned. In that respect Latvia leads Europe, along with Portugal and Lithuania.[3]

The political parties in Latvia are still small groups which resemble and quarrel with one another and which have gathered around wealthy populist *bosses*. They are more akin to economic interest groups than to political organizations. The representatives routinely desert one group for another, often apparently being bought out. The Parliament, *Saeima*, has lost its significance partly through its own fault: it busies itself with trifles, plays politics in a populist fashion before TV cameras, and rushes through strange laws at the government's request, which later have to be amended. Before the midsummer 2006, the President of the republic declared that she was happy because the *Saeima* summer vacation was beginning. "I dread to think how many more too hastily drafted laws it would otherwise have time to pass."[4]

The parties promise the sun and the moon, and after every election the electorate is disappointed and switches its support to another, often completely new power bloc. Economic growth has indeed been strong and unemployment has decreased in recent years, but many people are still living in worse conditions than at the end of the Soviet era. The growth has a reverse side. There are serious imbalances in the Latvian economy: it has the highest inflation rate in the EU, the biggest current account deficit in the EU, a tremendous borrowing binge and a sizzling real estate market – in a nutshell: it is over-heating. And the government is unwilling or unable to act.[5]

Trust in the parties and in politicians is almost nil.[6] A UNDP study in 2002 stated that 79 percent of Latvians trust their leaders "very little" or "not at all."

Furthermore trust in other public institutions such as the justice system, the police, and the customs and tax collectors is alarmingly small. The public does trust those newspapers and television programs which have tried to uncover wrongdoing and corruption. Politicians, on the other hand, criticize editors and try to silence them. New scandals are exposed almost daily. For one who follows Latvian politics, it is difficult to know where simple stupidity ends and provocation, crime, and underhanded activities begin.

In addition to this lack of trust, Latvians doubt their ability to influence political decision-making or to oppose corruption.[7] There would be help from citizens or non-governmental organizations (NGO), Transparency International among them. But of late the same kind of attack as in Russia against such organizations has begun to appear.[8] According to a recent listing of Transparency International, Latvia has the Baltics' most corrupt society: it is at the bottom of the EU list along with Poland.[9]

In 2006 Latvia did, however, improve its standing on the list of countries surveyed, rising from 57th to 49th place in the world. It was then tied with Slovakia and almost even with Lithuania. At the same time, the World Bank improved Latvia's rating in a survey in which it asked thousands of firms in 26 transitional countries how badly corruption affects them. Latvia's figures had improved slightly since 2002, with just four countries doing better than Latvia.[10]

It is difficult to measure corruption accurately – the statistics tell us only what opinion people have of the situation. They are based on polls of business people, academics, country analysts, and residents, both local and expatriate.[11] They are surely indicative of the truth. Foreign investors admit to bribery, even if they themselves would not bribe; intermediaries pay the bribes, which wind up in the coffers of the party involved. The bribery shows up in the cost of things, for example, in construction costs.[12]

According to informed sources, the problem in Latvia is *state capture* – the fact that the government and parliament make decisions and laws which profit certain interested circles.[13] The establishment of an anti-corruption office (KNAB) a few years back was indeed a step forward.[14] It has helped by initi-ating a number of court cases. Some experts conjecture, however, that the KNAB is unlikely to step on "politically large toes,"[15]

In March of 2007 the President told the press that the government and parliament had "opened the door to very serious political manipulations" which enabled "so-called oligarchs" to influence matters. She conjectured that this was an attempt to impede the investigations of officials, investigations which concerned certain political groups or their economic supporters.[16]

The prices of land and real estate in Latvia have in some places risen to insane heights, on a level with those on the French Riviera. Most likely foreign laundered money is being invested in building lots and real estate. Ordinary people will have to pay the price, for property taxes are based on the usual prices of real estate in a neighborhood.

In my opinion people should not suffer or be blamed if they happen to have bad leaders. The "servants of the people" become drunk with power. The problem is that "too large" sums of money are loose in political circles – they break almost anyone's political backbone. One election cycle is enough to make municipal politicians and state representatives rich. They need no longer care about the voters. One defect is that there is no mechanism by which voters can recall their representatives. The political good-brother organization will not punish those accused of wrongdoing – that has often been often been seen.

Many shed the last of their illusions when a new turn in the so-called *Jūrmalgate* was revealed in 2006. It was viewed as one of the worst scandals of the independence era. Latvian television broadcast for all the people to hear a police wiretap in which the country's best known and richest politicians were speaking in the slang of the Russian underworld with shady automobile dealers and other *bizinesmen* about a political coalition and about what was apparently bribe money. Among them were Šķēle, the then minister Ainārs Šlesers, both of them millionaires, party founders and leaders, and ministers for many terms. Neither should have had any direct dealings with Jūrmala's municipal politics, nor with the businessmen with whom they were negotiating. Not one of them would even discuss leaving office, but accused the journalists, officials, and competing parties of persecution.

The Jūrmala politician Ilmārs Ancāns revealed to the police in advance the huge bribe he was paid in the election of 2005. Because of threats, he and his family have been under police protection, along with the prosecutor of the case.[17]

Lost Trust

Something odd happened in the 1990's. Popular leaders were good at encouraging the spirit of independence and the singing revolution, but problems arose when they had to begin leading the independent country. They forfeited the trust of the people.

In the autumn of 2001, *The Economist* wrote that after ten years of independence, the leaders of the three Baltic countries could not adapt to the post-cold-war era. "The former dissidents often showed themselves to be quarrelsome and ineffectual when they got into power, and the former Soviet types brought their own bad habits with them from the past: greed, bossism, and secrecy." According to this publication, corruption and inefficiency stemming from these factors have to a great extent exhausted the trust of the public. The achievement of independence has too obviously enriched politicians, "and their inability to communicate with the electorate is alarming."

All in all, I have come to the conclusion that the deepest division in Latvia is perhaps not between the Latvians and the Russians, but between the successful and prosperous and the losers. "Two separate countries" live side by side in this country.

Is there hope in the next generation? How can the young change everything if no one sets them an example of high moral standards?

Free press, independent judiciary and honest politicians are indispensable if Latvia is to succeed. That is not to say that in Latvia there are no honest, moral and wise politicians. There are. I myself know some of them. But one has to ask: are there statesmen in Latvia, or only politicians?

And will the voice of the new president continue to be a voice crying in the wilderness when Vīķe-Freiberga retires in 2007? Will there be anybody to speak up then? I really cannot believe so. It is doubtful that the Latvian political structure would tolerate another "mistake," which would bring to power an independent, educated, critical and outspoken national leader, a true leader of the people who would dare criticize the present politico-economic system.[18]

Acknowledgements

How and Why this Book Came to Be

I became interested in international disinformation as far back as a quarter-century ago. In my books and newspaper columns I played a part in correcting the most mindless assertions about Finlandization, which were disseminated by even the most respectable research institutes, history books, and newspapers – for example that "Donald Duck was forbidden in Finland," (probably the most widely disseminated news about Finland since WWII), that "President Kekkonen was a KGB agent," that "Finland's rail, highway, and service-station network was built to serve the Red Army's strategic needs," that "Finland returned to the East all refugees and defectors from the Soviet Union, but on the other hand, did not dare expel Soviet intelligence agents." And so on. Not to speak of the strange picture that numerous history books in the West give about wartime Finland – very few seem to realize, for example, that Finland was at all times a democracy and that Finland was never occupied.[1]

In 1986, the book *The Rise and Fall of the Bulgarian Connection*,[2] taught me how interesting, important, and rewarding a subject the revelation and refutation of accepted disinformation about countries could be, and how careful the documentation should be. (The authors hold the view that the participation of Bulgaria's Secret Service, and through it, Moscow's, in a plot to murder Pope John Paul II in 1981 was an example of a Western disinformation campaign.)

An example of Eastern disinformation at the same time was the "fact" disseminated by the Soviet Union, especially in the media of Third World countries, that AIDS had begun to spread into the world as a result of secret disease tests by the United States.[3]

In 2005 certain Latvian-Americans, who followed the international transmission of information closely, first suggested that I write a book on Latvia. "You'll be dealing with facts, not fanciful constructs," one of them wrote to me.

"Take the bull by the horns. Find the worst things said about Latvia and the Latvians and deal with them. Don't whitewash, just show what and why."

I discovered that for some time there had been active in different corners of the world an unofficial group of twenty-five Latvians. These mainly academic volunteers prescribed as their duty: "To defend and polish the image of Latvia." They monitored what was written about Latvia in the mainstream media and the internet web pages, kept in contact with one another, and sent letters and corrections to newspapers with varying success. I sent a letter to all of them. About one-half of them answered, and a number of them later gave me welcome hints, information, and comments.

Some of them suggested that *The Case for Israel*, a work by Professor Alan Dershowitz of the Harvard Law School, and a *New York Times* best-seller published in the United States in 2003 could be a model for my book.[4]

There are thirty-two chapters in his book, all of which follow the same pattern: (1) The Accusation, (2) The Accusers, (3) The Reality, and (4) The Proof. According to the book's introduction, Dershowitz is one of the nation's brightest minds and most effective advocates. He "passionately and conclusively refutes, with the skills of a top lawyer" the slurs, slanders and misrepresentations from recent years and "proves that Israel is innocent of the charges leveled against it."[5] This promise, along with the aggressiveness and self-assuredness, even the arrogant tone of the introduction, aroused my doubts. Latvians generally are not categorical, unconditional and aggressive by nature. This type of discussion is foreign to them – nor does it suit me as a defender of Latvia.

Dershowitz uses very harsh language about the critics of Israel. "Bigots" in the Western countries, especially the students, are "forces of evil" and on the side of Hitler. Dershowitz writes of Israel: "I point out Israel's mistakes but argue that they were generally made in a good-faith (although sometimes misguided) effort to defend its civilian population."[6]

Israel to him is the world's most unjustly treated and most misunderstood of countries, "the Jew among nations." (See the same characterization of Russia in my prologue!) He forgets that the American press and television, which are followed and borrowed from elsewhere in the world, are for the most part especially favorable to Israel. Latvia has no such friend; the media paint it black both in the West and the East, as well as in the liberal democracies of Europe. And further, Israel's own information apparatus has the upper hand in the publicity game, and is supported by the partiality, intentional or not, of the media in many other countries.[7]

Fortunately, the situation in the Baltic countries is not as critical as in the Near East, nor has the imminent threat of force – at least not yet – put its stamp on life in Latvia. For that reason Dershowitz's angry and impassioned book does not serve as a model for a book on Latvia, except for the question-and-answer structure. Nor was the name of his book a bad one.

Atis Lejiņš, the director of Latvia's Foreign Policy Institute, recommended the name of *Latvia the Miracle Land* for the book. "If you go back to history and geopolitics, it is a miracle that we are still around as a nation. We could have gone the way of the unfortunate old Prussians. This is one of the most intriguing questions – what saved us?"

I can only note, with some degree of envy, that in his introduction Dershowitz thanks a group of assistants, research assistants, temporary assistants, editors, and agents. Someone writing about Latvia cannot even dream of such assistance. I neither have received, nor did I at all *want*, such help from the Latvian government institutions. I am an independent journalist, not anyone's propagandist, and would wish to write this book just exactly as I myself want it done. Journalistic integrity demands that I be independent and immune to direction and pressure.

I conjectured that being an outsider (yet one who understands the Baltic languages) and a professional journalist from a small, neutral country, one who in many political questions takes a stand on the left, might facilitate my difficult task and give the text credibility.

A number of Latvians also warned me before I took on the task and urged me to abandon the whole project. I will present (without permission) the basis for their position with the following citations in concise form from a letter sent to one of my friends:

That there is a great deal written about Latvia that maligns its history and the people of the country is indisputable. However, a "defense" or an attempt to refute the various accusations is more likely to backfire – make the situation worse – than to advance the cause of the image of Latvia and Latvians. For example, defense requires a compendium of the accusations. Such a compendium can only serve as a convenient recapitulation for anyone wishing to continue the attacks.

While the book might make Latvians feel better, whom would the book persuade? Those that are attentive to such accusations or are receptive to them are not likely to be receptive to counterarguments.

Furthermore, who would be fooled by the author's (self-righteous) refusal of government support? Of what significance is the refusal of government funding while inviting funding from the Latvian community? If Latvians support the project it could not be viewed as anything but self-serving – it would not and could not be viewed as disinterested and objective.[8]

Finally, deeds, not words, rule public-relations wars. One legionnaires' march in Rīga is a thousand times more effective as an image than any number of books explaining what good people Latvians are. That Latvia's war veterans have a right to march is true, but politically it is disastrous.

Thus writes a Latvian-born scholar in her letter, which in my opinion is clearly thought out and wisely framed. This letter caused me to hesitate. On the other hand I was encouraged by Edward Lucas from *The Economist* who was kind enough to read parts of my manuscript. He wrote – and I quote with his permission: "I think this is an excellent book idea. I have looked at the chapters and so far I agree with every word!"

I decided that one must always strive, even in difficult circumstances. One must not lose heart in the face of wrong and force. I find it sad that a small country is often robbed of its independence and in addition, of the right to its own history. As Paul Goble has noted, more than most nations, Latvia and Latvians have seen their history written by others.

The Finnish professor Seppo Myllyniemi warns of the dangers of disinformation and says he understands where the difficulty discussing the theme (the Balts' historical guilt) lies.

> On these questions there is no cool, scientific discussion, where facts decide, but political objectives dictate how things are looked at. In such a situation writings based on facts do not necessarily convince the mainstream media. There is a danger that massive repetition of false claims in public give the general public an impression that there must be some truth in claims like these.[9]

In other words: the Big Lie is effective. Historian Andrejs Plakans wrote from Iowa that he has had great admiration for the historians from Sweden, Norway, Finland, Germany, the Netherlands, England, and even Russia with whom he has had scholarly relations. But:

> I have always had the impression that their interest in the eastern Baltic littoral has never been very deep or abiding. Even when the histories of their own countries have been directly connected to the eastern Baltic – as is the case with Sweden, Germany, and Russia – the information my colleagues have about the twentieth century in Latvia is often very superficial, and therefore vulnerable to the acceptance of stereotyping. I wonder, though, if laying out the "facts" to them will change their minds. ... My own view is that the easy acceptance of negative stereotypes about Latvia (or any other nation) doesn't have much to do with

Picture 23. An example of Soviet disinformation according to Washington: the news that AIDS began to spread from secret tests financed by the Pentagon. Agayev, Pravda 31.10.1986; USA Foreign Ministry Foreign Affairs Note,
July 1987.

facts, but is deeply rooted in individual and collective agendas, involving basic political proclivities and the will to believe. To destroy stereotyped ideas requires the destruction of so many filters that the task may be impossible.[10]

I am fully aware that my task will not be an easy one. The occupiers' version of history, of the "truth" about the Baltic countries, was effectively spread to the world and even into the minds of the Latvians themselves. Historical evidence was either ignored or twisted to fit the ends of the occupiers.[11] For decades Latvian historians were not able to research their own country's history and write about it; it was not only forbidden but also dangerous. But is it not so that if we forget our past or allow someone else to steal it, we will be condemned to repeat it?

The situation is extraordinary in that Latvia has continually had to apologize for and explain its own history to others.[12] It is becoming hard to see through the veil of propaganda. Fewer and fewer eyewitnesses to Latvia's fateful years are still alive, and they are truly anxious and concerned to preserve the truth: What, for example, will children learn of their country's history both in school and from their parents? "Latvia today does not know her own history," wrote historian Heinrihs Strods in 1991, "and Latvian history writing cannot fulfill its tasks, because during the last 50 years Latvian history was written and taught as an assignment from the conquerors."[13]

People do not know history, not even their family's history, because the occupiers succeeded in destroying memory, says the Estonian documentarist Imbi Paju.[14] The writer Sofi Oksanen has studied, like Paju, the fate of Estonian women. She says: "Silence is one form of terrorism. When people are forced into silence, they are not given even a chance to survive."[15]

Large countries have always considered it their right to decide and dictate matters for the Baltic lands. I do not believe that such a natural right exists. Small countries have as much right to life and freedom as large ones.

It was also suggested to me that I adopt a larger perspective and write about all three Baltic countries; but that, however, would be too broad a subject, and I don't know if it would be necessary. I do mention Estonia and Lithuania often in this book; nevertheless, I consider a book dealing with Latvia a sufficient and satisfactory example. Latvia is the central Baltic state, and it has always been of strategic importance to Germany and Russia. The international image of Latvia is more problematic than that of its neighbors, and its internal situation has also been more strained.

I will be pleased if someone who reads this book will understand Latvia better, and even more so if it kindles an interest in the country among some readers – be they students, journalists, tourists, or anyone interested in history and in the world around us.

As I have noted in this book, "Latvia" was dropped from the *Encyclopaedia Britannica* in the 1970's; for that book the history of Latvia began only in 1940, with the founding of "Soviet Latvia."[16] George Orwell in his novel 1984 wrote of "memory holes" through which censors drop unpleasant historical facts to be burned in a big furnace; altering past records was officially "rectifying." I should like to see if I can help save Latvia from a memory hole and its history from rectifiers.

It is the absolute truth that even the best of writers can do nothing if Latvian politicians and officials, through their own unwise decisions and actions, render the writer's efforts fruitless in advance. Black does not become white with the wave of a magic wand.

I have never promised to defend Latvia unconditionally when it does anything I consider wrong. I understand that in politics different points of view clash. Latvian political life, however, appears particularly contentious. Also, the Parliament, Saeima, which sent Latvian soldiers to Iraq in 2003 after a few hours of consideration, apparently against the will of the majority of the people, and without any public discussion, can spend a lot of time and energy in arguing about useless, trifling matters.

I witnessed one shameful moment shortly before Christmas in 2005. The members of parliament suddenly decided that same-sex marriages should be prohibited in the Constitution although a law forbidding them already existed. The president was of a different opinion, but she had to bow to the almost unanimous Saeima. The change in the Constitution was approved by an over-whelming majority vote. Only five of the one hundred in the Parliament dared to hold a different opinion. When the chairperson read (which is usually not done after voting) their names, the Parliament, which never boos at even the greatest of crimes or injustices, burst out in chorus: "Boo-oo!" Also shouts of "Shame!" were heard – something quite unusual in the Latvian parliament.

"That was a perfect example of bolshevism," remarked the internationally experienced political scientist Vita Matisa of this majority treatment of the minority.[17]

A foretaste of this occurred the previous summer, when the first interna-tional meeting of homosexuals and lesbians was held in Rīga. Some leading politicians fanned the flames of hostility toward the visitors and warned that they were not welcome. The result: a riot during which the police were forced to defend the visitors physically from the angry demonstrators. There were more demonstrators (thousands) than people attending the conference (fifty).[18]

Even after joining the EU the Latvians want nothing to do with the admis-sion of refugees and those seeking asylum. They find it impossible to conceive that in the future they will, because of a shortage of labor, be forced to admit, even to recruit, workers from less developed countries, most likely from the East. Probably because of their recent history, Latvians are generally wary of foreigners. According to recent research, Latvia is the most averse to immigra-tion of all the European countries, although the Latvians themselves have always gone abroad in large numbers as refugees and emigrants.

Many Latvian politicians do nothing to change this situation; on the con-trary, they use xenophobia and populist prejudice to gain support. And in the cities harassment and abuse with racial overtones have begun to appear.

In the spring of 2005, the chairman of Saeima's foreign affairs committee warned Latvian Jews, some of whose representatives had demonstrated in the streets along with other Russian speakers, that they should learn a lesson from what had happened 60 years earlier (a veiled reference to the Holocaust). At that time, in his opinion, the Latvian Jews themselves were partially to blame for what happened to them.

On that occasion I announced publicly that although I had defended Latvia in the international forum, it was impossible for me to do so in the "current situation." Soon afterwards this politician was expelled from both his party and his chairman's position (of course not because of what I had written).[19]

Every now and then I have to remind myself that Latvia has been independ-ent for only sixteen years and that it was part of a totalitarian system for decades. Democracy there is not as developed as in the "old" Western European lands. I became aware of that again when in 2005–2006 I founded, along with my friends and neighbors, a defense organization for my new home city of Jūrmala. The object of this independent local citizens' organization is democracy and transparency in communal politics, the preservation of nature and of historical buildings, and opposition to corruption.

Many joined with us enthusiastically, but there were other kinds of reactions from "ordinary people." First: "Is another organization necessary?" Second: "In any case, you won't be able to influence the powers that be." Third: "Aren't you afraid?" Fourth: "Only political parties can have an effect."

Inhabitants of Latvia are skeptical about civic activities and remain alienated from the state. Most have no membership in any voluntary association.[20] Trust in nongovernmental organizations (NGOs) remains low and so does belief in one's ability to influence government or municipal politics.

It is distressing, although hardly surprising, that many leading politicians react antagonistically to free action by citizens and want to restrict the freedom and financing of such organizations – just as in Russia. Extraordinary suspicion and enmity have been aroused recently in the Baltic countries and Russia against the Soros Foundation, which has done so much to advance freedom of speech, and to promote culture, integration, human rights, and democracy. And it was only outside initiative that gave birth to the Latvian Anti-Corruption Agency KNAB. Part of the Latvian press even attacks the Save the Children as a "foreign" organization.

There is a saying that in democracy people have exactly the type of politicians and government they deserve. Now that I know the Latvians, I am not really sure of it anymore.

One further example of the difficulty in defending Latvia: Although I believe that Latvian war veterans have as much right as others to visit memorials and cemeteries and to remember their fallen comrades, I have told the Latvians that the rest of the world – both the East and the West – neither understands nor will they come to understand these "marches" no matter how often they are explained. The "problem" will of course solve itself when in time the last of the veterans is gone. Russians may celebrate their soldiers and their victories, and they also expect gratitude and praise from that part of Europe which the Soviet Union subjugated to its rule for nearly a half century. Unfortunately the reality is that the Latvians are forbidden to remember. In that regard, I agree with the writer of the letter quoted above. Nevertheless, I try in this book to explain what the issue is. (See Chapter 8).[21]

I began this book with the choice of fourteen often repeated claims, misinterpretations, and questions regarding Latvia. I have arranged the book so that reading can begin with any chapter at all. Thus there may be some repetition in chapters where the subject matter is similar to that in another. Each chapter relates not only to the present circumstances in Latvia but also the past. As Latvia's foreign minister declared recently: "Many issues topical in our country today, which are related to the social situation of national minorities, and to our relationship with Russia, can be understood only within the context of Latvia's 20th century history."[22]

In doing this work I have read dozens upon dozens of books and hundreds of articles, mainly on Latvian history, I have interviewed a lot of people, and also spent time in archives. The sources are listed at the end of the book.

The Latvian Historians' Commission, appointed by the President, has worked since 1998 and published seventeen volumes, which deal *inter alia* with anti-Semitism and the Holocaust during the German occupation, and with oppression and resistance while under the Soviets. Those who do not read Latvian may be interested in the fourteenth volume, *The Hidden and Forbidden History of Latvia under Soviet and Nazi Occupations 1940–1991* (Rīga 2005). In this rewarding English-language book are gathered a number of the most significant articles from the previous volumes. According to its editors, there was an "urgent need to respond to Western misconceptions and official Russian positions that are still based on Soviet ideological myths."

As many as ten years ago the then future President Vaira Vīķe-Freiberga said that "Latvia should have published a 'White Book' which would have explained clearly the horrors and destruction practiced by Nazi Germany and the Soviet Union during the occupations."[23]

A new *History of Latvia, The 20th Century*, written by members of the presidential Latvian Historians' Commission, has appeared in Latvian, Russian, English, and French, and is expected to appear in Finnish also.[24] According to its preface "attention has been paid to dispelling myths created by Nazi and Soviet propaganda." Few books are likely to have created such an emotional furor in Europe during recent years (see my Chapter 13).

A collection of original Latvian language documents from the years 1939–1991, almost 600 pages, edited by Elmars Pelkaus (Okupācijas varu politika Latvijā) is useful. A more recent similarly wide ranging collection of documents in English translation edited by the historian Andrejs Plakans is indispensable (*Experiencing Totalitarianism: The Invasion and Occupation of Latvia by the USSR and Nazi Germany 1939–1991: A Documentary History*, 2007). I found the relevant official documents of Latvian foreign policy and occupation in French and English on the net page http://www.letton.ch and in the U.S. Congressional records.

Collaboration with the Germans and the destruction of Jews in Latvia have been dealt with in pioneering studies particularly by Professor Andrew Ezergailis of Ithaca College in the state of New York, whose books are available in English (for instance, *The Holocaust in Latvia 1941–1944*, 1996).

Exceptionally lively discussion of history goes on continually in the Latvian press – a discussion that I have tried to follow closely. My own book dealing with Latvian history has appeared only in Latvian and Finnish, so out of consideration for those who read neither language, I borrow from it text translated into English.

Many thanks to the following: Edward Anders, Uldis Bluķis, Frank Gordon, Erland Uldis Gustavs, Jānis Krēsliņš, Sr., Paulis Lazda, Valters Nollendorfs, Andrejs Ozoliņš, Jānis Peniķis, Andrejs Plakans, Andris Priedītis, Claudia Spekke, Maruta Voitkus Lūkina, Ģirts Zeidenbergs and Anna Žīgure. Without you this book would probably never have been born.

The original Finnish language version of this book was published in 2007 in Finland. A Latvian translation is due in 2008 along with this one in English.

Jūrmala, Latvia, October 2007.
Jukka Rislakki

Basic Facts About Latvia

The Republic of Latvia became independent in 1918, was previously part of the Russian Empire for less than 200 years. Occupied by the Soviet Union 1940–1941. Occupied by Germany 1941–1944/45. Again a part of the Soviet Union from 1944/45 until August 1991, when independence was restored. A member of the United Nations, the European Union, and NATO.

Population approx. 2, 295,000 (2007 est.). Population growth 0,65% (2007 est.).

Official language Latvian.

Latvians 58.7 % (1,356,000), Russians 28.8 %, Belarusians 3.9 %, Ukrainians 2.6 %. (Figures from the year 2004.) Russian speakers about 36 % of the population.

Latvian citizens 77 %, non-citizens 21 %, former Soviet Union or Russian passport-holders and citizens of other countries 2.5 %. (2003). In Spring of 2007: non-citizens 17 %.

Area 64 589 km² (bigger than Belgium, Denmark or Holland). Capital city: Rīga.

Women of child-bearing age give birth on the average to 1.2 children.

Economic growth in 2006 11,9 %. Inflation about 9,5 % in summer of 2007. GNP/capita (PPP) 16,000 US dollars (2007 est.). Most important exports: wood, textiles.

The parliament *Saeima* is unicameral and composed of one hundred members, elected every four years. The president: Vaira Vīķe-Freiberga (1999–2007): Valdis Zatlers from July, 2007.

Table 2. Total inhabitants of Latvia, and their number by nationalities, (in thousands)

Year	1935	1959	1989	2000
Total	1905.4	2093.5	2666.6	2375.3
Latvians	1467.0	1297.9	1387.8	1369.4
Russians	168.3	556.4	905.5	702.5
Belarusians	26.8	61.6	119.7	87.1
Ukrainians	1.8	29.4	92.1	63.6
Poles	48.6	59.8	60.4	59.5
Lithuanians	22.8	32.4	34.6	33.3
Jews	93.4	36.6	22.9	10.4
Roma	3.8	4.3	7.0	8.2
Tatars	–	1.8	4.8	3.2
Germans	62.1	1.6	3.8	3.4
Estonians	6.9	4.6	3.3	2.6
Other	4.4	7.1	24.7	16.8

Source: Pārsla Eglīte 2007

Table 3. Migration to and from Latvia, 1951–2000 (in thousands)

Years	Arrived	Departed	Net Migration
1951–55	212.0	161.8	50.2
1955–60	165.2	145.8	19.4
1961–65	180.6	119.0	61.6
1966–70	146.8	101.8	45.0
1971–75	202.0	141.0	61.0
1976–80	187.2	149.6	37.6
1981–85	171.3	131.7	39.6
1986–90	149.8	122.9	26.9
1991–95	30.8	168.2	−137.3
1996–2000	12.2	47.0	−34.8

Source: Central Statistical Bureau of Latvia

Table 4. Citizenship and ethnicity in Latvia, 2006

Ethnicity	Citizens	Non-Citizens	Foreign Citizens	Total
Latvians	1,348,354	2,053	1,082	1,351,489
Russians	351,876	278,213	22,115	652,204
Belarusians	29,238	55,254	2,102	86,594
Ukrainians	14,637	39,633	3,905	58,175
Poles	40,685	14,385	612	55,682
Lithuanians	17,828	11,799	1,680	31,307
Others	31,644	17,103	6,547	55,314
Total	1,834,282	418,440	38,043	2,290,765

Source: Muižnieks, 2006, 17

Table 5. Ethnic composition of Latvia, July 2004

Ethnicity	Total	Percentage
Latvians	1,356,081	58.7%
Russians	664,092	28.8%
Belarusians	88,998	3.9%
Ukrainians	59,403	2.6%
Poles	56,798	2.5%
Lithuanians	31,840	1.4%
Others	52,127	2.1%
Total	2,309,339	100.0%

Source: Citizenship and Migration Affairs Board, 2004

Table 6. Percentages of ethnic Russians in Latvia's cities, 2000

City	Latvians	Russians
Rīga	38.8	43
Daugavpils	14.3	54
Liepāja	45.3	31
Jelgava	52.8	31
Jūrmala	57.1	27
Rēzekne	37.0	50
Ventspils	47.6	31

Source: Census data, 2000, Central Statistical Bureau of Latvia

Notes

Prologue   (Pages 11–31)

1. What we call the center point of Europe depends on the method of measurement (if the Atlantic islands are included in the calculation or not). The Balts think it is either in Lithuania or on the shore of Courland Province in Latvia. However, the location is extremely contentious. *Transitions Online*: Ukraine, etc.: Total Immersion by Adrian Ivakhiv, May 11, 2006.

2. In Ivar Ivask 2001

3. Jānis Krēsliņš 2004 376.

4. Juka Rislaki 2004. The book's Finnish version is: Jukka Rislakki, Latvian kohtalonvuodet [Latvia's Fateful Years] (Helsinki: SKS, 2005). The book on Finland is Juka Rislaki, *Kluso slēpotāju zeme Somija* [Finland, the Land of Quiet Skiers] (Rīga: Valters un Rapa 2003). In 2007 a book of my cartoons on Latvian themes was published in Latvia.

5. *Helsingin Sanomat*, January 13, 2006.

6. Ibid., May 1, 2006.

7. "Russia Prepares for Economic Conquest of the Baltic Countries," AIA, August 7, 2005.

8. *Le Monde Diplomatique* (Finnish version) 1/2007, 19–21.

9. *The Baltic Times*, March 23–29, 2006.

10. Pauls Bankovskis, "The Joy of Small Places," *Baltic Outlook*, February/March, 2006. Also on Eurozine: http://www.eurozine.com/articles/2005-11-30-bankovskis-en.html

11. *Natsizm Po-Pribaltijsky* ("Baltic Nazism"), shown on Russian television on March 16, 2006. At the time Latvia's foreign minister announced that the Latvian government would provide the funding if Latvian cinematographers and historians would make feature films and documentaries that would show the nation's history in an objective light. Within two short months, it was announced that Latvian documentary filmmakers were starting work on a "rebuttal film" financed by the defense ministry

and the city of Rīga.—On how political atmosphere changed in 1998, see Visvaldis Lācis 2006, 5–7.

12. Kemiläinen 2005.

13. *Helsingin Sanomat*, December 18, 2005. On the other hand, the foreign media survey of Finland's foreign ministry for the year 2005 reports that Finland received abundant praise: "Finland was the economic tiger of the Arctic," her ability to compete, her technology and the achievements of her students were absolutely tops, there was no corruption, health care was exemplary, its diplomacy skillful, the land was clean and pleasant, the people courteous, and even the food was good... The editorial writer for the Swedish *Dagens Nyheter* declared that Finland was the "coolest" country and could serve as a model for Sweden.

14. Klinge, 2000.

15. "The influence of propaganda may be strongest and longest lasting in literature and movies, where the Western point of view has clearly been predominant." Pekka Visuri 2006 313.

16. *New EU Countries and Citizens. Latvia* (London: CherryTreeBook, 2006. The rights to the book belong to KIT Publisher, Netherlands.

17. Edward Lucas in the Estonian Foreign Ministry's Year Book 2001; *Helsingin Sanomat*, August 18, 2001.

18. The company answered the criticism stressing that the home page was not quite ready yet and that it was being developed continually.

19. *Latvijas Avīze*, April 5, 2007.

20. Darren Moorby, Travelmag.com, April 4, 2001.

21. Julia Pascal in *New Statesman*, November 20, 2006.

22. "Latvijas tēls nav spožs salūts," [The Image of Latvia is not a Splendid Fireworks] *Latvijas Avīze*, February 12, 2006.

23. The website for Latvians to work in Sweden is http://www.hyrlett.nu (hirealatvian.now). It has had a "Campaign offer! All October, personnel only 95 Crowns per hour!" Order now, because "det är lätt med en lett" (it is easy with a Latvian).

24. Hollender's film *Buy Bye Beauty* was co-financed by the Swedish Film Institute and was shown on Sweden's TV 3 in February 2001 and also at film festivals. The director has not allowed showing the film in Latvia, if only because the women lying with him in the film are identifiable. Hollender has not visited Latvia since the completion of the film.

25. Zarembas Maciej: "I landet Nenozimigs är det inte så noga," *Dagens Nyheter*, November 15, 2005. The businessman who ran over and killed the policewomen was not arrested, tried, or extradited; and a year and a half passed before Swedish authorities considered that there was sufficient reason even to interrogate him. Their finding was that "taking extenuating circumstances" into account, his deed was considered "of little importance."

26. *The Baltic Times*, March 2–8, 2006. Recently I heard a Finnish man on the streets of Rīga say into a cell phone, "Guess where I am! I'm in Lithuania!"—In 2006, Lithuania began an expensive official campaign to find ways and distinguishing marks to differentiate itself from Latvia. "The saddest part of it all is that the word Lithuania awakens no association at all in a foreigner," declared the director of the Lithuanian Institute. *Diena*, February 15, 2006.

27. Some years ago, at a international festival of light music in Jūrmala, Latvia, where the main language of the soloists and performers was Russian, one of the happy and enthusiastic German singers announced into the microphone: "I've never before appeared in Russia!"

28. Davies, 1996, 1017. This book says very little about Finland, too. However, it does say, for example, that the Winter War lasted five months (should be a little over three months), that Finland was under Soviet occupation at the end of World War II (Finland was never occupied), and that Finland had to accept the permanent presence of Soviet bases (there was one base on the coast for 10 years).

29. *Mājas Viesis*, March 11–17, 2006.

30. Lieven 1994; Jānis Krēsliņš 2007; Anatol Lieven, "To Russia with Realism. The White House senselessly risks a new Cold War," *The American Conservative*, March 26, 2007.

31. Henry Cavanagh, "Overlooking Nazi Past," *The Daily Freeman*, May 17, 2005.

32. However, let the following be stated here: Bush did not give the speech at the soldiers' cemetery, but in downtown Rīga. The state of Latvia pays a pension to all seniors. The soldiers the writer refers to were neither SS-men nor volunteers, but soldiers of the Latvian Legion who were ordered to serve on the front lines attached to the Waffen-SS. The special unit recruited by the Germans, which executed Jews, was not under the SS but under the security service, the SD. It has not been proven that local civilians murdered Jews on their own initiative. There are no special decrees regarding the citizenship of Jews or the right to work of Russians in Latvia. "De-Nazification" in the Baltics, carried out by Soviet authorities after the war, was more thorough and more violent than in Germany, for example.

33. Frank Gordon's and Edward Anders' statements to the author.

34. *Diena*, January 30, 2006.

35. Andris Teikmanis in *Republika.lv*, January 12–18, 2007.

36. *Helsingin Sanomat*, May 10, 1998; Muižnieks 2006, 121.

37. *Reporteurs sans frontières* Web page, October 23, 2006; *Diena*, October 24, 2006. Finland shared the first position with Iceland, Ireland and the Netherlands.

38. *The Baltic Times*, February 23, 2002; "Russia launches repatriation

program in Latvia," en.rian.ru/russia/20070411. At the beginning of March 2006, President Putin signed a decree establishing a commission that would facilitate "the voluntary resettlement of our compatriots residing outside of Russia." The world's largest country is suffering a demographic crisis involving a catastrophic drop in population (about 700 000 people every year), for both birthrates and male life expectancy have fallen sharply since the demise of the Soviet Union; Russian economists have suggested inviting ethnic Russians in the "nearby countries to return." The invitation particularly involves Latvia and Estonia, which together have 1.2 million Russians.—At least one immigrant from independent Latvia has claimed political asylum in the United States because of threats to her life in Latvia.

39. www.delfi.lv news, June 5, 2006. Also in 2005 Latvia was number one with 49 percent. Muižnieks 2006, 94. In June 2007, the Juri Levada sociological centre told that Estonia was thought by the Russians to be the most hostile nation towards them (Estonia 60%, Georgia 46%, Latvia 36%.) The interviews were made in mid-May, when the dispute about the Soviet war monument in Tallinn was at its hottest. *Diena*, June 2, 2007.

40. The image of Latvia was positive for 37 % of the respondents, negative for 30 %, and 33 % had no opinion. The image of Finland, for example was: positive 78 %, negative 1 %, no opinion 21 %. *Suomen Kuvalehti* May 18, 2007.

41. Jörg Mettke in spiegel.de January 2006.

42. Russia is seen largely in a negative light, and more negative as before, as was shown in a major international survey made by the BBC World Service at the start of 2006. Russia was one of the most unpopular countries, ranked third following Iran and the U.S. Mosnews.com, February 3, 2006.—*Russia Today* transmits for 24 hours a day to Asia, Europe, and North America, and for 18 hours a day to Germany, the Czech Republic, Slovakia, and Hungary.—"The Kremlin's frantic attempts to improve Russia's image are somewhat reminiscent of the failed North Korean project," wrote *Moskovskii Komsomolets* (April 12, 2006). Despite the money and effort, the outside world's "opinion of Russia has dropped to a 15–year low."—The Moscow city government decided in 2006 to launch a large-scale PR campaign abroad. It will allocate 700 million rubles in order to "create a positive image" of Moscow. The bureaucrats were offended because recent international surveys ranked the Russian capital as one of the most expensive, dangerous, unfriendly, and uncomfortable cities in the world. *Pravda.ru*, July 24, 2006.

43. Johan Bäckman, *Saatana saapuu Helsinkiin* [Satan Arrives in Helsinki], manuscript, 2006.

44. BC Monitoring Service, March 4, 2007.

45. E-mail from Johan Bäckman, December 24, 2006.

46. Andrew Ezergailis, "Letter to *The Nation*," dated May 16, 2005, to my knowledge not published.

47. Eksteins 2000, 31.

48. Tomas McGonigle, "The Bloody Crossroads," *Washington Post*, August 10, 1999; *The Gazette*, August 21, 1999.

49. Eksteins 2000, 97. He considers Hitler's Germany a clear prototype of president Kārlis Ulmanis' Latvia, although Ulmanis was actually more interested in Mussolini's corporate system in Italy.—Devastating review of Eksteins' book: Jānis Krēsliņš, "Rētu uzplēšana Latvijas vēsturē" in *Latvijas Okupācijas Muzejs* 2000, 276–283.

50. Eksteins 2000, 148, 151.

51. During World War II, Finnish officials did, however, turn over to Germany some dozens of other Jews—refugees from elsewhere in Europe and captured members of the Red Army.

52. ...unless Sandra Kalniete's book *With Dancing Shoes in Siberian Snows*, published in several languages, is already as popular.

53. Agate Nesaule, 1995; Jānis Krēsliņš in *Jaunā Gaita*, March 2006 and *Laiks*, October 4, 1997. The book is described as "politically correct" and "just the kind that appeals to present-day Americans." At the start of the book, Nesaule writes that she trusts her own memory and has not wished to research the events of her childhood, and that "I have had to speculate and guess, even to invent." Her great idol is the Pole, Jerzy Kozinski, who achieved fame and a Princeton professorship in the U.S. by writing supposedly of his youthful experiences at the time of the Holocaust in Europe. After his suicide it was revealed that his autobiography was imaginary and that he had not even written much of his book.

54. Arnolds Spekke, 1959.

55. Akten zur Deutschen Auswärtigen Politik 1918–1945, Serie D: 1937–1941, Band XIII, 835–838; Andrew Ezergailis and others 2005, 9–10; Andrew Ezergailis, "A Letter to German Journalists," 2005, to my knowledge not published.

56. Andrew Ezergailis, 1996, xvi.

57. Eksteins 2000, 85–86, 150.

58. Rosenberg Alfred, "Bolschewismus, Hunger, Tod," in *Flugschrift aus der Bildwerk Pest in Russland* (München: 1922). Quoted in Valters Nollendorfs and Erwin Oberländer 2005, 320–321; Krēsliņš 2000, 276–283.

59. Yourcenar emphasized that in her book she wanted neither to idealize (verherrlichen) nor degrade (in Verruf zu bringen) any group of people or country. The book "is not to be judged as a political but as a human document." Endnote to the German edition Yourcenar 1986. See also Eksteins 2000, 69–70.

60. Sruoga 2005.

61. *Kultūras Diena*, 12/2006.

62. Deighton 1965, pp 129–130.

63. Salisbury, 1969, 159–167. For a description of what really happened in Latvia at the time, see for example my books (Rislaki 2004, 173–196, 207–242; Rislakki 2005, 177–.) or Treijs 2006, 226–229.

64. Kalniete, 2006, chapter 12.

65. Ochsner, "Thicker Than Water," *The New Yorker*, August 22, 2005. References: *Jaunā Gaita*, December 2005, and *Baltic Outlook*, February/ March 2006.

Chapter 1   (Pages 35–52)

1. *The Baltic Times*, February 9–15, 2006. For example, among the Finnish-related people living in the Russian republic of Mari, there are serious deficiencies in human rights, but Russian officials dispute such reports. They will not even agree to discuss human rights in Chechnya. *Helsingin Sanomat*, February 2, 2006.—From January 2007, non-citizens in Latvia have had the right to visa-free travel to EU countries.

2. BNS, October 24, 2006.

3. Muižnieks 2006, 50.

4. "Tapis pētījums Latvijas nomelnošanai," [A Study Has Been Made to Slander Latvia] *Latvijas Avīze*, April 28, 2006.

5. Latvian Parliament minutes, December 15, 2005.

6. http://faculty.ed.umuc.edu/~jmatthew/articles/langmin.html. Re Sudeten Germans: Latvia never denied citizenship and residence rights to its "Sudeten Russians," nor suggested their expulsion. Only the colonists sent to Latvia by the Soviets during the occupation have been a problem for Latvia.

7. *Göteborgs-Posten*, February 22, 1996. The amendment, which would have made the law more stringent, was defeated by referendum in Latvia the same year.

8. Ted Galen Carpenter, "America's Baltic Time Bomb," *South China Morning Post*, May 24, 2007.

9. All these examples come from Jukka Rislakki, "Baltia on häviöllä sana-sodassa. Lännessä leviää näkemys, että Latvia, Liettua ja Viro ovat kansallis– ja rotukiihkon pesiä" [Baltics are Losing the War of Words. In the West the Opinion Spreads that Latvia, Lithuania and Estonia Are Nests of Nationalist and Racial Bigotry], *Helsingin Sanomat* March, 19, 1993. All quotes (except from *Life*) are retranslated from Finnish.

10. Edward Barnes (text), Wayne Sorce (photos), *Life*, December 1992;. Attempts to get permission to use some of this material for this book were unsuccessful.

11. According to Soviet statistics, the flow of immigrants to Latvia was especially high in 1953 and 1956. *Migranti Latvijā 1944–1989. Dokumenti* 2004, 38, 142, 243.

12. Latvian law requires that in order to get citizenship, one must have a legal source of income; have lived in Latvia for five years; swear a loyalty oath; know the national anthem, the flag, the constitution, and the basic facts of Latvian history; and understand and be able to speak relatively simple sentences in Latvian. One can prepare for the two-hour test with the help of a special booklet that includes questions and material for the answers.

13. "There are few countries in the world that have been subject to such intense international monitoring—the United Nations sent a mission to investigate the status of Russian-speakers in 1992, the Organization for Security and Cooperation in Europe had a mission in Latvia from 1993 through 2001, the OSCE High Commissioner on National Minorities has visited Latvia more times than almost any other country … , the Council of Europe stopped human rights monitoring in 2001 and continues a post-monitoring dialogue with Latvia to this day, and the European Union pays much attention to integration policy and Latvia's Russians." "Russians in Latvia—History, Current Status and Prospects," lecture by the Minister for Social Integration Nils Muižnieks (Tübingen University, Germany, November 8, 2004). Muižnieks had been the director of Latvia's Center for Human Rights and Ethnic Studies.

14. Mark Ames, "Bush's Bitburg?" *Nation*, May 23, 2005. As far as I know, the magazine did not publish rebuttals that I and several others who know Latvia sent in; nor did it correct the errors.

15. More of this book in Chapter 7 and in the Acknowledgements.—It could be said, of course, that presenting the book to Putin at an Auschwitz memorial event was not a very diplomatic move. Whoever advised the Latvian president should have known better.

16. It must be remembered that Latvia's Russians are not a homogenous group; part of their community has deep roots in Latvian society. Among the largest subgroups of Russians were the Old Believers, descendants of a group that split off from the Orthodox Church in Russia in the 1700's and moved to Latvia as refugees. A second subgroup was composed of soldiers and refugees who fled the Bolshevik revolution. The post-WWII period saw the mass influx of Russians and russified Ukrainians and Belarusians into Latvia.

17. 77 percent in 1939 just before the war. *Migranti Latvijā* 2004, 48.

18. Bleiere and others, 2006, 419; Leo Dribins in *republika.lv* 5–12. April 2007.

19. Heinrihs Strods, "Sovietization of Latvia 1944–1991," in Nollendorfs and Oberländer 2005, 219; Pārsla Eglīte in *Yearbook of the Museum of the Occupation of Latvia* 2001, 94–109.

20. Jānis Riekstiņš, "Colonization and Russification of Latvia 1940–1989," in Nollendorfs and Oberländer 2005, 228–241.

21. Elmārs Pelkaus (ed.), 1999, 361.

22. In January 1945 it was ordered that in Rīga 29 percent of flats were to be given to immigrants from other Soviet republics, 16 percent to soldiers and military families, and 5 percent to war invalids. *Migranti Latvijā* 2004, 153.

23. *Museum of the Occupation* ... 2002, 93; Rislakki 2004 and 2005, 284. In 2005, the share of Latvians in Rīga rose to the same percentage as the Russian. Latvians now make up 42.4 percent of the inhabitants of Rīga and are the largest single group but still clearly an overall minority.

24. On the same sort of condition the Russian army agreed to leave Estonia in 1994.

25. In Jelgava, where proportionally more Latvians lived than in other cities, their share was 49.7 percent.

26. On the threshold of Latvian independence in 1989, the number of ethnic Latvians did not reach the level of 1935 (previous census), although Latvia's population had increased 1.4 times. There were 5.4 percent fewer Latvians than in 1935 (1.47 million in 1935 and 1.39 million in 1938), while the number of Russians had grown 5.4 times, Belarusians 4.5 times, and Ukrainians over 50 times. *Migranti Latvijā* 2004, 243; *Mājas Viesis*, March 4, 2005.

    The proportion of ethnic Latvians in Latvia has been as follows:

1935	76 %[*]	
1959	62 %	(*Latvijas Padomju Enciklopēdija*
1970	57 %	[Soviet Latvian encyclopedia],
1979	54 %	5th printing)
1989	52 %	

    [*]75,5 %, or 77 % inside Latvia's present borders, which makes the figure comparable to later ones.

    Proportion of Latvians and Russians in the largest cities in 2000: see Table 6

27. See for example *Museum of the Occupation...*, 2002, 89; Nollendorfs and Oberländer, 2005; *Mājas Viesis*, June 17, 2000; Markku Leppänen: 2002.

28. Mela and Vaba (eds.) 2005, 96.

29. Eglīte 2001, 101; Bleiere and others, 2006, 418.

30. Ibid., 349.

31. Rudīte Vīksne, "Soviet Repressions against Residents of Latvia in 1940–1941: *Typical Trends*," and Bergmanis and others in Nollendorfs and Oberländer, 2005, 53, 279. Davies 2007, 20. See also Bleiere and others, 2006. Some estimates have recently been made. The following comes from many different sources: From 1939 to 1941, over 60,000

Baltic Germans left Latvia. 7,600 prisoners were taken to Russia during the first occupation, and most of them were executed; in Latvia 1,500–1,800 were killed. In June of 1941, 16,563 were deported to the East, of whom 4,844 or altogether one-third died there. The Red Army took with it over 3,000 people, and in addition, tens of thousands of refugees and soldiers were evacuated. Some 90,000 civilians were killed during the Nazi regime; nearly 70,000 of them Latvian Jews, along with 18,000 communists and 2,270 gypsies and mentally ill. At least 115,000, maybe even 165,000 Latvians wound up in German military units and perhaps some 100,000 in the Soviet army—together about 10 percent of the Latvian population. Of those in the German army, about 60,000 were killed; and of those serving in the Soviet army, at least 36,000 lost their lives—in addition to which large numbers of civilians died in the war. Some 4,000–5,000 Latvian and *Reich* Jews were deported to Germany in 1944. Tens of thousands of Latvians were taken to Germany for forced labor, and 6,000–7,000 of them were sent to concentration camps. Along with the Abrene area in 1944, 35,000 people were transferred to Russia. At the end of the war, 91,000 Latvian soldiers and civilians wound up in the Soviet "filtration" and prison camps. During 1944–1945, almost 300,000 civilians and soldiers fled to the West; over 100,000 of them returned or were sent to the East from central Europe. Thousands of refugees died. Thousands are counted as suffering "repression" during the new Soviet occupation. Roughly 47,000–49,000 were sentenced for political crimes against the Soviet State. In 1949, some 44,200 were transported to the east for periods that varied in length, and over 5,000 of them died during the banishment. Some 3,000 "forest brothers" died in the resistance, and another 3,000 on the opposite side. Even after 1954 there were some 2,450 political imprisonments. In addition some 24,000 *Reich* Jews were brought to Latvia, of whom most were murdered, or died of other causes. Hundreds of Hungary's Jewish women and at least several hundred Jewish refugees from Lithuania died in Latvia. During the war thousands of Soviet prisoners of war died on Latvian soil, starved to death by Germans. Regarding other oppressive measures practiced by the occupiers, one can note that about 600,000–700,000 people (about a third of the population) suffered as a result of Soviet occupiers' efforts to restrict the career and educational opportunities of "the socially dangerous elements."

32. Among the 1939 inhabitants of Latvia there were 1.49 million native Latvians, but in 1989 there were 1.39 million and in 2000 only 1.37 million. In 1914 the Latvian population was around 2.55 million. During the same period, the population in Finland, for example, which has suffered from war and emigration, has risen from 3.1 million to 5.3 million. For more accurate tables: Eglīte 2001, 95; *Latvija citu valstu saimē* [Latvia in the Family of Nations] 1990; Bleiere and others 2006, 37; Rislakki 2005, 377.—The number of Estonians in Estonia is now 10 percent smaller than at the start of the 20th century. *The White Book.* 2005.

33. In Latvia in 1989, 42.0 percent were Slavs (Russians, Belarusians, Ukrainians), in Estonia 35.2 percent, and in Lithuania 12.3 percent. *Migranti Latvijā* 2004, 49, 98.

34. Dzintra Hirša in *Latvijas Avīze*, November 23, 2005; *Helsingin Sanomat*, September 29, 2006.

35. Latvian Inhabitant Register, August 2006. 386,322 are noncitizens in 2007. That is 17 percent of population.

36. According to Eurostat, there is one country in EU where proportionally more foreigners live—Luxembourg, almost 40 percent (mainly Portuguese guest workers).

37. Russian scholar Aleksandr Pogorelskis in *Latvijas Avīze*, March 6, 2007; *Latvijas Avīze*, January 9, 2006.

38. Paul Kolstoe in 1996, quoted in Muižnieks 2006, 130.

39. The first date refers to the first occupation by the Soviets and the second to Latvia's renewed independence.

40. Muižnieks 2006 15.

41. Muižnieks 2006, 17. See Table 4, Basic Information about Latvia

42. *Baltic Guide*, August 2005. Latvian is an East Baltic language-group tongue; the only surviving related language is Lithuanian. They are almost as closely related to each other as the Finno-Ugric Finnish and Estonian. Old Prussian is related to Latvian, but is extinct, it is being revived by a few devotees. Latvian is, however, an Indo-European language, like Russian, so that its grammar should not cause Russians any special difficulties. To a slight extent, the same is true of vocabulary and phrasing. "I can call you today at a quarter to three" is in Russian: *Ja magu pazvanitj tebje sevodnja bez pjatnadsati tri* and in Latvian: *es tev varu piezvanīt šodien bez piecpadsmit trijos*.

43. Bleiere and others, 2006, 454; Muižnieks 2006, 14, writes that 90–95 percent of ethnic Latvians supported independence, while the figure for non-Latvians was 38–45 percent.

44. *Delfi* portal, July 30, 2006.

45. *The Nation*, May 23, 2005; "Baltic Grudge Match," Newsweek, September 12, 2005; *Latvijas Avīze*, September 12, 2005; *Helsingin Sanomat*, November 1, 2005 and May 5, 2006. In Britain, an applicant must know English and pass a test in which he is examined on his knowledge of history, political organization, and the way of life in general. One can repeat the test, but each time it costs 50 euros. Britain, alarmed at how poorly some groups of immigrants have become integrated into society, now promises to tighten up its laws on immigration, citizenship, and deportation. The French government is introducing a new immigration law which makes it more difficult to get a residence permit and makes language and culture courses compulsory for immigrants. The applicant must speak French and approve of "the French basic values." Immigrants into Holland must get a teaching package which costs 64 euros, must

pass a test costing 350 euros, and watch a two-hour educational film. In the United States, an applicant must prove that he understands American government, basic laws, and society and speaks English well; allegiance and loyalty are required as well as compliance with laws. Germany is planning to require immigrants to take a language and citizenship course. In some German states the applicants are asked about Goethe's and Schiller's works. In Finland, a citizenship application alone costs 400 euros, and the language test, in which one must demonstrate a good command of Finnish, 70 euros. An immigrant who wishes to serve in any public (communal or state) office or job must learn two languages well: Finnish and Swedish. Even someone married to a Finn must live in Finland for four or five years without long periods of absence before he or she can apply for citizenship; during that period all travel abroad must be explained. In Denmark, immigrants who speak Danish and have lived in the country for nine years may take a citizenship test, where they have to give the right answer to at least 28 questions on Danish history, culture and society. Merely as a matter of interest, without applying for citizenship, I took the Estonian citizenship test, which is of the same type as the Latvian. The oral and the written tests lasted several hours and were demanding but not impossible. One was allowed to have written source materials with him. I passed the test the first time, as did almost all the 20 Russians and Ukrainians in the group.

46. *Diena*, April 22, 2006; *The Baltic Times*, April 27 and May 3, 2006. Although naturalization has increased more rapidly in Latvia than elsewhere, Ekeus still wants to speed it up further. He hopes that Latvia will help aged and uneducated noncitizens who are not interested in citizenship, or for whom citizenship would be too difficult to acquire. He indicated support for educational reform, on the condition that Latvia check to see if the results in Russian schools are worse after the reform.

47. One party, For Fatherland and Freedom (TB/LNNK), proposed before the elections in 2006, that rather than speed up naturalization it be discontinued on the first of January 2007 because so many who lacked the language skills and were disloyal to the country had become citizens, some with the help of bribes. Commentators saw this as an election gambit: although such a proposal would surely not pass (it did not), it would divide society more profoundly than before and would make those who were disloyal even more so. *Diena*, May 6, 2006.

48. Muižnieks 2006, 22.

49. Ibid., 23–25.

50. *Latvijas Avīze*, April 23, 2007.

51. Strods, 2004, 16.

52. Ibid., 31; Language expert Dzintra Hiřša in *Latvijas Avīze*, November 23, 2005.

53. The next BBC camera crew also came to Rīga from Moscow. The journalists had an interpreter who knew Russian with them. They went to

the Castle to interview Latvia's president on the subject of sex-slavery. The President's name was not mentioned at all in the article, which was written by the BBC's "fixer," a foreign journalist living in Rīga. The president was referred to only by her first name, "Vaira." She was declared to have uttered "banalities" in the interview, and finally to have left it, apparently offended. Tims Oksers, "Stāsts par ļaunuma banalitāti," *Rīgas Laiks*, February 2006.

54. Muižnieks 2006, 60.

55. Visvaldis Lācis' statement.

56. Muižnieks 2006, 57. The figure is from the year 2005.

Chapter 2   (Pages 53–64)

1. *Helsingin Sanomat*, August 21. 2006

2. Latvian is the world's 150th most spoken language

3. *Daily Telegraph*, January 3, 2006.

4. About 6 percent of the population in Finland is Swedish speaking. According to the constitution, Finland is a bilingual country. A municipality is officially bilingual if the minority language (in practice, Swedish) is spoken by eight percent of the population or at least 3,000 people. In the north, the Saami language also has an official position. All public officials must know both of the country's languages, and all school children must learn both.

5. In addition, the Livonian language, which is related to Finnish, has an official status in some Courland communities. The language law also establishes a special position for the Latgali (Lettgallian) dialect (a separate language in the opinion of some). Governmental records and correspondence are to be in Latvian according to the law. Place names, street names, road signs, advertisements, announcements, package and price labels are to be written in the State language. If information is given in other languages, Latvian has to be "visually dominating." The organizers of public activities should provide translation into the official State language, and TV programs must also be interpreted. The language law also dictates what kinds of names Latvians may have and that the first and last names of persons – also of Russians and other foreigners – "shall be written in accordance with the accepted rules of Latvian spelling." A long-standing principle established in the 19th century is that foreign person and place names are spelled phonetically. For example, I am not Jukka Rislakki, but Juka Rislaki. This rule causes a huge amount of work for linguistic officials and inspectors and confuses readers of newspapers and books. An "s" is always added to male names ending in consonants. In Latvia, James Bond is Džeimss Bonds. *Valsts valoda Latvijā / Official State Language in Latvia / Gosudarstvennyi jazyk v Latvii* (Rīga: 1992). The fire department, police, and ambulance corps can be contacted in Russian. Enterprises, of which the state or local government owns at least a half, are to use Latvian as the in-house language; that is not always the case. In the autumn of 2000, the PCTVL

party urged the flouting of the language law and the boycotting of businesses which used Latvian and a refusal to watch Latvian television programs. It also urged foreign businessmen to boycott Latvia, and the EU not to take Latvia as a member.

6. Tunne Kelam in *Linnaleht*, January 12, 2007.

7. Māris Ruks, "Latviešu valodas izredzes" [Latvian Languages Prospects] *Latvijas Avīze*, January 8, 2007.

8. According to the last Soviet census in 1989, 62.4 percent of the population were able to speak Latvian and 81.6 percent Russian. *Migranti Latvijā* 2004, 96.

9. *The Baltic Times* 21.12–10.01, 2007.

10. Krēsliņš 2006, 233; The 17 Latvian Communist Protest Letter (1971), http://www.letton.ch/lvx_17com.htm

11. Silvija Veckalne, "Latvieši vai krievi. Kurš kuru?, [Latvians or Russians. Who whom?] *Rīgas Balss*, January 12, 2007.

12. Ibid. Over a third of Latvians claim that they already know English.

13. Research done in 2003 reveals that knowing only Russian, one can get along in Latvia. The question asked was: "What language do non-citizens living in Latvia use in their everyday life?" The results: mainly Russian, 73.6 %, both Russian and Latvian, 20.8 %, mainly Latvian, 3.8 %, other languages or no answer, 1.8 %. *Latvijas Avīze*, January 3, 2004.

14. Journalist Tekla Šaitere's statement.

15. *Helsingin Sanomat*, December 28, 2005.

16. Ibid, August 31, 2006

17. David Lucas, "Estonia is Right and Amnesty is Wrong," *The Economist*, December 14, 2006.

18. Philologist Dzintra Hirša in *Latvijas Avīze*, November 23, 2005.

19. Mārtiņš Kālis in *Latvijas Avīze*, May 3, 2006.

20. *Latvijas Avīze*, May 9, 2006. Edward Anders comments that some of these pollsters "have totally failed to recognize that the situation is highly asymmetrical. If the Russians in Latvia after a few generations become assimilated to the point where they forget their language and culture, that's no loss to the world as there is the huge Russian federation with 140 million Russian speakers. But if the Latvians become so assimilated, then the Latvian language and culture vanish, like three other Baltic cultures before them. The world recognizes this principle for endangered animals and plants; that's why catching of whales is severely restricted, but catching of herring is not. Can the world grant such protection to animals and plants but deny it to humans?" Anders' e-mail, August 17, 2007.

21. *The Baltic Times*, April 27 and May 3, 2006.

22. "Quiet Revolution in the Classroom," *Transitions Online* Net magazine, October 30, 2006.

23. Ruks 2007.
24. Muižnieks 2006, 80; *Latvijas Avīze*, May 19, 2007.
25. L'Enciclopedie 2003, 2005 entry *Lettonie*.
26. *Latvijas Avīze*, February 8, 2006.
27. PCTVL home page, January 27, 2006.
28. *Latvijas Avīze*, January 28, 2006.
29. *Kultūras Diena*, March 10, 2006.
30. Radio Finland news, May 4, 2006; *Helsingin Sanomat*, May 5, 2006; *Latvijas Avīze*, May 8, 2006.
31. *Kabinets*, January 2006.
32. *Latvijas Avīze*, June 16, 2006. Russians often call Latvians by the name of gansi (Hanses, a subliminal reference to the Nazis). As a man recently said in Russian to his son at the Jūrmala indoor swimming pool, referring to my feminine acquaintance: "Oh how tired I am of these stinking gansi!"
33. Ibid., April 28, 2006.

Chapter 3　　　(Pages 65–77)

1. Tacitus, 1952, 70.
2. Diamond 1997, 181.
3. *Linguafranca*. Le Bulletin des Interpretes du Parlament Européen, vol. 8, Number 7, July 4, 2005; Krēsliņš 2006, 281; *National and Ethnic Groups in Latvia* (Rīga: Ministry of Justice, 1996); Bleiere and others 2006, chapter I; Rislaki 2004, 15–19. Later on, "Livonia" came to mean only northern Latvia and southern Estonia.
4. *Henrikin Liivinmaan kronikka/Heinrici Chronicon Livoniae* 2003, 8–40. In Latin and Latvian: *Indriķa Hronika* (*Heinrici Chronicon Livoniae*) 1993.
5. Imants Lancmanis' interview, *Kultūras Diena*, February 2007.
6. Butler 1988, 4–5.
7. Of the inhabitants of Latvia, 6.2 % were Germans in 1897. Of the ethnic Latvian inhabitants, only 0.4% then belonged to the manor owning class, as did 5.8 % of all Latvia's Germans. Krēsliņš 2006, 38, 292, 296.
8. Uldis Kauliņš, "Mīti un īstenība. Pastrīdēsimies?" [Myths and Reality. Shall We Argue?] in *Republika.lv* May 12–18, 2006.
9. Hvostov 1999; Krēsliņš 2006, 287; *republika.lv*, April 20–30, 2007..
10. Bleiere and others 2006, 70; Krēsliņš 2006, 47.
11. "Skats pa pils logu" [View from a Castle Window] in *Kultūras Diena*, May 26, 2006.
12. Krēsliņš 2006, 37–57.

13. The Museum of the Occupation of Latvia, 2002, 15.

14. Medijainen and Made 2002, 11.

15. Bormane Anita, "Rusifikācijas ēra" [The Russification Era] in *Mājas Viesis*, December 13, 2002.

16. Dunn 1966; *The New Yorker*, August 19, 1944. Krēsliņš 2006 writes (p. 273), that Dunn depicts the Latvians as some kind of African tribe, with whose members it was impossible to communicate.

17. Jukka Rislakki, "Latvia – a Country Europe Does Not Understand," in *10 uutta tulijaa. Euroopan unioni – erilaisia yhdessä* (Ulkoministeriö, 2004). The quotation is from the diaries of Klinge, published by Otava.

18. Goltz, 1920.

19. Tuompo 1918, 7–11.

20. Kemiläinen 2005.

21. Eksteins 1999; Bleiere and others 2005, 94, 312.

22. Pumpurs 2006; Project Gutenberg www.gutenberg.org/etext/17445

23. *Riga. Ein Führer für deutsche Soldaten.*1941. Cited in Angrick and Klein 2006, 93.

24. "Ostlandes reihskomisariāta…" in *Yearbook of the Museum of the Occupation of Latvia* 2002, 303–306.

25. Uldis Neiburgs, "Western Allies…," in Nollendorfs and Oberländer 2005, 141.

26. Spekke 1959.

27. See, for example, Beschloss and Talbott 1993.

28. Vitols Dixon 2006, 171.

29. *Linguafranca*, op. cit.

Chapter 4 (Pages 79–85)

1. *Latvijas Avīze*, February 7, 2006

2. He also said: "What are the Russian people guilty of? A Pole, Dzerzhinsky, headed the Cheka; of the revolutionary council's 44 members, 38 were Jews, four were Latvians, only one was a Russian." Jukka Rislakki, "Latvian-Russian Relations at a New Low" in Rozentals-seuran vuosikirja (Helsinki: 2005.)

3. Sociologist Renald Simonjon in *Latvijas Avīze*, January 5, 2006.

4. *Helsingin Sanomat*, February 26, 2006.

5. Aleksandr Chapenko, "The Red and White Latvian Riflemen during the Civil War in Northern Russia 1918–1920," in the *Yearbook of the Latvian War Museum II* (2001), 85.

6. Bleiere and others 2006, 89–90; Krēsliņš 2006, 91–92.

7. Detlef Henning, "Wir warfen Feuer in jedes Haus," *Baltische Briefe*, April-May 1998. He explains the election results in part by the fact that many Russian army soldiers took part in the voting. In addition, according to him, this temporary phenomenon is explained by the people's unfamiliarity with elections and the Bolsheviks' heated agitation and manipulation of the election. Henning also observes that the workers', soldiers', and farmers' soviets at the time cannot be described simply as bolshevik.

8. Interview with Aimo Minkkinen. Dr. Minkkinen runs the world's only Lenin museum in Tampere, Finland. Recently a museum has been opened in the house in Rīga which Lenin visited in 1900. See also: Juka Rislaki, "Rokas augšā – latvieši nāk!" in *Diena*, November 20, 1998, and my article in Marja Niiniluoto and others, Suomi, suuriruhtinaanmaa [Grand Duchy Finland] (Hämeenlinna: Tammi 1991).

9. Bleiere and others 2006, 93–94; Salomaa 1992.

10. *The Irish Times*, March 11, 2006; Frank Gordon, "Maskava–Berlīne" in Jaunā Gaita, September 2004.

11. Ilgvars Butulis in *SestDiena*, July 17, 1999.

12. See especially Draudins 1961.

13. *Diena*, November 12, 2005. Dissenting opinion: Edward Anders' e-mail, August 18, 2007.

14. Latviešu strēlnieks 3/1994.

15. Jānis Krēsliņš, "Rētu uzplēšana Latvijas vēsturē" [Opening up of wounds in Latvian history] in *Yearbook of The Museum of the Occupation of Latvia 2000*, 279.

16. Tanskanen, 1978 132–133; Rislakki 2005, 52; Šalda (ed.) 2007.

17. Mannerheim, 1951, 456.

18. Ēriks Ingevics letter March 2007.

19. Some memoirs record that Finnish workers for Cheka made home searches, arrested people, transported prisoners, and "shot and stole." Rislakki 2004, 323.

20. Stranga, 2002, 241; Nollendorfs-Oberländer 2005, Rislakki 2004, 52.

21. *Yearbook of the Museum of the Occupation of Latvia 2000*, 279; Bangerskis 1922.

22. Gunita Nagle, "Latviešu strēlnieki. Sarkanie?" [Were the Latvian Riflemen Reds?] in *SestDiena*, October 13, 2001.

23. Applebaum, 2003, 96–97, 108–109; Gordon 2004.

24. *The Museum of the Occupation of Latvia 2002*, 56; Ruta Ozoliņa, "Latviešu operācija" in *Mājas Viesis*, December 9, 2000. Krēsliņš 2006 presents the conjecture that some 70,000 Latvians were liquidated in the Soviet Union from 1929–1938. Other researchers' figures are smaller. (See the following footnotes).

25. Aivars Beika, "Latvians in the Soviet Union: The Victims of Communist Terror, 1929–1939" in *Yearbook of the Museum of the Occupation of Latvia 1999*, 89–91. Beika writes that from 1926 to 1939, the number of Latvians in the Soviet Union fell by 23,065 people, or that 15 percent of them disappeared. The loss of Soviet Estonians was 15.3 percent and that of Lithuanians was 21.31 percent. So the Latvians were not the most hated group in Stalin's Russia?

26. Aivars Stranga, "Contributions of the Latvian Commission of Historians to Holocaust Research," in *Yearbook of the Museum of the Occupation of Latvia 2001*, 281–282.

27. Radzinsky 1992, 462; Eksteins 1999, 53. For a historian's comment: see The *Yearbook of the Museum of the Occupation of Latvia 2000*, 279; *Latvijas Avīze*, February 28, 2006; Nagle 2001.

Chapter 5   (Pages 87–94)

1. *Rīgas Balss*, November 7, 2003. A slight shock was experienced at the Latvian War Museum, for the article had come into being with "the help of Latvian War Museum employees."—11.11. commemorates the 1918 Armistice Day in many European countries. The origin of the Latvian date is the liberation of Rīga in 1919.

2. Ibid, November 12, 2004.

3. Eglīte 2001, 101.

4. Butler 1988 ; Mullingar 1988, 5; Bleiere and others 2006, 76–77, 118.

5. Medijainen and Made 2002, 10, 15, 19.

6. Marko Lehti, "The Baltic League and the Idea of Limited Sovereignty" in *Jahrbücher für Geschichte Osteuropas*, Band 45, 1997, Heft 3.

7. Krēsliņš 2006, 68–73.

8. Aivars Stranga, "Bermontiādes ugunīs šķīstītā Latvija" [Latvia Purified in the Fires of Bermontiade] in *Latvijas Avīze*, November 10, 2004.

9. *Kultūras Diena*, January 26, 2007. The first news of the recognition was received on the morning of January 27th, when word of Finland's recognition arrived by wire in Rīga and brought about a huge celebration in the streets.

10. *Latvija citu valstu saimē* 1939, 20, 76. The 1935 census showed a steep drop in the male/female ratio for the age group 30–49 (who were 13–32 years old in 1918):

Age	Men	Women	M/F
30–34	76325	86148	0.886
35–39	53634	79209	0.677
40–44	51879	68238	0.760
45–49	49544	64319	0.770

On the other hand, there were more males than females in the 0–16 year
age group (ratio 1.014–1.047). Edward Anders' letter, January 20, 2006;
Darbiņš–Vītiņš: *Latvija, Statistisks Pārskats, 1947.*

11. For Latvia's war of independence in general see also Pētersone 1999.

12. Interview with Paulis Lazda. Wikipedia: Walter Duranty. Duranty
     became a propagandist for Stalin, and he downplayed the famine in
     Ukraine in the 1930's.—The "Latvian red" is magenta or cherry color.

13. Muižnieks 2006, 12; Darbiņš–Vītiņš, 26–27. 13.5% worked in manufac-
     turing, 5.3% in commerce.

14. Of Latvia's 231,055 farms, in 1929, 20 percent were very small, under 5
     hectares, and 19 percent were from 5 to 10 hectares. 94 percent of the
     farms were privately owned. Production was quite inefficient, less per
     hectare than in Finland, which is farther north. There were more horses,
     pigs, and sheep than in Finland, which is a much larger country. *Etat de
     l'agriculture en Lettonie en 1936.* Rīga: Bureau de Statistique de L'Etat,
     1937, 1, 252.

15. Bleiere and others 2006, 37; Rislaki 2004, 91.

16. Krēsliņš 2006, 52, 308.

17. *Kultūras Diena*, May 26, 2006.

18. Juris Pavlovičs, "Change of Occupation Powers in Latvia in Summer
     1941," in Nollendorfs–Oberländer 2005, 94.

19. Edward Anders' e-mail, August 18, 2007.

20. Thus for example in the memoirs of Edmunds Johansons, 2006.

Chapter 6   (Pages 95–108)

1. Edward Lucas in *The Economist*, translation in *Diena*, July 8, 2000.

2. *Latvijas Avīze*, February 7, 2006.

3. *We were liberators: so the bands played, / Ice on the mouthpiece and the
    fingers ... / And the bodies stiff like logs / Are freed at last from the loud-
    speaker ...* wrote Graham Greene in his ironic poem "Finland," with
    which he won the *Spectator* poetic competition during the Winter War.
    The Spectator, March 8, 1940.

4. Dr. Veli-Pekka Leppänen in *Helsingin Sanomat*, February 19, 2006.

5. Alexander V. Berkis, "Soviet Russia's Persecution of Latvia, 1918 to the
    Present" in *The Journal of Historical Review*, Vol 20, 2001, reprinted from
    Vol 8.

6. It is interesting to note that in a report of the US Congress from the year
    1954, Ulmanis' coup is understood and defended. It was a question of a
    "moderate authoritarian regime," and Ulmanis was "temporarily" to
    concentrate power in his hands "because of the communist threat;" the
    congressmen believed that he planned to return to a democratic and
    constitutional organization. *Report of the Select Committee to Investigate*

Communist Aggression and the Forced Incorporation of the Baltic states into the U.S.S.R. 1954, 116–117.

7.   Political scientists Veiko Spolītis and Andris Sprūds of the University of Latvia write that Prime Minister Ulmanis made himself president illegally in April of 1936 and that the presidents' portrait gallery in the castle in Rīga was not the proper place for his portrait. *Diena*, October 16, 2006.

8.   Myllyniemi 1977, 131; Ezergailis 1996, 45.

9.   Ilgvars Butulis in *SestDiena*, July 17, 1999.

10.   "Baltic States and Revisionism. Among the three Baltic States of Estonia, Lithuania and Latvia, the latter is perhaps the worst offender." *http://english.pravda.ru* 2006. Perhaps!

11.   Ulmanis proclaimed, 25 years before J.F. Kennedy: "Ask not what your country can do for you – ask what you can do for your country."

12.   Butulis op. cit.; Juris Čiganovs in *Tēvijas Sargs*, August 8, 2000.

13.   At the end of the 1930's there were some 94,000 Jews and some 62,000 Germans in Latvia. There was a significant number of Jews among the commercial, medical, and legal professions.

14.   Myllyniemi 1997

15.   Ibid; *Ruotuväki* 21/1996; Rislakki 2005, 118. The strength of the Baltic countries' military (with reserves) was calculated at about 360,000. They had some 173,000 soldiers in arms, and 120 artillery pieces, 147 tanks and armored cars, three submarines, and 300 airplanes in use.

16.   Myllyniemi 1997; Rislakki 2005, 179. In the 1930's, Finland's military expenses were some 20 % of the budgets passed by parliament and some 4 % of the GNP.

17.   Tannberg 2003, 159. Andersons 1983, 25.

18.   Soviet-German treaties of 1939 plus the secret protocols and supplementary protocols in English: *Report of the Select Committee...* (1954), 291–292; Also Plakans 2007, 3.

19.   Strods 2004, 38–41; Rislakki 2004, chapter XIII.

20.   The entire text of the agreement between Latvia and the Soviet Union: *International Affairs* 4/90 "The Baltic States Join..." This Soviet journal offers in English all the relevant documents of 1939; Elmārs Pelkaus (ed), 1999, 68. This book contains documents concerning Latvia's becoming socialist and joining the USSR – but only in Latvian. In English see Plakans 2007, 6, 8.

21.   Heinrihs Strods, "The Disorganized Retreat of the Red Army from Latvia in 1941," *Yearbook of the Museum of the Occupation of Latvia* 2001, 93.

22.   Taken from Soviet Union and Soviet Latvian textbooks of the 1980's: Strods 2004, 14.

23. Ibid., 16; Ilmjärv 2004, 733; Rislakki 2005, 205.

24. Bonifācijs Daukšts, "Kā briedināja okupāciju [How the occupation evolved] in *Mājas Viesis*, April 8, 2000.

25. The Soviet Union's note clearly states that it was literally a question of an "ultimatum."

26. The whole Russian note in English: *Report of the Select Committee...* 1954; Plakans 2007, 25.

27. http://en.wikipedia.org/wiki/Occupation_of_Latvia offers a good explanation of the events which led to the occupation of 1940, as well as its immediate consequences.

28. Iosifs Šteinmanis 2002, 117–123.

29. Lācis 2006a 380; Rislaki 2004, 230.

30. Ojārs Niedre, "Vai armija domāja par pretošanos?" [Did the Army Consider Resistance?] in *Mājas Viesis*, June 16, 2001.

31. It is striking that the name of Vyshinski and his activities in Latvia in 1940 have been purged in Soviet Latvian sources. There is no mention of him in *Latvijas Padomju Enciklopēdija* (1987), *Latvijas PSR Mazā Enciklopēdija* (1972), I couldn't find him in *Latvijas PSR vēsture* [The History of Soviet Latvia, red. A. Drīzulis, 1967] and E. Žagars' *Sociālistiskie pārveidojumi Latvijā* [Socialist Changes in Latvia] *1940–1941* and any other Soviet books that cover the same period. Still his presence was conspicious at the time, his picture was in the papers, and he gave public speeches (on June 21 1940, at the end of the speech from the balcony of the Soviet embassy, Vyshinski exclaimed in Latvian, "Long live free Latvia" and "Long live the friendship between the Republic of Latvia and the Soviet Union.") Any mention of Moscow's proconsul would not suit the later party line which is still useful in Moscow.

32. Professor Seppo Zetterberg in *Kanava* 8/2006.

33. Myllyniemi 1977, 146.

34. Zunda in *Latvijas Vēstnesis*, March 17 and March 23, 2005; Ojārs Niedre, "Vēlēšanu traģikomēdija" [Tragicomedy of the Elections] in *Mājas Viesis*, July 21, 2001; Aivars Stranga, "Latvijas okupācija un iekļaušana PSRS" [Latvia's Occupation and Annexation to the USSR] in *Latvijas Avīze*, August 2–4, 2004; Henry Kissinger; *Diplomacy* (New York: Touchstone, 1994), 347. In one election district the percentage of voters was, according to newspaper reports, 102! Danute Dūra and Ieva Gundare, "Okupācijas vara un Latvijas cilvēks" [Occupation Power and Latvians], in Ērglis 2004, 110. The official results of the election were published in Moscow before the polls had closed in Latvia.—It has been estimated that only less than half of the Latvians voted; nevertheless the percentage was probably quite high, for mandatory internal passports were stamped at the polling places and an unstamped passport implied opposition to the regime and serious trouble later on. In Estonia, the similar statistics (according to official reports 84.1 percent voted and of

them 92.8 percent supported the only party's candidates) were quite close to the truth, writes an international group of historians which published an extensive study of Estonia during World War II. By checking election documents, they concluded that the percentage voting was 80.1 and that 91.1 percent of them voted for the "workers slate." *Estonia 1940–1945. Reports of the Estonian International Commission for the Investigation of Crimes against Humanity* (Tallinn: Estonian Foundation for the Investigations of Crimes Against Humanity, 2006).

35. Pelkaus 1999, 86. This occurred on July 21, 1940.

36. Bleiere and others 2006, 156.

37. Bleiere in Nolledorfs and Oberländer 2005, 246; Šteinmanis 2002, 117–123.

38. Ulmanis died in September of 1942 in the Krasnovodsk jail. That information was obtained only after decades, and his body has still not been found.

39. Rislakki 2005, 233; Cielēns II, 188; Bērziņš 1959, 229. *Diena*, March 21, 2003; Ērglis 2003, 7; Ilmjärv 1998, 253–255; Aivars Stranga in *Latvijas Avīze*, August 2, 2004.

40. Ilmjärv 2004, 666, 804, 809; Juris Čiganovs in *Tēvijas Sargs*, August 8, 2000.

41. *International Affairs* op. cit.; Rislakki 2005, 225.

42. Stranga op. cit. (August 2004); Bleiere and others 2006, 245.

43. Krēsliņš 2006, 36; Aivars Strangas' statement.

44. The list is mainly from Edward Anders' letter of Oct. 18, 2005. In Lithuania there were about 1500 communists, in Latvia according to different estimates 400–1000, and in Estonia 150.

45. Šneidere, "The First…", 36–37, and Ivanovs Aleksandrs: "Sovietization of Latvian Historiography 1944–1959" in Nollendorfs–Oberländer 2005, 258–260. Historians also argued that "very large masses" of Latvian society, workers and peasants particularly, were eager to see the Soviet power restored as soon as possible after the war. Antonijs Zunda, "Resistance against Nazi German Occupation in Latvia," Ibid., 149.

46. Gogol 1993, 22.

47. Askolds Rodins in *Atmoda*, March 16, 1991.

48. Ilmjärv claims that Konstantin Päts, the president of Estonia, had earlier been an expert on the Soviet embassy, had used his position to advance his business affairs and secretly received a salary as a legal consultant to a Soviet oil firm. Also Ulmanis, his party, and his business enterprises had Russian connections which raised questions. Ilmjärv 204, 108–114. Rislakki 2005, 115.

49. Inesis Feldmanis in *Latvijas Avīze*, November 7, 2006.

50. Šneidere, op. cit., 35.

Chapter 7   (Pages 109–126)

1.   Over 62,000 Baltic Germans heeded Hitler's *Heim-ins-Reich* call and moved from Latvia in 1939–1941. The Soviet Union approved the operation, which was a preparation for war.

2.   For Holocaust in Latvia generally, see e.g. Ezergailis 1996; Eksteins 1999; Angrick and Klein, 2006; Arnolds Spekke, 1957; Elmārs Pelkaus (ed.), 1999; *Museum of the Occupation…*, 2002, 64–66; Leppänen 2002; Margers Vestermanis, 1998; Documents in Plakans 2007, 113–120. Ezergailis and Eksteins, for example, have somewhat different conceptions of the nature of the Holocaust in occupied Latvia. Briefly, Eksteins lays the blame on the shoulders of the Latvians, Ezergailis asserts the German responsibility and guilt. Ezergailis' sources seem solid and his research is the most inclusive on the topic. He does not gloss over local participation in the killings, but has no patience with German and Russian disinformation, either.

3.   From 1934 to 1936, Jews filled 39 percent of leadership positions in the NKVD. By the beginning of 1938 that percentage had dropped to 21.3, and by 1940 only 3.4 percent of those in leadership position were Jewish. N.V. Petrov, K.V. Sorokin and others, eds., 1999, 495; Galina Ivanova, 1997, 153–54, 159–60; Aivars Stranga 2002, 241.

4.   Irēne Šneidere, "The First…" in Nollendofs and Oberländer 2005, 40–41.

5.   That the Jews were over-represented among deportees, is testified to in Edward Anders' footnote references to the book, *History of Latvian Jews*. See also *Aizvestie* 2001; *Represēto saraksts*, [The List of the Repressed] 1995; *Lauku Avīze*, February 24, 2002; *Kultūras Diena*, May 7, 2005; *Mājas Viesis*, June 12, 1999; Eksteins 2000, 147–8, 154.

6.   A former prime minister of Latvia said in a newspaper interview in 2006 that although "seven thousand" (!) dead Jews undeniably is a tragedy, we should remember, that "tens of thousands" Latvians had to suffer from the occupations. His mistake was soon corrected by angry readers. Let us hope that it was a printing error and that he said or meant to say "seventy thousand Jews." *Neatkarīga*, March 30, 2006.

7.   Even Aleksandrs Lavents, who is a suspect in Latvia's biggest bank swindle, has been portrayed abroad as a persecuted Jew. His bank, which promised totally unrealistic interest rates on deposits, took with it the funds of thousands of people and organizations when it crashed in 1995. Israel and Jewish organizations followed his case closely. Lavents lodged a complaint about his treatment with the European Court of Human Rights, which ordered that he be retried.

8.   Anders' e-mail to the writer, September 8, 2006; Edward Anders, "Amidst Latvians during the Holocaust," manuscript; Wikipedia: Righteous Among the Nations.

9. Anna Polyanskaja and others, "Commissars of the Internet," September 2006, posted on LR Translations February 24, 2007. http://lrtranslations.blogspot.com/2007/02/commissars-of-internet.html

10. Ezergailis 1996, 65; Rislakki 2005, 120.

11. Paulis Lazda's e-mail to the writer, October 21, 2006.

12. Edward Anders' e-mail to the writer, September 8, 2006; Bleiere and others 2006, 219–220; Vitols Dixon 2006, 102.

13. Ezergailis 1996, 80.

14. *Museum of the Occupation...*, 2002, 60; Edward Anders' letter, January 20, 2006., http://www.jewishgen.org/yizkor/Pinkas_latvia/lat_00119.html

15. Aivars Stranga, "Holocaust in Occupied Latvia," in Nollendorfs and Oberländer, 2005, 173.

16. Kilpinen, 2002; Margers Vestermanis, "Es geht um das Warum und das Wie," *Die Tageszeitung*, June 22, 1991.

17. Yad Vashem has a number of survivors' reports claiming killings during the interregnum or very early in the German occupation. Most of them are in Yiddish or Hebrew. Dov Levin claims that a number of them are true. He has been challenged publicly to translate them so they could be scrutinized.—The intensive research in recent years by the Latvian President's Commission of Historians has failed to uncover a single proven instance of spontaneous mass murder of Jews by the local population. Letter from commission member Valters Nollendorfs to the writer in August, 2006.

18. Juris Pavlovičs: "Change of Occupation..." in Nollendorfs and Oberländer, 2005, 100–103; Vestermanis 1991; Stranga 2005, 168; Dr. Juris Pavlovičs' interview, *Lauku Avīze*, November 25, 2003; Ezergailis 1996, 17.

19. Boris Sokolov in *Latvijas Avīze*, June 20, 2005.

20. *Kultūras Diena*, May 7, 2005.

21. Major B. Nordlund reported that the Germanization of Latvia began immediately, that Baltic-German aristocrats returned, confiscations of property began, labor was demanded for Germany, and there was no promise of independence. "100% of the people are anti-communist and 95% of the people are opposed to the Germans." Ignoring the prohibition, many listened to British radio. Mannerheim Archives, National Archives, Helsinki, Nordlund, September 12, 1942.

22. Helmut Heiber published important *Generalplan Ost* documents about Latvia in *Vierteljahreshefte für Zeitgeschichte* (July 1958, pages 280–325). Their writing was supervised by Himmler in 1941.—According to some memoirs, there were plans to liquidate non-Aryan Latvians after the Jews.

23. The Russian *MosNews.com* had a not-so-subtle slant in their news item in February 2006, telling of the Latvian president's visit to Israel. The title was: "Latvia's President Regrets Her Country's Role in Holocaust." And the first sentence: "Latvia's president has apologized for her *country's* [my emphasis] behavior during World War II." The *Jerusalem Post* wrote that the president asked pardon for the Holocaust in Latvia. The Latvian *Latvijas Avīze* asked why the president said: "We are deeply sorry about the participation of Latvia in the atrocities of Holocaust." In fact, according to the official text, the president had said: "I regret the *participation of Latvians* [my emphasis] in the extermination of Jews during World War II. Regrettably, there were people in Latvia who took part in the Nazi campaign to annihilate the Jewish population in Europe." *MosNews.com*, February 22, 2006; *Latvijas Avīze*, March 10, 2006.

24. *The Nation*, May 23, 2005.

25. Kilpinen 2002.

26. Ezergailis 2001.

27. Stranga, op. cit., 165–166; Ezergailis 1996, 13, 17, 51, 154; *Yearbook of the Museum of the Occupation of Latvia* 2002, 172.

28. Ezergailis and others 2005, 27.

29. Andrew Ezergailis in *Diena*, April 9, 2005; Edward Anders' e-mail to the writer, September 8, 2006.

30. Ezergailis in *Rīgas Laiks*, December 2000. Eksteins 1999, 147–148.

31. Kaufman 1947; Press, 1988 and 1992.

32. Goldhagen 1996, 407.

33. Lipstadt 1993, 7.

34. Eskin 2002. Wolkomirski turned out to be Bruno Grosjean, the Protestant son of a Swiss factory worker. He had chosen a new identity after meeting the Polish violinist Wanda Wilkomirska.

35. Angrick and Klein 2006, 8–9.

36. Kārlis Kangeris: "Closed Units of Latvian Police—Lettische Schutzmanschafts-Bataillone," in Nollendorfs and Oberländer 2005, 107, 116; Hilberg 1992, 96–101; Edward Anders's letter to author, January 20, 2006. For the books mentioned in the text and the discussion they aroused, see also Heikki Länsisalo's article in *Kanava* 2/2006.

37. Heinrihs Strods in *Kultūras Diena*, May 7, 2005; Ezergailis 1996, 6.

38. Stranga, op. cit., 163.

39. The mass killing in Ukraine began on September 29, 1941, in Babi Yar near Kiev, where over 100 000 people were shot, mainly Jews. In Belarus the Nazis began on October 18, when about 7,000 were killed at Borissow.

40. Rudīte Vīksne, "Members of the…," Nollendorfs and Oberländer 2005, 202, 206.—Professor Ezergailis, on the other hand, writes that he would not necessarily say that the participating Latvians were marginal people.

Letter to the author, August 18, 2006.—Edward Anders would like to add that there were a number of students from fraternity Lettonia, too. E-mail to the author, September 8, 2006.

41. Ezergailis 1996 173–175; Stranga, op. cit., 167; *Museum of the Occupation...* 2002, 66; Eksteins 1999, 150.

42. Aivars Stranga in *Diena* June 8, 2005. Edward Anders' letter, January 20, 2006. Arājs was first captured by the British after the war, and their prosecutors had gathered considerable material against him for a trial. Inexplicably he was soon freed and arrested only 30 years later.

43. *Yearbook of the museum of the Occupation of Latvia* 1999, 210; Pelkaus 1999, 191. In these translations from German Stahlecker tells of 31,868 executions in a document that seems to be dated *August 17, 1941*. In the following sources the date is October 15, 1941: Bleiere and others 2006, 283; Ezergailis 1996, 222. In fact it seems to be a report compiled on October 25, about a period ending October 15.—At the end of January 1942, Einsatzgruppe A reported the killing of 229,052 Jews in the Baltics. Kilpinen 2002.

44. *Einsatzgruppe A*, General Report up to October 15, 1941. Part II: Cleansing and securing the area of operations. (1) Encouragement of *Selbstreiningungsaktionen* [Self-cleaning operations]. Thanks to Paulis Lazda, who got this document in the Wannsee Museum Archive in Berlin and gave me a copy; see also Ezergailis 1996, 145, 203.

45. *Einsatzgruppe A*, General Report up to October 15, 1941.

46. Ezergailis 1996, 272.

47. In the Soviet Union Rumbula, the scene of Latvia's largest mass murder, was neither remembered nor paid any heed to until the 1960's. When a memorial was finally placed in these woods, its inscription read "To the victims of Fascism 1941–1945" with a hammer and sickle emblem. Nor did the Soviet regime emphasize on other memorials that the victims were Jews. During Brezhnev's time, the Jewish "Zionists" were accused of complicity in their own tragedy. Surviving Jews were automatically suspected of being spies or of having collaborated with the Nazis.

48. USHMM manuscript RG–18.002M, file 83–1–22.

49. Scheffler-Schulle, *Buch der Erinnerung an die ins Baltikum deportierten deutschen, österreichischen und tschechoslowakischen Juden* [Memorial Book on German, Austrian and Czech Jews deported to the Baltics] (Saur: 2003) lists about 31 000 names and is thought to be virtually 100% complete.—This mass destruction was not kept secret from the outside world for long. The physician of Himmler, Felix Kersten, visited the president of Finland, Risto Ryti, on July 31, 1942, and told him, according to the diary of Ryti: "Jews are being sent from Germany to Latvia and Poland, where they are being murdered in cold blood." Ryti thought this to be "terrible," and Kersten also said he disliked "this kind of butchering of people." Professor Seikko Eskola in *Kanava* 6/2006.—Already in October 1941 Olavi Viherluoto, an officer of the Finnish secret police

(Valpo) visited the German officials in Tallinn and wrote for his supe-
riors a detailed report on the murder of Jews and Communists in
Estonia. This document, which I found in Kansan Arkisto, Helsinki, is
also printed in Suominen 1979, 53–56.

50. Ezergailis 1996, 25.

51. Ibid, Introduction.

52. *Lauku Avīze*, July 23, 2002.

53. Bleiere and others 2006, 351–352.

54. Nollendorfs and Oberländer 2004, 13; Vīksne, op. cit., 190–204.

55. Of these twelve, one (Martin Bormann) was sentenced in absentia, and
another (Hermann Göring) committed suicide.

56. Burleigh 2004, 822–825; *Der Spiegel*, February 10, 2003; May 2, 2003;
Helsingin Sanomat, January 22, 2005; Internet: Nuremberg Trials
1945–1949.

57. Lauku Avīze, July 23, 2002.

58. Latvian aviator and former deputy of Arājs Herberts Cukurs was kid-
napped and murdered in 1965 in Montevideo, Uruguay, by Israeli
Mossad agents. Many survivors have accused Cukurs of involvement in
murders but as he was not brought to trial there has been no systematic
examination of the evidence.

59. Angrick and Klein 2006, 259.

60. Avotiņš and others 1963, 29, writes that "hundreds of thousands of prisoners" died in Salaspils in 1942–1944. About this book see chapter 8.

61. *The Nation*, March 23, 2005. Also the Finland-Latvia Friendship Society
year-book of 2005 stated that over one hundred thousand died. The Russian newspaper *Pravda* likewise wrote in 2005 that "over 100,000" died
in Salaspils. According to one Soviet era encyclopedia, the dead numbered 110,000. *Eesti Nougokude Entsüklopedia IV* [Soviet Estonian
Encyclopedia] (Tallinn: 1972), p, 544.

62. Angrick and Klein 2006, 269.

63. Ezergailis 2005, 154.

64. Heinrihs Strods, "Salaspils koncentrācijas…," in *LOM Yearbook 2000*,
87–153; *SestDiena*, February 18, 2005. *Museum of the Occupation…* 2002,
74; *Rīgas Balss*, February 2, 2006; Uldis Neiburgs, "Salaspils, mazāk
zināmās epizodes" [Less Known Episodes] in *Mājas Viesis*, April 28,
2006.

65. Angrick and Klein 2006, 269.

66. Strods, 2006, 38; documents of Vyatlag in *Yearbook of the Museum of the
Occupation of Latvia 2003*, 137–156; Ainārs Bambals in *Yearbook of the
Museum of the Occupation of Latvia 1999*, 158; Kalniete 2006, chro-
nology; Heinrihs Strods in *Mājas Viesis*, April 8, 2005; Bleiere and others
2006 327.—Vyatlag held about 3,500 Latvians 1938–1945, and of them

2,373 died (67.8 %). In 1941–1945 alone there died 2,318 Latvians (95.3 %). In Buchenwald 1938–1945 the death rate was 14.2 %.

67.		Viesturs Sprūde, *Latvijas Avīze*, July 27, 2006; Diena, July 28, 2006. On the U.S. Army picture showing Elie Wiesel see http://en.wikipedia.org/wiki/Image:Buchenwald_Slave_Laborers_Liberation.jpg

68.		Davies 2007, 13, 312; Davies 1996, 1004–1005; Daukšts 2006; internet Encyclopedia *Wikipedia* Katyn article; Šneidere in Nollendofs and Oberländer 2005, 33–34. Bonifācijs Daukšts in *Mājas Viesis*, April 8, 2000. *Diena*, September 13, 2006. A fourth mass grave, with about 2 000 bodies, was found near Kiev in 2006.—The decision for the mass execution was made on a high level (i.e. Stalin) in Moscow on March 5, 1940. Prison camps were emptied, since space was needed for Estonian, Latvian, and Lithuanian prisoners of war, of whom some 50,000–60,000 were estimated to arrive (no prisoners arrived as the Baltic countries did not resist the occupation in June 1940). The murders occurred in April, May and June. There has also been conjecture that plans were to use the camps for Finnish prisoners of war; the Winter War against the Finns was still going on in March and the Finnish resistance was on the verge of collapse.—Moscow for 50 years laid the responsibility for the Katyn bloodbath on the Germans. Of the Soviet leaders, only Mikhail Gorbachev fully admitted its occurrence. Today's Russia still fails to recognize the Katyn victims as victims of Stalinist's repression and of genocide.

69.		*Estonia 1940–1945. Reports of the Estonian International Commission for the Investigation of Crimes Against Humanity* (Tallinn: 2006). The conclusions in English, Estonian and Russian: http://www.historycommission.ee

## Chapter 8		(Pages 127–142)

1.		*"Ich befehle die Aufstellung einer Lettischen SS-Freiwilligen Legion"* (February 10, 1943). According to this order, the legion's size will depend upon the number of Latvian men available. Indulis Kažociņš, *Latviešu karavīri zem svešiem karogiem 1940–1945* [Latvian Soldiers under Foreign Banners] (Rīga: Latvijas Vēstures fonds, 1999), 93. Copy of the order: *Mājas Viesis*, February 7, 2003; Bleiere and others 2006, 286. A copy of the conscription order sent to men: the exhibition of the War Museum in Rīga; also in *Latvijas okupācijas muzejs, 1998*, 66.

2.		Atis Lejiņš, "16. marts un 39. gads" [March 16 and the Year 1939], *Diena*, March 15, 2006; Uldis Neiburgs, "Kāpēc Lietuvā nebija leģiona? [Why There Was No Legion in Lithuania?]," *Mājas Viesis*, March 12, 2004. On Dankers and Valdmanis: Krēsliņš 2006, 138–139.

3.		Professor Seppo Myllyniemi's e-mail to the author, February 10, 2007. He writes also: "The collaboration in German-occupied Western Europe was ideological in its nature, but collaboration in occupied Baltic

countries was rather tactical in nature; this collaboration was characterized by partial collaboration and partial resistance."

4. "It is forbidden to compel the inhabitants of occupied territories to swear
allegiance to the hostile power." Mirdza Kate Baltais, 1999, 41; Inesis
Feldmanis, "Waffen-SS...," in Nollendorfs and Oberländer 2005, 125;
Museum of the Occupation... 2002, 79; Nollendorfs and Neiburgs: Latvians in the Armed Forces of Germany in World War II. Briefing Paper
1, Museum of the Occupation of Latvia; Ezergailis 1996, 127.

5. Baltais 1999, 30.

6. Mauno Jokipii, "Suomalaisen SS-pataljoonan erikoisuus," [The special
character of the Finnish SS Battallion] *Kanava* 1/2001.

7. Kreslins 2006, 131, 137; *Museum of the Occupation...* 2002, 82; Jēkabsons
and Ščerbinskis 1998, 45.—When Waffen-SS was at its largest, it had
910,000 soldiers, 57 percent of the non-German foreigners.

8. Lācis 2006, 20–21. "The Waffen SS was the combat unit of the elite Nazi
paramilitary force that ran German concentration camps", wrote
Bloomberg in "Putin Urges EU to Crack Down on Nazi Backers in
Estonia, Latvia," Bloomberg.com, October 11, 2007. (Putin attacked these
countries at a meeting with members of the European Jewish
Congress.)

9. John Keegan 1970, 156–159. The only German division included among
the *Waffen-Divisionen der SS* was the 36th – originally Dirlewanger's
Brigade that was a "penal brigade composed of poachers, professional
criminals and men under the sentence of courts-martial." Heinz Höhne,
1969, 465.—The Latvian Legion's Inspector-General Bangerskis was
informed that he had been promoted to SS Lieutenant-General (*Grup-
penführer*), but the bearer of the message told him that even he did not
belong to the SS. Andrew Ezergailis in *Diena*, June 26, 2004.

10. Jokipii 2001.

11. Keegan 1970, 143.

12. Feldmanis, "Latvia under...," in Nollendorfs and Oberländer 2005, 87;
Edward Anders' letter, October 18, 2005.—In the 1960's an opinion poll
was carried out by the German historian Hans Werner Neulen among
Waffen-SS veterans of various ethnic backgrounds. 70 percent of the
Finns and 100 percent of the Latvians interviewed acknowledged their
anti-Communist sentiments as the main reason for fighting on the
German side. Feldmanis, "Waffen-SS...," in Nollendorfs and Oberländer
2005, 128; *The Baltic Times*, February 22-March 1, 2006.

13. Mannerheim 1952, 456.

14. Krēsliņš 2004, 372. The quoted sentences were translated into English by
the author himself.

15. Arturs Silgailis, *Latviešu karavīrs Otrā pasaules kara laikā* [The Latvian
Soldier During WWII] (Stockholm: 1974).

16. Kažociņš 1999, 96.

17. Colonel Voldemārs Veiss said that the battle for freedom demands weapons and "now we are being offered them. It doesn't matter what kind of uniform we wear; the main thing is that we now have weapons." Veiss was fatally injured in a battle in Russia.

18. Uldis Neiburgs in Nollendorfs and Oberländer 2005, 145.

19. Reuters, March 15, 2006. In the same Reuters news dispatch Efraim Zuroff said he found it tragic that the Latvians had chosen the wrong heroes for themselves.

20. Lācis 2006, 28, 56–57; Baltais 1999, 14–15.

21. Ibid., 26–27; *The Baltic Times*, November 5–11, 1998; Inesis Feldmanis, "Latvia under...," in Nollendorfs and Oberländer, 2005, 88.

22. Many examples of what the intelligence services knew: Lācis 2006, 6, 9, 13, 25, 29, 36, 37, 38, 41, 43.

23. *Mājas Viesis*, March 15, 2002 and March 14, 2003.

24. Neiburgs: "Western...," in Nollendorfs and Oberländer 2005, 143. Quisling is the common name for collaborators.

25. Ibid.; Jokipii 2003, 47.

26. For example, Jokipii 2003, 90, 145, 148.

27. About 57 000 Latvians served in the Legion, wrote J. Feldmanis in his report to N. Rosenfield in August 2, 1950. Plakans (ed.) 2007, 139; Inesis Feldmanis, "Latvia under...," in Nollendorfs and Oberländer 2005, 86

28. Foreign Office coded telegram to Berlin 817/252/59 (February 4, 1946), quoted in Lācis 2006, 7–8.

29. Brukfelds and Levins 2000, 81.

30. Feldmanis, "Waffen-SS...," in Nollendorfs and Oberländer 2005, 127; Bleiere and others 2006, 293; Edward Anders' letter to the author, October 18, 2005; Ezergailis 1996, 42–43; *Diena*, January 25, 2006.

31. Rudīte Vīksne: "Members of the Arājs Commando in Soviet Court Files," in Nollendorfs and Oberländer 2005, 189; *Museum of the Occupation...* 2002, 193; Andrew Ezergailis and others, 2005; Edward Anders' statement to the writer; *Baigais gads* (Rīga: Zelta Ābele, 1942. Reprint: Rīga: Tēvija, probably 1999). Daugavas Vanagi or The Hawks of the Daugava was an aid and cultural agency for former Latvian soldiers and their families established at Western European POW camps after the war, and later the largest Latvian exile organization in the West.

32. Frank Gordon, Sine ira et studio in http://centropa.org/index.php?page=r details&rtype=report&id=51&land=Latvia

33. Howard Blum, 1958 asserts that "the Latvians heartily collaborated with the German invaders in 1941 and committed the most bastardly acts against the helpless Jews" and "the behavior of the Latvians ... is one of the most inhuman and darkest pages in the history of man." (In exactly the same way some Latvian émigré circles have accused the whole Jewish community of Latvia of crimes committed by the Bolsheviks.) Howard Blum writes: "A Latvian SS regiment ... formed a group called Daugavas

Vanagi ... . The hawks would be a brotherhood of exiles bound by their complicity in common crimes. They would protect each other, hoping to survive until the day Latvia was again a fascist, anti-Jewish, anti-communist state. And then, in triumph, they would return." In 1980's great controversy was caused by another book with a similar theme, Allan Ryan's *Quiet Neighbors* (Harcourt Brace Jovanovich, 1984). In this book Ryan, among other things, confuses Latvians and Lithuanians. With great satisfaction he recounts that in 1980, in Moscow, he was received personally by the chief prosecutor of the USSR, the late Roman Rudenko [an old Stalinist], who promised to cooperate with him in identifying Nazi war criminals in the United States and in collecting evidence. Between 1948 and 1952 about 400,000 displaced persons arrived in the United States, of whom about 10,000 were under suspicion of being Nazi war criminals. That is 2.5 per cent.

34. Ibid, 86; Ezergailis 1996, 321; Uldis Neiburgs, "Latviešu leģions – apmelots bez faktiem" [The Latvian Legion Slandered Without Facts], *Latvijas Avīze*, March 10, 2007. John Loftus, former attorney in the U.S. Justice Department Office of Special Investigations (OSI), published a book in 1982 in which he explained how certain government agencies, in the aftermath of World War II, smuggled into the USA hundreds of Nazi collaborators from Eastern Europe and protected them from investigation and deportation. However he writes mainly of Belarusians and says nothing of the Balts. John Loftus, *Belarus Secret* (New York: Alfred A. Knopf, 1982). Alexander Berkis writes under the heading "Useful Idiots" that the OSI entered into collaboration with the Soviet secret police and that some Baltic refugees were deported from the U.S. on the basis of forged evidence. According to him, Allan A. Ryan's book *Quiet Neighbors* (1984) with great zeal justifies the activities of the OSI, characterizing Latvians, Lithuanians and Estonians in general as collaborators with the Germans and engaging in character assassination of the three peoples. Berkis 2001.

35. *Yearbook of the Occupation Museum of Latvia* 1999, 280.

36. Klas-Göran Karlsson, "Holocaust, Soviet Terror...," in *Yearbook of the Museum of the Occupation of Latvia* 2003, 24. To Karlsson, "the silence on the Soviet terror and on the Holocaust is in my opinion a problem not only for Russia, but also for the world that wishes to integrate Russia into a community of European values."

37. Dzintars Ērglis, "A Few Episodes...," Nollendorfs and Oberländer 2005, 176. Steven Springfield, the president of the New York organization "Jewish Survivors of Latvia," which at times has been fairly hostile to Latvians, writes in the September 2006 newsletter: "Regrettably, the work of foreign researchers in the state archives of the Russian Federation has been severely hindered until now. At the same time, the Russian authorities have selectively used archival material to cultivate a one-sided interpretation of history for propaganda purposes, e.g. to incite ethnic hostility and discredit Latvia in the eyes of the international

community." *From the President. "NO" to the Misuse of Tragic Pages From Latvian Political History!* September 2006 Newsletter.

38. Interview of Ilgvars Dižgalvis who served with the US counter-intelligence in Germany after the war; Blum 1977, 222, 228.

39. Heikki Matiskainen, *Kanava* 9/2005; *Museum of the Occupation...*, 2002. Sweden turned over to the Soviet Union more than 2,000 German soldiers, and soon afterwards, in January of 1946, some Balts too, of whom the greatest number, 152, were Latvians. There was widespread protest in Sweden, and some Latvians committed suicide. Many consider Sweden to have violated the Geneva Treaty and the Hague Convention. Sweden publicly apologized to the Baltic countries in 1994, but did not wish to grant reparations to the victims. It is still written that the Balts were "volunteers" in German forces and "probably" took part in murdering Jews. See Matiskainen 2005.—This episode was of course only a drop in the bucket, for the West forcibly sent back a total of two million refugees to the East from 1944 to 1947. See Julius Epstein, 1973; Mark Wyman, 1998, 64.

40. According to this statement, the Nazis had killed 300,000 people in Rīga and its environs, in addition to which 200,000 Jews brought from elsewhere to Latvia and 40,000 children were said to have been killed. In every figure there are one or two extra zeros, in other words, the errors are more than tenfold. *Mājas Viesis*, October 17, 2003 and February 3, 2006. In the same class of accuracy is the "data" that 20,000 Red partisans were said to have been active in the Latvian area during the war. Documents have revealed that there were only around 800. Heinrihs Strods in *Mājas Viesis*, April 8, 2005.

41. At the Velikaya River in March of 1943, both Latvian divisions were fighting to stem the advance of the Red Army toward the west. One might say that at the outset the date for the anniversary was not chosen too wisely, for Velikaya is Russian territory, and thus it is difficult to present the battle as only a defensive one. The event was first celebrated in exile. The unthinking way in which the day was declared a national holiday in Latvia and then rescinded is, unfortunately, a typical example of hasty decisions by the government and parliament in newly independent Latvia.

42. *Latvijas Avīze*, December 29, 2005 and February 1, 2006. The news and analysis service AIA recently wrote that the Russian foreign ministry and intelligence service had begun "a black propaganda campaign" to discredit the Latvian president and prevent her choice as the UN Secretary General. According to the article, "Information about Vaira Vīķe-Freiberga's alleged neo-Nazi and revanchist views is being diffused through confidential contacts, without any reference to the official Russian sources." "The Kremlin Crosses out Candidates for UN SG Post," AIA, April 10, 2006.

43. *Helsingin Sanomat* and *Diena* October 13, 2006.

44. *Diena*, March 20, 2006.

45. Feldmanis and Kangeris, "Patiesība par latviešu SS brīvprātīgo leģionu," [Truth about the Latvian SS Volunteer Legion] *Latvijas Avīze*, March 15, 2004; Ezergailis 1996, 8. In addition (according to old Soviet statistics) 240,000 people from elsewhere in Europe would have been brought to Latvia to be killed. Among the rest, 39,831 children and 330,632 Soviet prisoners of war would have been murdered in Latvia.—The number of victims was exaggerated all through the USSR by factor of three or more. Edward Anders, a Jew who lived in Liepāja in 1941, says the following about the first mass murder in Liepāja on July 3, 1941: the 43 victims were exhumed and reburied a few days later. The Soviet extraordinary commission report for Liepāja claims 1,430 victims for that date, a 33-fold exaggeration.

46. *Lauku Avīze*, July 28, 1998.

47. *Latvijas Avīze*, March 14, 2006.

48. Ibid., Februay 2, 2007.

49. Martin Séamus in *The Irish Times*, March 11, 2006.

50. Latvian television news, February 24, 2006.

51. Certain Russian-Latvian politicians helped in the making of the film. One of them, a member of the parliament, also arranged for its showing in the parliament's quarters in Rīga and praised it for its truthfulness. He was dismissed from his post on the foreign affairs committee after a two-hour discussion by a vote of 64–18, after which his party members announced in the EU parliament that in Latvia, those opposed to Nazism were persecuted.—Let the following testify to the "rise of neo-Nazism:" Jack Hunter, a special agent of the U.S. State Department and head of an anti-terrorist unit, commented on the accusations against the Latvians in an interview in January 2006. He was concerned about the recent racist attacks on and murders of dark-skinned people in Russia, and he said this among other comments: "In my opinion, Russia is the state in which there are the most neo-Nazis, neo-fascists, and skinheads." *Latvijas Avīze*, January 28, 2006, and March 10, 2007; *The Moscow Times*, "Fighting past battles," March 24, 2006.

52. *Latvijas Avīze*, April 27, 2006.

53. I have seen only the trailer of the film (in fact, the final version of the film was not even ready yet). It seems to me that the film-makers have somehow found and interviewed all the worst and best-known Latvia-bashers – and only them. There were so many half-truths and distortions, that I did not have time write them all down while looking at it. This is the trailer's last comment on Latvia: "Hitler would be proud!" Experts told me the film had "obscure origins" or was "a Russian job." Bradford says his ideas come just from British thinking. He says that nationalistic laws annoy him. "The more I learn about Latvia the more my dislike of the nationalistic movement there is re-affirmed. ... Latvia

today is behaving, in my view, like it is on a vendetta … ." E-mail to Andrejs Ozoliņš, July 16, 2007.

54. See Lācis 2006 on what a former legionnaire thinks and how the outside world has seen the Legion at different times. With regard to the Latvian legionnaires in general, see also Kažociņš 1999; Mirdza Kate Baltais 1999; Jēkabsons and Ščerbinskis 1998, 45–46; Eksteins 1999, 158; Kārlis Kangeris in *Latvian War Museum Yearbook 2000*.

Chapter 9   (Pages 143–156)

1.   This is in essence what the Russian ambassador thought after taking a tour in the Museum of the Occupation of Latvia in 2005. He was not impressed by what he saw, and reminded others that the Russians had also suffered. And that materially Latvia had gained a lot from the Soviet Union.

2.   For example, in November 19, 1998, the Russian Duma passed a resolution to "remind deputies of the Latvian *Saeima* that Latvia's being a part of the Soviet Union was grounded in fact and by law."

3.   *Latvijas Avīze*, May 9, 2006.—The Russian born ballet dancer Mikhail Baryshnikov, Rīga's most famous living native son, calls his parents "occupiers" in Rīga. The minute he returned to Rīga in 1998, he "realized that this was never my home. My heart didn't even skip one beat." *The New Yorker*, January 19, 1998.

4.   *Mājas Viesis*, March 17, 2006; Muižnieks 2006, 53.

5.   Bleiere and others 2006, 332–334.

6.   Kultūras Diena, May 7, 2005.

7.   *Le Nouvelle Revue d'Histoire*, quoted in *Latvijas Avīze*, March 6, 2006.—In 2006, however, in the preface of a new book by Russian and Lithuanian researchers, prominent historians from the Russian Academy of Science seem to admit the fact of occupation: "[in 1940] the Soviet Army took over much of Lithuania. Thus the Soviet Union began the occupation and the subsequent annexation process in Lithuania and other Baltic States." *Diena*, August 10, 2006.

8.   *Eurasia Daily Monitor*, Jamestown Foundation, May 21, 2005; *RIA Novosti* May 10, 2005. A bit earlier, the Russian Foreign Ministry had issued a statement which similarly claimed that the USSR could not possibly have occupied what it already possessed. *Interfax*, May 2, 2005.

9.   Irēne Šneidere, "The First Soviet Occupation Period in Latvia 1940–1941" in Nollendorfs and Oberländer 2005, 33.

10. Strods 2004, 17.

11. Treaties which were broken: http://letton.ch. Many of the relevant treaties between Latvia and the USSR dealing with the occupation in 1940 can be found in English in a very thorough (537 pages) compilation of documents in *Report of the Select Committee … 1954*.

12. Magnus Ilmjärv, who is very critical of Ulmanis' actions, writes of the strange relations between Ulmanis and the Soviets in his book *Hääletu alistumine* [Quiet Submission] (Tallinn: Argo, 2004).

13. Jüri Ants, "Eriti salajane" [Top Secret]. *Postimees*-series of newspaper articles in 1999.

14. Editorial, *Diena*, March 18, 2006; *Financial Times*, March 28, 2005.

15. *Latvijas Avīze* December 12, 2005 and December 27, 2005. In December 2006 the Ambassador said that it is "childish" to speak about occupation now that Latvia together with the USA has occupied Iraq.

16. Davies 1996, 1004–1005; Ants 1999; Inesis Feldmanis, "Latvia under the Occupation of National Socialist Germany 1941–1945" in Nollendorfs and Oberländer 2005, 78; Bonifācijs Daukšts, "NKVD un Gestapo sadarbības..." [The Cooperation of the NKVD and the Gestapo...], *Kultūras Diena* 15/2006; Burleigh, op. cit., 823; Inesis Feldmanis, "Lai mēs paši un arī pasaule izprot..." [So That We and Also the World Would Understand...], *Latvijas Vēstnesis*, October 3, 2000. The chief American prosecutor wrote in his diary that the "Russian list of sins does not look much smaller than the German."—In Britain the truth was known almost from the beginning, but every effort was made to suppress the facts about the Katyn massacre because London was committed to the alliance with Stalin. As late as 1989 the Foreign Office proclaimed that it was unclear what had happened at Katyn.—In March 2006 the Russian chief Military Prosecutor's Office failed to recognize Katyn victims as victims of Stalinist's repression and victims of genocide. According to the representative of the Polish president, the decision was "shocking." News agency PAP, March 5, 2006. In a similar fashion, the foreign ministers of Russia and other former Soviet republics decided, after voting at a CIS meeting in the spring of 2006, not to treat as ethnic murder the famine which raged in Ukraine during Stalin's rule in 1932–1933 and killed millions of people. Several Western countries have recognized the famine as genocide.

17. *Cīņa*, December 28, 1989; Fredén 2005; Ants 1999. At that same time the Yugoslavian jurist Konstantin Obradovich wrote: "If it could be proved that the voting in the Baltic States [in 1940] had been carried out under duress and that unification with the USSR was not in accord with the will of these peoples, 'the incorporation into the USSR' would at the very least become open to question from the aspect of international law," because "any territorial alteration effected in defiance of the right of self-determination would have to be considered unlawful and illegitimate." "The Hitler-Stalin Pact...," *Review of International Affairs*, Belgrade, Vol. XX, No. 949 (1989)

18. One Latvian party (TB/LNNK) proposed in 2007 a new law that would make it a crime to either deny or to publicly exhort to denial of "the fact of occupation of Latvia." The model was the "Holocaust denial law" of some European countries.

19. Professors Viesturs Sprude and Antonijs Zunda in *Latvijas Avīze*, October 17, 2005.

20. Uldis Bluķis, 2002, 3 (47).—Walt Disney already took the side of Latvians in his movie *Bernard and Bianca* in 1977: in the "United Nations of the Mice" one can see representatives of "Latvia" seated.

21. Welles in July 23, 1940 (right after the Soviet-organized elections in the occupied Baltics): "The people of the United States are opposed to predatory activities no matter whether they are carried out by the use of force or by the threat of force. They are likewise opposed to any form of intervention on the part of one state, however powerful, in the domestic concerns of any other sovereign state, however weak." Statement by the Undersecretary..., www.letton.ch.

22. Heinrihs Strods, "Sovietization of Latvia 1944–1991" in Nollendorfs and Oberländer 2005, 213; Strods 2004, 33; Krēsliņš 2006, 240.

23. Churchill understood that the Soviets needed a "buffer zone," and he recommended to Roosevelt that they should not be denied the borders they had in 1941. On the other hand he criticized the way Soviet occupiers treated the Balts. In October of 1939, when Russia was pressuring the Baltic countries for an agreement on bases, Churchill (not yet Prime Minister) said to the Soviet Ambassador: "Only a few sentimental liberals and Labour politicians are in tears because of the Soviet protectorate in the Baltic area." Ilmjärv 2004, 662; Medijainen and Made 2002, 109; Rislaki 2004, 184; Eksteins 1999, 164–165; Antonijs Zunda in *Latvijas Vēstnesis*, March 23, 2005; *Museum of the Occupation...*2000, 84; Nollendorfs and Oberländer 2005, 331.

24. Ezergailis and others 2005, 199–200.

25. Krēsliņš 2006, 102–103.

26. Roosevelt added with a smile that of course "the USA was not going to go to war against the Soviet Union because of the Baltic republics;" he could not speak in this manner publicly because, according to his words, he had to think of the voters of Baltic ancestry living in the USA. The Balts "wished to join the Soviet Union," but Roosevelt hoped "that the opinion of people supporting it could somehow be made manifest." Stalin said he understood Roosevelt's position and declared: "They will have many opportunities to express their desires according to the constitution of the Soviet Union." Later he said that the Balts had already voted (in 1940) on joining the USSR. *Foreign Relations of the United States* ...1961; Baltais 1999, 81; Tuomo Polvinen, *Teheranista Jaltaan* [From Teheran to Yalta] (Porvoo: WSOY 1980); Harriman & Abel, 1976, 278–279; *Museum of the Occupation...*, 84; Eksteins 2000, 195–196. A.E. Senn, "Baltic Battleground;" Feldmanis, "Latvia under the Occupation..." and Uldis Neiburgs, "Western Allies..." in Nollendorfs and Oberländer 2005, 28, 89, 137; Bleiere and others 2006, 323.

27. Churchill 1983.

28. Churchill was "absolutely euphoric" at the end of the conference and spoke in glowing terms of the Soviet desire to cooperate. American public opinion was highly favorable to the Soviet Union, too. Soviets, however, refused to hold the free elections in Poland Stalin had promised, and arrested the leaders of the Polish underground. This was the issue that soon led to the break between East and West. Gerhard Weinberg 1994, 809.

29. *The New Encyclopaedia Britannica*, 15th edition, 1976, 10:706. In the 1967 edition there was still an article on the history of Latvia starting in 1918 – factual and quite objective.—Of the errors in the 1976 edition: Latvia was proclaimed a Soviet Socialist Republic *in July* 1940, and *in August* it became one of the republics of the Soviet Union.—Russian history had not disappeared from the encyclopedia in 1976: there was still an entry called *Russia* in addition to the *Soviet Union.*

30. Rudīte Vīksne: "Soviet Repressions...," in Nollendorfs and Oberländer 2005, 55 ; Aivars Stranga, "Latvijas okupācija un iekļaušana PSRS (1940–1941)" [The Occupation of Latvia and Its Joining the USSR], *Latvijas Avīze*, August 2–4, 2004.

31. Pelkaus 1999, 127; Ainars Bambals, 1999, 92–158.

32. Senn, op. cit., 21–22. As mentioned before, the Latvian Reds proclaimed in Latvian Livland (except for Rīga) a Bolshevik dictatorship that lasted from November 1917 to February 1918.—According to the Russians, Germany's defeat in WW II meant that Soviet Russia had regained its rights over the Baltic provinces that had belonged to the Russian Empire. Russia annulled the 1918 treaty of Brest-Litovsk interpreting this act as the reinstatement of its legal power over the region. Bleiere and others 2006, 129.

33. Seppo Myllyniemi, "Consequences of the Hitler-Stalin Pact for the Baltic Republics and Finland" in *From Peace to War* (New York: 1966); Stranga, "Latvijas okupācija..." in *Latvijas Avīze*, August 2–4, 2004.

34. *Museum of the Occupation...*, 202–204.

35. *Diena*, May 21, 2004. Again, one might ask: what then about some European countries occupied by Nazis, where local quislings took part in governing under varying degrees of autonomy?

36. Bleiere and others 2006, 146; Convention on the Prevention and Punishment of the Crime of Genocide Approved by General Assembly resolution 260 A (III) of 9 December 1948, entry into force 12 January 1951. Also Article 6 of the International Criminal Court defines Genocide as a crime.

37. Nevertheless, when the Latvian justice system tried to sentence KGB veterans who had participated in deportations and old Red partisans who had murdered civilians, Moscow conducted a propaganda campaign on behalf of the accused and offered them legal aid in the form of money and attorneys.

38. According to Strods, everything went like this: occupation, annexation, incorporation, colonization. Strods 2004, 17.—In 2007, professor Strods was refused a visa to visit Russian archives.

39. *Diena*, March 25, 2003 and March 31, 2004.

40. Strods 2005, 210.

41. *Latvijas Avīze*, December 6, 2004; Bleiere and others 2006, 160; Aivars Beika, "Latvians in the Soviet Union: The Victims of Communist Terror, 1929–1939," in *Yearbook of the Museum of the Occupation of Latvia* 1999, 89–91; Aivars Stranga, "Contributions of the Latvian Commission of Historians to Holocaust Research," in *Yearbook of the Museum of the Occupation of Latvia* 2001, 281–282. Stranga writes that "only" 23,065 Latvians, most of the repressed, disappeared in the Soviet Union at the end of the1930's, and furthermore that Russians "did not love the Latvians" because of the role they had in the Russian civil war and in the secret police. Instead Stranga would be ready to use the term genocide speaking of Latvia in the 1940's. Aivars Beika (see chapter 4), who has calculated that 15.23 percent of Russia's Latvians were eliminated, speaks of genocide.

42. *Museum of the Occupation…*2002, 108.

43. Bleiere in Nollendofs and Oberländer 2005, 255. To her "social genocide" was what happened to the Latvian countryside.

44. Edward Anders' E-mail to author, October 29, 2006.

45. Again one may ask, was it a "hostile army," taking into consideration Ulmanis' speech. If Czechoslovakia did not resist Hitler, was there no occupation? What about Denmark in 1940?

46. Bergmanis, Jansons, Zālīte, "The Activities and Tasks of LSSR Agencies of National Security" in Nollendorfs and Oberländer, 277. This would apply if Latvia was an occupied country and the partisans were thus considered members of the Latvian military, for which there is ample evidence.

47. *Kultūras Diena*, May 7, 2005; On January 13…, www.letton.ch.

48. Congressional Record Vol 112, No 183, Washington DC, 22 October 1966.

49. The European Court of Human Rights, Grand Chamber Judgment Ždanoka v. Latvia (58278/00), March 16, 2006. Tatjana Ždanoka, a member of the European Parliament, a Latvian citizen, and a parliament member during the Soviet era, had sued the state of Latvia for refusing to accept her as a candidate in the parliamentary elections of 1998 and 2002, and she had also had to give up her membership on the Rīga city council. Ždanoka had been a member of the "Interfront," that opposed Latvian independence. She had not resigned from, but continued to be active in the Communist Party after the bloody acts committed by the Soviet troops in January 1991. The party was outlawed for opposing the

Latvian constitution. The court decided by a vote of 13–4 that Latvia had not violated Ždanoka's human rights (rights to free elections, freedom of assembly and association, freedom of expression), nor did it need to pay her reparations. The court decided that Ždanoka had played "an active and leading role in a party which was directly linked to the attempted violent overthrow of the newly-established democratic regime" and which aimed at the "restoration of a totalitarian regime." The court added that the Latvian decision can be considered acceptable in a country like Latvia, in view of the historico-political context, but that in old and established democracies such a measure could scarcely be considered acceptable.—A little earlier, in January 2006, the Court rejected as groundless a complaint made by a Russian military pensioner against the government of Estonia, which ordered him to leave the country after 20 years of residence. RIA-Novosti, January 24, 2006.—In the year 2005 alone, the Court received 345 claims from Latvia. *The* Baltic Times, April 20, 2006.

50.   To be precise, the last of the Russian troops left Latvia only in 1998, when they vacated the giant radar station at Skrunda and American engineering troops demolished it.

Chapter 10   (Pages 157–171)

1.   In the 1940's Latvia lost 30 % of its population, Estonia 25 % and Lithuania 15 % see Misiunas and Taagepera 1993, 329. For recent estimates by Latvian investigators, see my chapter 1.

2.   Davies 2007, 86

3.   Krēsliņš 2006, 391. Latvians were killed elsewhere as well. In the opinion of historian Oto Lācis the Soviet state's "greatest crime against the Latvians" was their liquidation in the USSR in 1937. Thousands were murdered in a short time – every third Latvian man, for example. *Latvijas Avīze*, October 22, 2002.

4.   For a more accurate table: *Yearbook of the Museum of the Occupation of Latvia* 2001, 95.

5.   Wyman 1998, 162.

6.   Data from Mirdza Kate Baltais and Valters Nollendofs. Part of these Latvians were former forced labourers and KZ inmates. Alexander Berkis writes that there were at least 134,000 Latvian political refugees in 1947, the overwhelming majority of them in West Germany, "and this is a minimum estimate." Berkis 2001. At Yalta, in February 1945, Americans, British and Russians signed a secret agreement on liberated prisoners of war and civilians. "Soviet citizens" (according to Moscow's interpretation, Balts were also included) were to be kept in separate camps until they would be turned over to Soviet officials, who were freely admitted to the camps, where hostile propaganda was prohibited. Soviet citizens were "subject to repatriation without regard to their

personal wishes." Balts and Ukrainians were soon not forced to return anymore, but in Western German refugee camps, Latvians were influenced and pressured to return home. Most of them, however, refused and preferred to wait in uncertain and deprived circumstances for years to get work in some western country. Ibid., 62–63: Mela and Vaba 2005, 98.

7. *Jaunā Gaita*, June 2005.

8. Ibid.

9. *Diena*, September 21, 2006.

10. Mela and Vaba 2005, 103.

11. William L. Shirer 1962, 1 041.

12. Heinrihs Strods, "Top Secret Operation 'Priboi'...," in Yearbook of the Museum of the Occupation of Latvia 1999, 186. See the books *Aizvestie* [The Deported] and *These Names Accuse*; Bleiere and others 2006, 264. On the same night there were large deportations from Estonia, Lithuania, and Moldavia. The deportations were recommended to the party leadership by the state's new people's national security director Vsevolod Merkulov on the 16 th of April. The deportees would live in the camps for 5–7 years, after which they would be banished to the far reaches of the Soviet land for 20 years. Jānis Riekstiņš, "The 14 June 1941 Deportation in Latvia" in Nollendorfs and Oberländer 2005, 65, 70–71.

13. *Chas*, June 14, 2005.

14. Interior Minister S. Kruglov's top secret communication to the Soviet Union's leadership, May 9, 1949 now in LVA (Latvian State Archive); Misiunas and Taagepera 1993, 94–107; *Museum of the Occupation of Latvia* 2002; *Mājas Viesis*, June 12, 1999; Senn: "Baltic Battleground" in Nollendorf and Oberländer 2005, 29, and Bleiere Ibid., 250, and Bergmanis and others Ibid., 278.; Bleiere and others 2006, 355.

15. Krēsliņš 2006, 391; Jānis Riekstiņš, "Die Befreiung der Deportierten...," in Ērglis 2004, 604.

16. "Psiholoģiskos zaudejumus naudā neizteikt" [Psychological Losses Cannot Be Measured with Money] in *Latvijas Avīze*, March 24, 2007.

17. Ibid., November 14, 2006. He tells of having asked Dutch editors and students – generally in vain – why they do not use the word "occupation" although they knew the Baltics were occupied; why they call the Baltic peoples nationalistic but not their own queen, who does not speak German to Germans; why they demand that the Baltic peoples forget the past and look to the future although they themselves celebrate the fact that Holland was freed from five years of German occupation 60 years ago.

18. Pelkaus 1999, 337.

19. The 17 Latvian Communist Protest Letter, http://www.letton.ch/lvx_17com.htm; *Republika.lv*, February 16–22, 2007; Edward Anders' letter, October 18, 2004.

20. Plakans (ed.) 2007, 240; *Migranti Latvijā* 2004, 126; Aldis Bergmanis, "Repressive System of Occupation," in Ērglis 2004, 432; Mela and Vaba 2005, 113; The 17 Latvian Communist Protest Letter, op. cit.

21. *Migranti Latvijā* 2004, 127–134.

22. Rislaki 2004, 283–284; *Museum of the Occupation of Latvia* 2002, 164–165, 169; Bleiere and others 2006, 394–403; Strods, Sovietization... Nollendorfs and Oberländer 2005, 225; Küng 1979, 69–73, 182–195; Pelkaus 1999, 361, 368, 541.

23. Kudu, 2004.

24. Inesis Feldmanis, "Waffen SS Units of Latvians and other Non-Germanic Peoples in World War II" in Nollendorfs and Oberländer 2005, 122; Jānis Riekstiņš, "Colonization and Russification of Latvia 1940–1989" ibid., 230; Inesis Feldmanis, "Lettische un andere nichtdeutsche...," in Erglis 2004, 350; Diena, March 25, 2003; Bleiere and others 2006, 332. It is in part just for this reason that some oppose the publication of the (incomplete) KGB archives left in Latvia: one cannot know about everyone why they were "agents" and what they did.

25. Leppänen 2002; Strods: "Sovietization..." in Nollendorfs and Oberländer 2005, 221, 238; *Eesti Entsüklopedia*: Läti, Eesti; Mauno Jokipii, 1992, 110; Bleiere and others 2005, 340–342.

26. Strods in *Diena*, January 31, 2004; Strods in Nollendorfs and Oberländer 2005, 290; Krēsliņš 2006, 36.

27. Krēsliņš 2006, 231.

28. Visuri 2006, 292.

29. Terras 1989; Anita Bormane, "Helsinkieši: Viņi bija sākumā" [The Helsinki People: They Were at the Beginning], *Mājas Viesis* July 7, 2006.

30. This has caused confusion later: many, especially abroad, believe Latvia to have become independent in May of 1990, not in August of 1991. Latvia adds to the confusion by celebrating only the May date and not the August one.

31. "Putin: Soviet collapse a genuine tragedy." msnbc News, April 25, 2005. According to the text of the speech Putin said: The collapse of the Soviet Empire "was the greatest geopolitical *catastrophe* of the century"

32. Visuri 2006, 292.

33. Berkis 2001, who on the other hand holds the view that Gorbachev's good reputation in the west is due to disinformation. Professor Berkis is a relative of General Krišjānis Berķis, the former Latvia's minister of war.

34. Sandra Kalniete in *Latvijas Avīze*, August 21, 2006.

35. Elizabeth Drew in *The New Yorker*, May 14, 1990.

36. Medijainen–Made 2002; Beschloss–Talbott 1993; Uldis Bluķis, 2002, 3(47).—In his August 1991 speech in Kiev George Bush, Sr. warned against the breakup of the USSR.

Chapter 11   (Pages 173–180)

1.   *Daily Telegraph*, January 3, 2006.

2.   Uldis Neiburgs, "Western Allies in Latvian Public Opinion and Nazi Propaganda" in Nollendorfs and Oberländer 2005, 135–136.

3.   Sherwood 1948, 979; Krēsliņš 2006, 103.

4.   Evolution des points de vue sur l'annexation de la Lettonie de 1940 á 1990. www.letton.ch.

5.   *Diena*, February 2, 2006. Some one thousand journalists took part in a press conference lasting for many hours. Putin said that "we have in Rīga" (u nas v Rige) 60 percent Russians. He demanded that their problems be settled according to norms generally approved by the world. He again offered Macedonia as an example. (In Macedonia 25 percent of the population is Albanian, which by an armed guerilla movement forced the granting of special privileges to their group, and the country became a dual nation.)

6.   In the same breath he admitted having drunk a lot of beer during his student days, but having nevertheless learned something by virtue of his good teachers.

7.   The *St. Petersburg Times*, March 11, 2005.

8.   Muižnieks 2006, 88; "Russia aims directly...," http://lettonie.ch.

9.   Solzhenitsyn wrote his world-renowned Gulag Archipelago in rural Estonia protected by brave Estonians, who saved his manuscript by hiding it. The KGB never managed to pick up their trail. When Estonia became independent and the writer returned from exile to Russia, they wrote to him that Estonia was being "smothered" by its former occupiers and asked him to help them as he had promised to. They told me in an interview in the year 2000 that his reply was harsh: the Estonians helped the communists by being the first to make peace in 1920; Estonians fought with the Red forces; Estonians submitted without resisting the occupation of 1940; Estonians hated the Russians and had founded an organization for the defense of the "oppressed Finno-Ugric" peoples. Jukka Rislakki, "Suden talo, Solzhenitsynin pesä" ["The Wolf House, Solzhenitsyn's Nest"], *Helsingin Sanomat*, February 27, 2000.

10. LETA–AFP, April 28, 2006; *The Guardian*, April 28, 2006.

11. *Latvijas Avīze*, March 9, 2006.

12. Medijainen and Made 2002, 138.

13. The Russians protested in 2005 when the city of Rīga would not give them permission to transmit this kind of television program from a central square. The cameras and the guests were taken to the roof of a Rīga house owned by Russia.

14. Lithuania is now the largest; it became larger in 1940 and Latvia smaller in 1944.

15. Rislaki 2004, 179.
16. Medijainen and Made 2002, 115–116, 134.
17. *Financial Times*, March 31, 2006. Among others, George Kennan, the expert on Russia, was first stationed in Rīga.
18. Tannberg 2003.
19. *Latvijas valstij 80*, exhibition catalog, LVVA 1998; Muižnieks 2006, 132.
20. *Diena*, January 6, 2007; Muižnieks 2006.
21. Pitkänen, 1998.
22. "Simon Araloff on the Baltic States Stuck Between Russia and the West" in AIA 9, May 2006 http://www.axisglobe.com/article.asp?article=841.
23. Pitkänen 1998.
24. *Kultūras Diena*, March 3, 2006.
25. Davies 2007, 85.
26. Ivanovs in Nollendorfs and Oberländer 2005, 263–4, 352.
27. Article in the *Nezavisimoje Vojennoje Obozrenije* newspaper, reference: *Latvijas Avīze*, April 26, 2006. The writer asserts that if Latvia demands Pytalovo, then Russia can demand the city of Tartu from the Estonians "because it was founded by a Russian prince, Jaroslav the Wise, in the year 1030."
28. "Documents of Soviet Intelligence: The Abrene Region is Latvian Territory" in AIA 5, November 2005. As the name makes clear, the article says that during the war Soviet intelligence reports treated the area as Latvian and used the name Abrene.
29. Muižnieks 2006, 131.
30. *Eesti Noukogude Entsüklopeedia* IV (Tallinn: 1972), 543.
31. Ivanovs op. cit, 263.
32. Visuri 2006, 296.
33. Medijainen and Made 2002, 117, 137.
34. Interview with Gundars Zaļkalns, the then secretary of the Latvian Security Council.

Chapter 12 (Pages 181–191)

1. Lars Fredén, "Shadows of the Past in Russia and the Baltic Countries," *Russia in Global Affairs*, No 3, July–September 2005.
2. *Latvijas Avīze*, November 11, 2006.
3. Ibid., December 12, 2005. Yearly some 12,000 more Latvians die than are born.
4. Erkki Toivanen, "Imperiumien paluu historiaan" [The Return of Empires to History] in *Kanava* 7/2006.

5. In 1930, Latvia was still even wealthier than Finland – Latvia's national income was (estimated) 620 lats per capita, Finland's 600 lats per capita. Professor Aivars Stranga in *Latvijas Avīze*, May 15, 2004. Professor Heinrihs Strods said recently: "If the occupation had not occurred, we would not be living on one hundred lats per month, but would be at the same level as Finland."

6. GNP per capita (on the basis of purchasing power). At the beginning of 2006 it was estimated that, thus calculated, Poland was slightly poorer than Latvia. In 2004, the GDP per inhabitant in Latvia was (according to purchasing power) 45.5 % of the EU's average. Eurostat, February 2007.

7. Kimmo Kiljunen, *Valtiot ja liput* [States and Flags] (Keuruu: Otava 2002). Purchasing power corrected GDP per capita in Finland was 2.6 times that of Latvia in 2004. Eurostat 2005.

8. In the Nordea Bank estimate of 2006. Latvia's economic growth at present is Europe's most rapid – for example, in 2006 it was over 11%.

9. *Latvijas Vēstnesis*, May 16, 2002; Mela and Vaba 2005, 128. GNP per capita fell 28.7 percent in 1990–2000 and the value of Latvia's imports 49 percent. GDP per capita on the basis of purchasing power was $ 5,094 in 1989 and $ 3,313 in 1995. The standard of living was higher even in the 1970's. The incomes of city dwellers declined until the year 2000 by 25% and of rural dwellers by about a half. Clearly less in the way of food products were bought than before.

10. *Latvijas Vēstnesis*, May 16, 2002; *The White Book 1940–1991*. Estonian State Commission's Examination of the Politics of Repression. Tallinn 2005, 169.

11. *Diena*, May 16, 2006; *Baltic Guide*, December 2006. The minimum monthly wage increased to 120 lats in 2007. In contrast, the State Employment Agency found that 170 lats a month before tax were needed to survive. 29 % of jobs offered in Rīga were paying lower or only slightly above the survival level.

12. Bleiere and others 2006, 40–41.

13. Ibid., 42–43.

14. Ibid., 53–54.

15. Gyllenbögel, 1946, 80–88.

16. Riekstiņš: The 14 June…, in Nollendorfs and Oberländer 2005, 74.

17. Pelkaus 1999, 242; Mela and Vaba 2005, 99.

18. *Diena*, June 14, 2002; *Mājas Viesis*, March 4, 2005.

19. *Latvijas Avīze*, November 14, 2005.

20. *Linguafranca* op. cit. Latvia's delegation to Moscow in 1940 petitioned for annexation to the Soviet Union on the basis, among other things, that the people were living in hunger. That astonished even some members of the delegation.

21. Total farmland in Latvia was 2.26 million hectares in 1939 and 1.67 mil-
     lion hectares in 1985. There were over 1.27 million head of cattle in 1939
     and under 1.22 million head in 1985. In addition to grain, the production
     of potatoes also crashed. *We Accuse*, Latvian National Foundation,
     Stockholm 1985; Bleiere and others 2006, 386–392.

22. Daina Bleiere, "Repression against Farmers in Latvia in 1944–1953" in
     Nollendorfs and Oberländer 2005, 243, 255.

23. *Latvija citu valstu saimē*, 26–27, 39–40, 60, 64, 70–71. In the 1930's there
     were proportionately more college students in Latvia than in the rest of
     Europe and Latvians were on the average the largest consumers of meat,
     milk, and butter. Only Denmark printed more books per capita than
     Latvia.

24. *Latvijas Avīze*, November 14, 2005.

25. *SNTL:n Korkeimman Neuvoston seitsemäs sessia* [Seventh session of the
     USSR Supreme Soviet] 1.8.–7.8.1940. Pikakirjoituspöytäkirja [Shorthand
     records], Moscow 1940.

26. *Diena*, April 27, 2002. An estimated 50,000 to 100,000 Latvian workers
     have left for Western Europe during Latvian membership in the EU,
     which in the opinion of some investigators is an even greater threat to
     the language and the culture than Soviet rule.

27. Quality of Life, http://www.worldbank.org/data
     08/01/05.

28. *Museum of the Occupation...* 2002, 181; Edward Anders' e-mail August
     18, 2007.

29. *We Accuse* 1985.

30. Eksteins 2000, 162.

31. Heinrihs Strods, "Resistance..." in Nollendorfs and Oberländer 2005,
     291.

32. Putin responded angrily to an Estonian journalist's question on the
     occupation in May 2005: "What else are we supposed to do, maybe
     condemn the Molotov–Ribbentrop pact every year? We consider this
     topic closed and will not return to it. It was denounced once, and that's
     enough." Jamestown Foundation, *Eurasia Daily Monitor*, May 21, 2005;
     RIA Novosti, May 10, 2005. Yeltsin mentioned "repression in Latvia" and
     the violent expulsion of many Latvian residents to Siberia in his brief
     speech in 1994 when the agreement on the withdrawal of the troops was
     signed; according to him, neither Russia nor the Russian people were
     responsible for what happened. Putin said in Slovakia in 2005: "We
     respect the opinion of those people in the Baltics who consider that the
     tragedy of the Baltic States' loss of independence was connected to the
     end of World War II." Fredén op. cit.

33. *Diena*, January 26, 2007; *Newsweek*, September 12, 2005. *Izvestija* con-
     ducted an opinion survey in which Russians were asked what they

thought of the Baltic demands for moral and economic compensation for the destruction wrought during the Soviet era. 26.3 percent said that Russia should apologize to the Baltic countries, 40.4 percent felt that Russia was not responsible. 33.3 percent replied: "They should apologize to us."

34. *The White Book*, Tallinn 2005. In preparing the book the researchers went through the damages during the occupation and the effects on the population, the economy, the environment, on health and culture. The occupiers directly caused the deaths of an estimated 90,000 Estonians. According to the book, the average life span before the occupation was longer than that of the Finns; now it is five-and-a-half years shorter. The damage to the environment caused by the Soviet Army alone is estimated at billions of Euros. In 2001 the Latvian refugee organization published the same sort of book, almost 600 pages long, about the occupation damages in Latvia: *Okupācijas varu nodarītie postījumi Latvijā 1940–1990* (Stockholm / Toronto / Rīga: Memento/Daugavas Vanagi, 2001).

35. *The Baltic Times*, March 30–April 5, 2006. In his visits to Hungary and the Czech republic, Putin expressed regret and claimed "moral responsibility" for the events of 1956 and 1968, when Soviet troops repressed democratic movements in these republics. A Russian presidential aide said that the Baltic States should follow the example of these two countries and not seek financial compensation. AFP, March 24, 2006.

36. *St. Petersburg Times*, March 11, 2005. On the other hand 77 % of Russians say they want to live in a free and democratic country. *Time*, April 10, 2006.

37. Paul Goble's column on the internet, March 6, 2006.

38. AIA, May 9, 2006.

39. Fredén op. cit.

Chapter 13   (Pages 193–203)

1. Russia's Council of Foreign and Defense Policy in 1997, quoted in Muižnieks 2006, 125.
2. Muižnieks 2006, 89.
3. *Helsingin Sanomat*, May 1, 2006.
4. Kennan, 1978, 115.
5. Muižnieks 2006, 89.
6. Ibid., 26, 119.
7. Interview in *Süddeutsche Zeitung* published on the Russian Foreign Ministry's web page, February 9, 2007.
8. *Latvijas Avīze*, January 21, 2006.

9.   Muižnieks 2006, 101. Sea, railroad, and road freight contributed a little over 3 percent to Latvia's 2005 GDP. As to trade, that same year 76 percent of Latvia's merchandise exports went to fellow members of the EU; Russia's share was 8 percent.

10. Ibid., 96.

11. Ibid., 92. The new policy concept is available on the web page www.mid. ru.

12. Carl Bildt, "The Baltic Litmus Test," in *Foreign Affairs* Vol. 73, No. 5 (1994), 72–85.

13. *The Baltic Times*, May 20–26, 2006. For more details on the 2005 crisis: Jukka Rislakki, "Fasisteja ja kuivattuja suolakaloja" [Fascists and Dried Salt Fish], *Kanava* 2/2005.

14. *Financial Times*, March 23, 2005.

15. Jukka Rislakki, "Latvian ja Venäjän suhteet aallonpohjassa" ["Latvian–Russian relationship at a low point"] in Rozentals-seuran vuosikirja, Helsinki 2005; Vitols Dixon 2006, 134–5; *The Baltic Times*, March 2–8, 2006.

16. Bush said in Rīga that the Yalta agreement was in the unjust tradition of the Munich and the Molotov–Ribbentrop pacts. According to him, it happened again that when the powerful governments negotiated, the freedom of small countries was shoved aside as a matter of secondary importance.

17. For examples see caricatura.ru.

18. Both official and unofficial Russia reacted angrily, when Estonia enacted a law prohibiting the public use of the Soviet and Nazi symbols – not to mention a law which permitted the moving of a Soviet soldier's statue from the center of Tallinn. The question was not one of "demolishing" the monument, as *The Guardian* wrote, or "tearing it down," as Associated Press wrote (March 3, 2007), but of dismantling and relocating it in a nearby military cemetery, as the Russian Interfax wrote in its cooler and more factual article. What followed when Estonia did move the statue in April 2007 is outside the scope of this book; another book could be written about it. Let us remember one thing: During the Soviet occupation the Russians destroyed every national monument on every military cemetery in the Baltic republics. As *The Baltic Times* wrote (May 3, 2007): "The extraordinary amount of errors, misinformation and abject lies in Russian reporting on the war monument removal ought to be documented by a team of journalism graduate students and used as a case study." To that newspaper, "the greatest lesson that will emerge will be the staggering hypocrisy and mass hysteria of Russian society and government, who have once again demonstrated their lack of preparedness for a place among civilized nations."

19. About two weeks after the fact, the majority of Saeima after a bitter debate finally voted to accept a somewhat watered-down resolution of support to Estonia.

20. *Helsingin Sanomat*, May 26, 2006; Muižnieks 2006, 95.
21. "Prime Minister and the 'Russians' of Estonia Rise in Arms Against AIA," AIA home page November 1, 2005.
22. Erkki Pennanen in *Helsingin Sanomat*, August 24, 2005.
23. *Diena*, January 2 and 19, 2007.
24. *Republika.lv*, January 12–28, 2007.
25. The Prime Minister thought that it would be enough to point to the August 1991 constitutional agreement on Latvia's continuity as a state; it in turn has a reference to the Latvian constitution of 1922 and to the Latvian Supreme Soviet's May 1990 declaration of the renewal of Latvia's independence, in which the Soviet occupation and the peace treaty of 1920 were mentioned.
26. *The Baltic Times*, March 9–15, 2006.
27. Jakobson 130.

Chapter 14   (Pages 205–210)
1. Vitols Dixon 2006, 64.
2. Valters Nollendorfs in *Museum of the Occupation...* 2002, 211.
3. *Diena*, March 28, 2007.
4. Latvian radio news, June 21. 2006.
5. " ... sound fiscal policy, wage moderation, reduction of inflation, containing credit growth and a reduction of the current account deficit. Not a single one of these recommendations have been met." Morten Hansen in *The Baltic Times*, January 25–31, 2007.
6. According to Eurobarometer, 9 percent of Latvia's inhabitants trust political parties, while the average in the EU countries is 17 percent. Apollo portal, January 9, 2007. The trust in the government and in the Saeima is well below the European average, too: 20 % and 18 % in 2007–a drop of 15 and 9 percentage points from 2005. *Diena*, July 20, 2007.
7. A survey in 1999 found that 78 percent of the respondents feel that "the bureaucratic system forces you to give bribes." In 2000 and 2001 surveys respondents were asked whether they personally could do anything to diminish corruption. 52 percent "could do nothing because the struggle is at the state level." When legislators, entrepreneurs, and high state and judicial employees were polled, 55 percent said that public officials should pursue their self-interest more than the good of the people. Karklins 2005, 63–64, 70–71. Kārkliņa, a well-known investigator of corruption, was a candidate to be Latvia's first ombudsman in 2007, but Saeima did not choose her because the prime minister did not support her.
8. The press has furiously attacked Transparency because it tried to reveal and oppose hidden media advertising in the elections of 2006.
9. In recent years, Finland has been rated the least corrupt country.

10. *Baltic Guide*, October 2006.

11. Karklins 2005, 12.

12. Interviews with Finnish businessmen working in Latvia.

13. Kārkliņš writes that *state capture* means *"de facto* takeover of state institutions, building personal fiefdoms, exploiting public institutions for enrichment." According to her, Latvia ranks low in administrative corruption but high in *state capture*, almost on a par with Russia. Karklins 2005, 29, 48, 50.

14. The Latvian Law Society president opposed the founding of KNAB and considered the agency to be "useless." Ibid., 2005, 64. KNAB has already exposed several cases of large-scale corruption.

15. Interviw with security expert Gundars Zaļkalns in 2006. However, the first millionaire-politicians were arrested in 2007.

16. The news agency LETA account of the press conference called by the president on March 10, 2007.

17. The intent of the bribe was to guarantee that the then mayor of Jūrmala stayed in office. He was finally sentenced to five years in prison in 2007, and his property was confiscated. Some of the accused impeded and evaded court trials and finally fled abroad. See for example Jukka Rislakki in *Helsingin Sanomat*, March 20, 2006.

18. That is exactly what happened. After I wrote this, the Saeima, with a practically unanimous coalition vote, elected as president an "independent" candidate, a physician, who was unknown and inexperienced in politics, was close to the biggest government party, was accused of corruption, and who had very little popular support. The government disclosed his name only just before the election – May 22 – while at the same time without explanations advancing the ballot from June 6 to May 31, 2007.

Acknowledgements   (Pages 211–220)

1. For the strange and mistaken news that circulated world wide that Walt Disney's Donald Duck was forbidden in Finland, see my articles in *Sarjainfo* 1/1978 and *Filmihullu* 7/1983. As I see it, this "information campaign" was begun by some Finnish right wing politicians and newspapers, which probably had no idea of the repercussions it would have. This is exactly the kind of stuff that the foreign news and entertainment pages in different countries love to spread.—For western history books' misconceptions about wartime Finland, see Professor Aira Kemiläinens article "Suomi puolusti läntisiä arvoja, mutta väärään aikaan" [Finland defended Western values, but at the wrong time] in *Kanava* 4–5, 2006.

2. New York: Sheridan Square Publications, 1986. See also Jukka Rislakki, "The Attempted Murder of the Pope, and The KGB. Investigative journalists, borrowing from one another, cooked up the story of the decade," *Helsingin Sanomat*, February 6, 1983.

3. "The USSR's AIDS Disinformation Campaign," Foreign Affairs Note. Department of State. July 1987.—The U.S. Department of State now runs a Web page called *Identifying Misinformation* (usinfo.state.gov/media/misinformation.html).—*The Economist* writes that Soviet propagandists planted specious stories in obscure corners of the media, and now Russia's interests are again being promoted by information sources that look plausible. An example is the International Council for Democratic Institutions and State Sovereignty (ICDISS), which has no address and no telephone number; its website is registered at a hotel address in Mexico and operated from a server in Latvia. *The Economist*, August 6–11, 2006.

4. Dershowitz 2003.

5. Ilan Pappe and Norman Finkelstein, known for their sharp criticism of Dershowitz and other "Zionists," consider that "Israel must be guilty in Dershowitz's mind, as becomes apparent in The Case for Israel, which defends his client's most obvious crime – its human rights record." According to Professor Finkelstein, Dershowitz has copied the thesis and the footnotes of his book from Joan Peters' work, *From Time Immemorial*, "which historians don't take seriously." *Bookforum*, February 2006; *Kanava* 2/2006, 118–122.

6. Dershowitz 2003, 6. It should be said, however, that he writes later in the same book: "Nor do I try to defend egregious actions by Israelis or their allies, such as the 1948 killings by irregular troops of civilians at Deir Yassin, the 1982 Phalangist massacre of Palestinians in the Sabra and Shatilla refugee camps, or the 1994 mass murder of Muslims at prayer by Baruch Goldstein."

7. Columnist Olli Kivinen in *Helsingin Sanomat*, September 6, 2005.

8. This point of the letter demands an answer. I asked the Latvians for help only in seeking information for my book; I did not request or expect funding help from anyone, either in official or private circles. However, Andris Prieditis, who now lives in Toronto, offered me a stipend from his deceased wife's private foundation for writing the book during the year 2006. I wish to express my gratitude to him.

9. Myllyniemi's e-mail to the author, February 10, 2007.

10. Plakans' e-mail to the author, September 1, 2006.

11. Nollendorfs and Oberländer 2005, Introduction.

12. The President of Latvia Vaira Vīķe-Freiberga has said: "It turns out that, after all, the victims are expected to ask the world for forgiveness for being inconveniently in the way of the great powers of the world."

13. Krēsliņš 2006, 35.

14. Imbi Paju in Radio Finland, November 25, 2006.

15. *Helsingin Sanomat*, January 6, 2007.

16. *The New Encyclopedia Britannica*. 15th edition (Chicago, London: 1976), Micropaedia, 74, Macropaedia, 10:706.

17. Latvian television, April 12, 2006.—In fact, *six* members of parliament voted "differently," but one of them declared that he had erred and wanted to vote with the majority. Minutes of Saeima, December 15, 2005.

18. The next summer the Rīga city council forbade the Pride procession and a court ruling upheld the decision citing "danger of violence" that the police would not be able to prevent. Visitors and passers-by were physically attacked and the police did practically nothing during the day to stop the abuse.

19. Juka Rislaki, "Grūti aizstāvēt Latviju," *Diena*, May 27, 2005.

20. Muižnieks 2006, 75.

21. Similarly it is said in the West that Finland got much sympathy during the Winter War (1939–1940) but "spoiled" everything by becoming allied with Nazi Germany in 1941. See, for example, Trotter, 2000, 265–267. He writes: "it was a tragic and cruel twist of history," that soon after the Winter War, Finland "should compromise its national image if not its honor. There was a disturbing aspect to the Continuation War in that a nation that only fifteen months before had been held up as a shining example of freedom and democracy should now make aggressive war at the side of one of history's most ruthless totalitarian regimes." Finland's worst mistake, clearly, was in choosing the losing side, as Trotter writes. Winston Churchill told Roosevelt and Stalin in Tehran in 1943, that he, like other Englishmen, felt sympathy for Finns during the Winter War. However, when Finns joined the German attack in 1941, "everybody in Britain turned against Finland." He thought the Finnish demeanor was "contemptible." (Translated from Finnish.) Visuri 2006, 321. In general histories Finland between the world wars is usually considered to be one of the rare democracies in Europe. However, when compared with Scandinavian countries it is often seen as a half-fascist nest of reaction. Mikko Majander, *Pohjoismaa vai kansandemokratia?* [A Nordic Country or People's Republic?] (Helsinki: SKS, 2004), 20.

22. Bleiere and others, 2006, 5.

23. Nadine Vitols Dixon 2006, p. 84. French original: Le Parcours de une vie: Vaira Vīķe-Freiberga, Présidente de Lettonie (Rīga: Pētergailis 2005).

24. Bleiere and others 2006. Unfortunately at least the first edition had errors, and the English version was not very readable or well adapted to the Western reader.

Bibliography

Aizpuriete, Amanda (2006) *New EU Countries and Citizens. Latvia.* London: Cherrytree Books & Amsterdam: KIT Publisher.

Aizvestie: 1941. gada 14. jūnijs (2001) [The Deportees]. Rīga: Nordik.

Andersons, Edgars (1983) *Latvijas bruņotie spēki un to priekšvēsture* [Latvian Armed Forces]. Toronto: Daugavas Vanagu apgāds.

Angrick, Andrej & Klein, Peter (2006) *Die "Endlösung" in Rīga: Ausbeutung und Vernichtung 1941–1944.* Darmstadt: Wissenschaftliche Buchgesellschaft.

Applebaum, Anne (2003) *Gulag: A History.* London: Penguin Books.

Avotiņš, E. & Dzirkalis J. & Pētersons, V. (1963) *Daugavas Vanagi: Who Are They?* Rīga: Latvian State Publishing House.

Baigais gads (1942) [The Year of Terror]. Rīga: Zelta Ābele.
New printing: Rīga: Tēvija, probably 1999.
Also: http://home.parks.lv/leonards/BaigaisGads/lat/saturs.htm

Baltais, Mirdza Kate (1999) *The Latvian Legion in Documents.* Toronto: Amber.

Bambals, Ainars (1999) In Memory of the Latvian Officers Repressed in 1940–1941. *Yearbook of the Museum of the Occupation of Latvia 1999.*

Bangerskis, Rudolfs (1922) *Latviešu strēlnieku ērkšķainā gaita* [The Thorny Road of the Latvian Riflemen]. Rīga: Valters un Rapa.

Beika, Aivars (1999) Latvians in the Soviet Union: The Victims of Communist Terror, 1929–1939. *Yearbook of the Museum of the Occupation of Latvia 1999.*

Bergmanis, Aldis (2004) Repressive System of Occupation. In Ērglis (ed.).

———. & Jansons, Ritvars & Zālīte, Indulis (2005) The Activities and Tasks of LSSR Agencies of National Security. In Nollendorfs & Oberländer (ed.).

Berkis, Alexander V. (2001) Soviet Russia's Persecution of Latvia: 1918 to the Present. *Journal of Historical Review*, vol 20.

Beschloss, Michael R. & Talbott, Strobe (1993) *At the Highest Levels.* Boston: Little, Brown and Company.

Bildt, Carl (1994) The Baltic Litmus Test. *Foreign Affairs*, Vol. 73, No. 5.

Bleiere, Daina (2005) Repressions against Farmers in Latvia in 1944–1953. In Nollendorfs & Oberländer (ed.).

———. and others (2006) *History of Latvia. The 20th Century.* Rīga: Jumava.

Bluķis, Uldis (2002) Valsts nepārtrauktība un ANO [The Continuity of the State and the UN], *Latvijas Vēsture* 2002, 3 (47).

Blum, Howard (1977) *Wanted! The Search for Nazis in America.* New York: Quadrangle/The New York Times Book Co.

Bruchfeld, Stéphane & Levine Paul A. (1999) *Om detta må ni berätta: En bok om förintelsen i Europa 1933–1945.* Stockholm: Regeringskansliet.

———.& ———. (2003) *Kertokaa siitä lapsillenne: Kirja juutalaisten joukko-tuhosta Euroopassa 1933–1945.* Helsinki: Opetushallitus.

Brukfelds, Stefans & Levins, Pols A. (2000) *Stāstiet par to saviem bērniem... Grāmata par holokaustu Eiropā 1933–1945.* [Tell Your Children]. Rīga: Nordik.

Burleigh, Michael (2004) *Kolmas valtakunta.* [The Third Reich]. Helsinki: WSOY.

Butler, Hubert (1988) *The Children of Drancy.* Mullingar: Lilliput Press.

Bäckman, Johan (2007) *Saatana saapuu Helsinkiin: Anna Politkovskajan murha ja Suomi* [Satan Arrives in Helsinki]. Helsinki: Russian Advisory Group.

Chapenko, Aleksandr (2001) The Red and White Latvian Riflemen during the Civil War in the Northern Russia 1918–1920. *The Yearbook of Latvian War Museum II.*

Churchill, Winston (1983) *The Second World War.* Vol. 6. Boston: Houghton Mifflin.

Cielēns, Fēlikss (1963) *Laikmetu maiņā* II [Changing Epochs]. Stockholm: Memento.

Darbiņš, Alfrēds & Vītiņš, Verners (1947) *Latvija. Statistisks pārskats* [Statistical Overview]. Stockholm: P. Mantnieks.

Davies, Norman (1996) *Europe: A History.* Oxford: Oxford University Press.

———. (2007) *No Simple Victory. World War II in Europe, 1939–1945.* New York: Viking.

Deighton, Len (1967) *Billion-Dollar Brain.* Paperback edition. New York: G.P. Putnam's Sons.

Dershowitz, Alan (2003) *The Case of Israel.* Hoboken, New Jersey: John Wiley & Sons.

Diamond, Jared (1997) *Guns, Germs and Steel. The Fates of Human Societies.* New York: W.W. Norton & Co.

Draudins, Teodors [Teodor Draudin] (1961) *Latviešu strēlnieku cīņu ceļā 1917–1920* [The Fighting Route of the Latvian Riflemen]. Rīga: Latv. Valsts izd.

Dunn, Stephen (1966) *Cultural Processes in the Baltic Area under Soviet Rule.* Berkeley: University of California Press.

Dūra, Danute & Gundare, Ieva (2004) Okupācijas vara un Latvijas cilvēks [The Occupying Power and Latvians]. In Ērglis (ed.).

Eglīte, Pārsla (2001) Changes in the Number and Ethnicity of the Inhabitants of Latvia during the Twentieth Century. *Yearbook of the Museum of the Occupation of Latvia 2001.*

Eksteins, Modris (1999) *Walking since Daybreak. A Story of Eastern Europe, World War II, and the Heart of the Twentieth Century.* Chatman: Papermac.

Epstein, Julius (1973) *Operation Keelhaul: The Story of Forced Repatriation from 1944 to the Present.* Old Greenwich: Devin-Adair.

Ērglis, Dzintars (ed.) (2004) *Occupation Regimes in Latvia in 1940–1959.* Rīga: Latvijas vēstures institūta apgāds.

———. (2005) A Few Episodes of the Holocaust in Krustpils: A Microcosm of the Holocaust in Occupied Latvia. In Nollendorfs & Oberländer (ed.).

Eskin, Blake (2002) *A Life in Pieces: The Making and Unmaking of Binjamin Wilkomirski.* New York: W.W. Norton & Co.

Eskola, Seikko (2006) Sota presidentinlinnasta nähtynä [The War Seen from the President's Castle]. *Kanava* no. 6.

Etat de l'agriculture en Lettonie en 1936 (1937). Rīga: Bureau de Statistique de L'Etat.

Ezergailis, Andrew (1996) *Holocaust in Latvia 1941–1944. The Missing Center.* Rīga: The Historical Institute of Latvia.

———. (2001) 'Juutalaiskysymyksen lopullinen ratkaisu' Latviassa ["The Final Solution of the Jewish Question" in Latvia]. *Kanava* no. 4–5.

———. and others (2005) *Nazi/Soviet Disinformation about the Holocaust in Nazi-Occupied Latvia.* Rīga: Latvijas 50 gadu okupācijas muzeja fonds.

Feldmanis, Inesis (2004) Lettische und andere nichtdeutsche Waffen-SS Einheiten in Zweiten Weltkrieg. In Ērglis (ed.).

———. (2005a) Waffen SS Units of Latvians and other Non-Germanic Peoples in World War II. In Nollendorfs & Oberländer (ed.).

———. (2005b) Latvia under the Occupation of National Socialist Germany 1941–1945. in Nollendorfs & Oberländer (ed.).

Fredén, Lars (2005) Shadows of the Past in Russia and the Baltic Countries. *Russia in Global Affairs*, No. 3.

Gogol, Valeri (1993) Bomba dlja Stalina. In Viktor Andrijanov, *Chetire portreta* [Four Portraits]. Moskva: Voskresenje.

Goldhagen, Daniel J. (1996) *Hitler's Willing Executioners. Ordinary Germans and the Holocaust.* London: Abacus.

Goltz, Rüdiger von der (1920) *Toimintani Suomessa ja Baltian maissa* [My Activity in Finland and in the Baltic Countries]. Porvoo: WSOY.

Gyllenbögel, Boris (1946) *Sotilaana ja diplomaattina Itä-Euroopassa: Entisen Moskovan-lähettilään muistelmia* [As Soldier and Diplomat in Eastern Europe]. Helsinki: Tammi.

Harriman, William Averell & Abel Elie (1976) *Special Envoy to Churchill and Stalin.* London: Hutchinson.

Henrikin Liivinmaan kronikka/Heinrici Chronicon Livoniae (2003). Helsinki: SKS.

Herman, Edward S. & Brodhead, Frank (1986) *The Rise and Fall of the Bulgarian Connection.* New York: Sheridan Square Publications.

Hilberg, Raul (1992) *Perpetrators, Victims, Bystanders. The Jewish Catastrophe 1933–1945.* New York: HarperCollins.

Hvostov, Andrei (1999) *Mõtteline Eesti* [Imaginary Estonia]. Tallinn: Vagabund.

Höhne, Heinz (1969) *The Order of the Death's Head.* London: Secker and Warburg.

Ilmjärv, Magnus (1998) Viron ja toisten Baltian maiden 1930-luvun ulkopolitiikan heijastuminen historiakirjallisuudessa [The Reflecting of Estonian and Other Baltic States' Foreign Policy in 1930's in Historiography]. *Ajankohta 1998. Poliittisen historian vuosikirja.* Turku.

———. (2004) *Hääletu alistumine. Eesti, Läti ja Leedu välispoliitilise orientatsioni kujunemine ja iseseisvuse kaotus: 1920. aastate keskpaigast anneksiooonini* [Quiet Submission]. Tallinn: Argo.

Indriķa Hronika (Heinrici Chronicon Livoniae) (1993). Rīga: Zinātne.

Ivanova, Galina (1997) *Gulag v sisteme totalitarnogo gosudarstva* [GULAG in the Totalitarian State System]. Moskva: Moskovskij Obshchestvennyj Nauchnyj Fond.

Ivanovs, Aleksandrs (2005) Sovietization of Latvian Historiography 1944–1959. In Nollendorfs & Oberländer (ed.).

Ivask, Ivar (2001) *The Baltic Elegies.* Rīga: Pētergailis.

Jakobson, Max (2006) *Tulevik* [Future]. Tallinn: Tänapäev.

Jēkabsons, Ēriks & Ščerbinskis, Valters (1998) *Latvijas armijas augstākie virsnieki 1918–1940* [The Highest Officers of Latvian Army]. Rīga: LVA & Nordik.

Johansons, Edmunds (2006) *Čekas ģenerāļa piezīmes* [Notes of a Cheka General]. Rīga.

Jokipii, Mauno (1992) *Baltisk kultur och historia.* Uddevalla: Bonniers.

———. (2001) Suomalaisen SS-pataljoonan erikoisuus [The Special Character of the Finnish SS Battalion]. *Kanava* no. 1.

———. (2003) *Hitlerin Saksa ja sen vapaaehtoisliikkeet* [Hitler's Germany and its Volunteer Movements]. Helsinki: SKS.

Kalniete, Sandra (2007) *Tanssikengissä Siperiaan* [With Dancing Shoes in Siberian Snows]. Helsinki: WSOY. Available in several languages, including English.

Kangeris, Kārlis (2005) Closed Units of Latvian Police – Lettische Schutz-manschafts–Bataillone. In Nollendorfs & Oberländer (ed.).

Karklins, Rasma (2005) *The System Made Me Do It. Corruption in Post-Communist Societies.* Armonk: M.E. Sharpe.

Karlsson, Klas-Göran (2003) Holocaust, Soviet Terror and Historical Consciousness: An Outline. *Yearbook of the Museum of the Occupation of Latvia 2003.*

Kaufmann, Max (1947) *Die Vernichtung der Juden Lettlands.* München: Selbstverlag.

Kažociņš, Indulis, (1999) *Latviešu karavīri zem svešiem karogiem 1940–1945* [Latvian Soldiers under Foreign Banners]. Rīga: Latvijas Vēstures fonds.

Keegan, John (1970) *Waffen-SS: The Asphalt Soldiers.* New York: Ballantine Books.

Kemiläinen, Aira (2005) Suomen ja suomalaisten kuva maailmalla [The Image of Finland and the Finns in the World]. *Kanava* no. 1.

———. (2006) Suomi puolusti läntisiä arvoja, mutta väärään aikaan [Finland defended Western values, but at the wrong time]. *Kanava* no. 4–5.

Kennan, George F (1978) *Soviet Foreign Policy 1917–1941.* Westport: Greenwood Press.

Kiljunen, Kimmo (2002) *Valtiot ja liput* [States and Flags]. Helsinki: Otava.

Kilpinen, Pekka (2002) *Ensimmäinen kerta* [The First Time]. *Kanava* no. 7.

Kissinger, Henry (1994) *Diplomacy.* New York: Touchstone.

Klinge, Matti (2000) *Eurooppaa – päiväkirjastani* [Europe—From my Diary]. Helsinki: Otava.

Krēsliņš, Jānis (2000) *Rētu uzplēšana Latvijas vēsturē* [Opening up of Wounds in Latvian History]. *Yearbook of the Museum of the Occupation of Latvia 2000.*

———. (2004) *Ceļi un neceļi* [Paths and Wrong Paths]. Rīga: Valters un Rapa.

———. (2006) *Raksti* [Writings]. Rīga: Valters un Rapa.

Kudu, Reet (2004) Die literarisch-politische Zeitbombe. Estland und die 'Russen' *Zwischenwelt*, Wien, 12/2004.

Küng, Andres (1979) *Unelma vapaudesta* [Dream of Liberty]. Tampere: Kustannuspiste.

Lācis, Visvaldis (2006a) *Latviešu leģions ārzemju vērotāju skatījumā* [The Latvian Legion as Seen by Foreign Observers]. Rīga: Jumava.

———. (2006b) *Latviešu zemes un tautas vēsture.* Rīga: Vieda.

Latvija citu valstu saimē [Latvia in the Family of Nations] (1939). Rīga. Reprint: Zinātne, 1990.

Latvija pod igom natsizma (2006) [Latvia under the Nazis]. Moskva: Evropa.

Latvijas valstij 80 (1998) [The Latvian State 80 Years], exhibition catalog. Rīga: LVVA.

Latvijas okupācijas muzejs, (1998) *Latvija zem Padomju Savienības un nacionālsociālistiskās Vācijas varas / Lettland unter sowjetischer und nationalsozialistischer Herrschaft.* Rīga: OMF

Lehti, Marko (1997) The Baltic League and the Idea of Limited Sovereignty. *Jahrbücher für Geschichte Osteuropas,* Band 45, Heft 3.

Leppänen, Markku (2002) Julkaisuja Latvian miehityksen 1939–1990 aikaisista asiakirjoista [Publications of Documents on the Occupation of Latvia]. Helsinki: Kansallisarkisto.

Levinson, Isaac (1958) *The Untold Story.* Johannesburg: Kayor.

Lieven, Anatol (1994) *The Baltic Revolution. Estonia, Latvia and Lithuania and the Path to Independence.* New Haven: Yale University Press.

Linguafranca (2005) Le Bulletin des Interpretes du Parlament Européen, vol. 8, number 7, July 4.

Lipstadt, Deborah (1993) *Denying Holocaust: The Growing Assault on Truth and Memory.* New York: Plume.

Loftus, John (1982) *Belarus Secret.* New York: Alfred A. Knopf.

Länsisalo, Heikki (2006) Norman Finkelstein – sionistisen "holokaustiteollisuuden" kriitikko [Norman Finkelstein – a Critic of the Zionistic "Holocaust Industry"]. *Kanava* no. 2.

Majander, Mikko (2004) *Pohjoismaa vai kansandemokratia?* [A Nordic Country or People's Republic?]. Helsinki: SKS.

Mankell, Henning (1994) *Riian verikoirat* [Dogs of War]. Helsinki: Otava.

Mannerheim, G. (1951) *Muistelmat,* I [Memoirs]. Helsinki: Otava.

———. (1952) *Muistelmat,* II. Helsinki: Otava.

Matiskainen, Heikki (2005) Ruotsin sotilaspakolaisten luovutukset Neuvostoliittoon [Deporting Refugee Soldiers from Sweden to the USSR]. *Kanava* no. 9.

McEvan, Ian (2005) *Lauantai* [Saturdady]. Helsinki: Otava.

Medijainen, Eero & Made, Vahur (ed.) (2002), *Estonian Foreign Policy at the Cross-Roads.* Kikimora: Helsinki.

Mela, Marjo & Vaba, Lembit (ed.) (2005) *Latvian historiaa ja kulttuuria* [Latvian History and Culture]. Helsinki: Rozentals–seura.

Migranti Latvijā 1944–1989. Dokumenti (2004) Rīga: Latvijas Valsts Arhīvs.

Misiunas, Romuald & Taagepera, Rein (1993) *The Baltic States: Years of Dependence 1940–1990.* London: Hurst & Berkeley: University of California Press.

Muižnieks, Nils (2006) *Latvian-Russian Relations: Domestic and International Dimension.* Rīga: University of Latvia.

Museum of the Occupation of Latvia 1940–1991 (2002). Rīga: Latvian Occupation Museum Foundation.

Myllyniemi, Seppo (1977) *Baltian kriisi 1938–1941* [The Baltic Crisis 1938–1941]. Helsinki: Otava.

———. (1997) Consequences of the Hitler-Stalin Pact for the Baltic Republics and Finland. In Bernd Wegner (ed.) *From Peace to War: Germany, Soviet Russia, and the World, 1939–1941.* Providence: Berghahn Books.

Neiburgs, Uldis (2005) Western Allies in Latvian Public Opinion and Nazi Propaganda. In Nollendorfs & Oberländer (ed.).

Nesaule, Agate (1995) *A Woman in Amber. Healing the Trauma of War and Exile.* New York: Soho.

Niiniluoto, Marja and others (1991) *Suomi, suuriruhtinaanmaa* [Grand Duchy Finland]. Helsinki: Tammi.

Nollendorfs, Valters & Oberländer, Erwin (ed.) (2005) *The Hidden and Forbidden History of Latvia under Soviet and Nazi Occupations 1940–1991.* Selected Research of the Commission of the Historians of Latvia. Rīga: Institute on the History of Latvia.

———. & Neiburgs, Uldis (2006) *Latvians in the Armed Forces of Germany in the Second World War.* Briefing Paper 1. Rīga: The Museum of the Occupation of Latvia. Also: http://www.li.lv/index.php?option=com_content&task=view&id=139&Itemid=452.

Okupācijas varu nodarītie postījumi Latvijā 1940–1990 (2001) [Devastation Caused by the Occupying Powers in Latvia]. Stockholm, Toronto & Rīga: Memento & Daugavas Vanagi.

Pavlovičs, Juris (2005) Change of Occupation Powers in Latvia in Summer 1941. In Nollendorfs & Oberländer (ed.).

Pelkaus, Elmārs (ed.) (1999) *Okupācijas varu politika Latvijā 1939–1991* [The Occupying States' Politics in Latvia]. Rīga: Nordik.

Pētersone, Inta (1999) *Latvijas Brīvības cīņas 1918–1920. Enciklopēdija.* [Latvian War of Independence]. Rīga: Preses nams.

Petrov, N.V. and others (ed.) (1999) *Kto rukovodil NKVD, 1934–1941: Spravochnik* [Who Led the NKVD]. Moskva: Zvenia.

Pitkänen, Veijo (1998) Baltia saranana 'sydänmaan' ja ulkomaailman välissä [The Baltics as a Hinge Between the 'Heartland' and the Outside World]. *Ulkopolitiikka* no. 1.

Plakans, Andrejs (ed.) (2007) *Experiencing Totalitarianism. The Invasion and Occupation of Latvia by the USSR and Nazi Germany 1939–1991: A Documentary History.* Bloomington: AuthorHouse.

Polpredy soobshchajut... Sbornik dokumentov ob otnoshenijah SSSR c Latvijei, Litvoi i Estoniei avgust 1939 g. – avgust 1940 g. [The Plenipotentials Inform...]. MID SSSR. Mezdunarodnyje Otnoshenija. Moskva 1990.

Polvinen, Tuomo (1980) *Teheranista Jaltaan* [From Teheran to Yalta]. Helsinki: WSOY.

Press, Bernhard (1988 & 1992) *Judenmord in Lettland 1941–1945*. Berlin: Veitl-Verlag.

Pumpurs, Andrejs, *The Bear Slayer*, transl. Arthur Cropley, 2006. Project Gutenberg www.gutenberg.org/etext/17445

Radzinsky, Edward (1992) *The Last Czar: The Life and Death of Nicholas II*. New York: Doubleday.

Report of the Select Committee to Investigate Communist Aggression and the Forced Incorporation of the Baltic States into the U.S.S.R. (1954). House of Representatives. 83. Congress. Washington: U.S. Government Printing Office.

Represēto Saraksts (1995) [The List of the Repressed]. Latvian State Archives (LVA).

Riekstiņš, Jānis (2004) Die Befreiung der deportierten Einwohner Lettlands von der Sonderansielung (1953–1959). In Ērglis (ed.).

———. (2005a) Colonization and Russification of Latvia 1940–1989. In Nollendorfs & Oberländer (ed.).

———. (2005b) The 14 June 1941 Deportation in Latvia. In Nollendorfs & Oberländer (ed.).

Rislaki, Juka (2003) *Kluso slēpotaju zeme Somija* [Finland, the Land of Silent Skiers]. Rīga: Valters un Rapa.

———. (2004) *Kur beidzas varavīksne. Krišjānis Berķis un Hilma Lehtonena* [Where the Rainbow Ends]. Rīga: Jumava.

Rislakki, Jukka (2004) Latvia – maa, jota Eurooppa ei ymmärrä. In *10 uutta tulijaa. Euroopan unioni – erilaisia yhdessä* [10 New Members of the EU]. Helsinki: Ulkoministeriö.

———. (2005a) *Latvian kohtalonvuodet*. [Latvia's Fateful Years]. Helsinki: SKS.

———. (2005b) Latvian ja Venäjän suhteet uudessa aallonpohjassa [Latvian-Russian Relations at a New Low]. *Rozentals-seuran vuosikirja*. Helsinki.

———. (2005c) Fasisteja ja kuivattuja suolakaloja [Fascists and Dried Salt Fish]. *Kanava* no. 2.

Ryan, Allan A. (1984) *Quiet Neighbors: Prosecuting Nazi War Criminals in America*. New York: Harcourt Brace Jovanovich.

Šalda, Vitālis (ed.) (2007) *Latviešu strēlnieki par un pret lieliniekiem 1915–1920* [Latvian Riflemen for and against the Bolsheviks]. Daugavpils: Saule.

Salisbury, Harrison (1969) *The 900 Days: The Siege of Leningrad*. New York: HarperCollins.

Salomaa, Markku (1992) *Punaupseerit* [Red Officers]. Helsinki: WSOY.

Scheffler, Wolfgang & Schulle, Diana (2003) *Buch der Erinnerung: die ins Baltikum deportierten deutschen, österreichischen und tschechoslowakischen Juden*. München: Saur.

Senn, A.E. (2005) Baltic Battleground. In Nollendorfs & Oberländer (ed.).

Sherwood, Robert E. (1948) *Roosevelt and Hopkins.* New York: Harper & Brothers.

Shirer, William L. (1962) *The Rise and Fall of the Third Reich: A History of Nazi Germany.* New York: Simon and Schuster.

Silgailis Arturs (1964) *Latviešu leģions. Dibināšana, formēšana un kauju gaitas Otrā pasaules kaŗā.* [The Latvian Legion]. Kopenhāgena: Imanta.

Simenon, Georges (1960) *Maigret ja latvialainen* [Maigret and the Latvian]. Helsinki: Otava.

Šneidere, Irēne (2005) The First Soviet Occupation Period in Latvia 1940–1941. In Nollendorfs & Oberländer (ed.).

SNTL:n Korkeimman Neuvoston seitsemäs sessia (1940) [Seventh session of the USSR Supreme Soviet] *1.8.– 7.8.1940.* Pikakirjoituspöytäkirja [Shorthand records]. Moscow.

Spekke, Arnolds (1957) *History of Latvia.* Stockholm: Zelta Ābele.

———. (1959) *Baltijas jūra senajās kartēs* [The Baltic Sea in Old Maps]. Stocholm: Zelta Ābele.

Sruoga, Balys (2005) *Forest of Gods.* Vilnius: Versus Aureus.

Šteinmanis, Iosifs (2002) *History of Latvian Jews.* Boulder: East European Monographs, No. 595.

Stranga, Aivars (2001) Contributions of the Latvian Commission of Historians to Holocaust Research. *Yearbook of the Museum of the Occupation of Latvia 2001.*

———. (2002) *Ebreji un diktatūras Baltijā 1926–1940* [Jews and the Dictatorships in the Baltics]. Rīga: University of Latvia.

———. (2005) Holocaust in Occupied Latvia. In Nollendorfs & Oberländer (ed.).

Strods, Heinrihs (1999) Top Secret Operation 'Priboi' for the Deportation of Populations from the Baltic Countries, 25 February–23 August 1949. *Yearbook of the Museum of the Occupation of Latvia 1999.*

———. (2000) The Concentration Camp at Salaspils October 1941 – September 1944. *Yearbook of the Museum of the Occupation of Latvia 2000.*

———. (2001) The Disorganized Retreat of the Red Army from Latvia in 1941. *Yearbook of the Museum of the Occupation of Latvia 2001.*

———. (2004) Latvijas okupācijas pirmais posms [The first phase of the occupation of Latvia]. In Ērglis (ed.).

———. (2005a) Sovietization of Latvia 1944–1991. In Nollendorfs & Oberländer (ed.).

———. (2005b) Resistance in Latvia 1944–1991. In Nollendorfs & Oberländer (ed.).

———. (2006) *Latvijas pilsoņu martiroloģijs Vjatlagā 1938–1956.* [Latvian Citizens as Martyrs in Vyatlag]. Rīga: Tēvijas Sargs.

Suominen, Elina (1979) *Kuoleman laiva S/S Hohenhörn* [The Death Ship S/S Hohenhörn]. Helsinki: WSOY.

Tacitus (1952) *Germaania*. Helsinki: Otava.

Tannberg, Tõnu (2003) Par Baltijas vietu Padomju Savienības militāros plānos 1920.–1930. gadā [About the Baltic States' Place in the Soviet Military Plans]. *Latvijas kara muzeja gadagrāmata* IV. (In Estonian in Eesti ajalooarhiivi toimetised 9. Tartu 2003.)

Tanskanen, Aatos (1978) *Venäläiset Suomen sisällissodassa vuonna 1918* [Russians in the Finnish Civil War]. Acta Universitatis Tamperensis, ser A, vol 91.

Terras, Aleksander (1989) Baltikumi rahvaste vaimse vabanemise lühikroonika [A Short Chronicle of the Spiritual Liberation of the Baltic Nations]. Stockholm: Eesti Rahvusnõukogu.

These Names Accuse: Nominal list of Latvians deported to Soviet Russia in 1940–41 (1982). Stockholm: Latvian National Foundation.

Toivanen, Erkki (2006) Imperiumien paluu historiaan [The Return of Empires to History]. *Kanava* no. 7.

Treijs, Rihards (2006) *Latvijas ģenerāļi*. Rīga: Latvijas Vēstneša bibliotēka.

Trotter, William R. (2000) *Frozen Hell*. Chapel Hill: Algonquin Books.

Tuompo, W.E. (1918) *Suomen jääkärit* [The Finnish Jäger-movement]. Jyväskylä: Gummerus.

Valsts valoda Latvijā/Official State Language in Latvia/ Gosudarstvennyi jazyk v Latvii (1992). Rīga.

We Accuse (1985). Stockholm: Latvian National Foundation.

Weinberg, Gerhard (1994) *A World at Arms: A Global History of World War II*. Cambridge: Cambridge University Press.

Verne, Jules (1983) *Tsaarin kuriiri* [The Czar's Courier]. Helsinki: WSOY 1983.

Vestermanis, Margers (1998) Retter im Lande der Handlanger. In Benz, Wolfgang & Wetzel, Juliane (ed.) *Solidarität und Hilfe für Juden während des NS-Zeit*. Berlin: Metropol.

White Book, The. Losses Inflicted on the Estonian Nation by Occupation Regimes 1940–1991 (2005). Tallinn: Estonian Encyclopaedia Publishers 2005. Also: http://www.parliament.ee/public/Riigikogu/TheWhiteBook.pdf

Vīksne, Rudīte (2005a) Soviet Repressions against Residents of Latvia in 1940–1941: Typical Trends. In Nollendorfs & Oberländer (ed.).

———. (2005b) Members of the Arājs Commando in Soviet Court Files. In Nollendorfs & Oberländer (ed.).

Wilkomirski, Binjamin (1995) *Bruchstücke*. Frankfurt am Main: Jüdischer Verlag.

Visuri, Pekka (2006) *Suomi kylmässä sodassa* [Finland in the Cold War]. Helsinki: Otava.

Vitols Dixon, Nadine (2005) *Le Parcours de une vie: Vaira Vīķe-Freiberga, Présidente de Lettonie.* Rīga: Pētergailis.

———. (2006) *Meripihkahelmi povella. Latvian presidentti Vaira Vīķe-Freiberga* [An Amber Jewel on Her Breast]. Rīga: Pētergailis.

Wyman, Mark (1998) *DPs. Europe's Displaced Persons.* Ithaca: Cornell University Press.

Yourcenar, Marguerite (1986) *Der Fangschuss.* München: Carl Hanser Verlag.

Yourcenar, Marguerite (1988) *Armonlaukaus.* Helsinki: WSOY.

Zetterberg, Seppo (2006) Ihmisyysrikokset Virossa 1940–1945 [Crimes against Humanity in Estonia]. *Kanava* no. 8

Zunda, Antonijs (2005) Resistance against Nazi German Occupation in Latvia. In Nollendorfs & Oberländer (ed.)

Index

A

Abrene 44, 144, 148, 179, 184, 199,
    202
Afanasyev, Yuri 178
Afghanistan 24, 95, 186
Aftenposten 139
Alexander II 69
Alexander III 176
Alksnis, Ingrida 28
Alksnis, Ivar 28
Alksnis, Jakov (Jēkabs) 83
Al-Qa'ida 13
Amis, Kingsley 29
Amnesty International 58, 63
Amnuel, Grigory 22
Ancāns, Ilmārs 209
Anders, Edward 110, 112, 206, 220
Andersons, Edgars 68
Angrick, Andrej 116
Anninsky, Lev 77
Arājs, Viktors 117, 118, 119, 120,
    121, 123, 134
Araloff, Simon 12, 177, 191
Associated Press 140

Atlantic Charter 149
Auschwitz 27, 197
Austria 21, 111, 190

B

Bäckman, Johan 24
Baltic German 20, 27, 69, 70, 72,
    90, 93, 157
Baltic Times, The 13, 202
Baltische Landeswehr 90
Bangerskis, Rūdolfs 82
Bankovskis, Pauls 13
BBC 51, 52, 137, 140
Beevor, Anthony 144
Belarus 45, 53, 113, 116, 117, 123,
    164, 187, 195, 221, 222, 223
Belgium 92, 221
Bellow, Saul 115
Bergs, Arveds 97
Beria, Lavrentii 163
Berklāvs, Eduards 163
Berlin 19, 30, 84, 108, 119, 130, 134
Bermondt-Avalov, Pavel 87, 88, 91
Berzarins, Nikolai 84

Berzins, Eduard 84
Bērziņš, Jānis 83
Bērziņš, Uldis 158
Biķernieki 120
Bildt, Carl 195
Bleiere, Daina 187
Bluķis, Uldis 220
Blum, Howard 135
Bradford, Richatd 142
Brazauskas, Algirdas 166
Brest-Litovsk 89, 144, 145, 174
Buchenwald 124, 125
Bush George Sr. 171
Bush, George W. 20, 21, 40, 197
Butler, Hubert 69, 181
Butulis, Ilgvars 81

C

Čakste, Konstantins 131
Cālīte, Aija 140
Canada 19, 25, 110, 135
caricatura.ru 198
Carpenter, Ted Galen 36
Castells, Manuel 5, 13
Cato Institute 36
Caucasus 134, 155
Cēsis 90
Charles, Prince 39
Cheka 24, 79, 83, 109
Chernobyl 168, 186
Chubais, Anatoli 12
Churchill, Winston 1500
Council of Europe 40, 49
Courland, Duchy of Courland 68,

72, 75, 84, 89, 111, 113, 120,
134, 176, 183, 184
CPSU, Commulist Party of the Soviet
Union 39, 152
Czechoslovakia 36, 95, 108, 111

D

Dagens Nyheter 19, 164
Daily Telegraph 53, 54, 173
Dankers, Oskars 114, 128
Daugava 20, 67, 91, 125, 135, 142,
186
Daugavas Vanagi 125, 135, 142
Daugavpils 20, 48, 119, 223
Davies, Norman 20, 157, 178
Deighton, Len 29
Denikin, Anton 83, 84
Denmark 146, 183, 190, 221
Dershowitz, Alan 212, 213
Dribins, Leo 63, 143
Ducmanis, Pauls 135
Dzerzhinsky, Feliks 83

E

Economist, The 59, 178, 206, 214
Eglīte, Pārsla 44, 162, 222
Ekeus, Rolf 50
Eksteins, Modris 25, 27, 85, 115
Encyclopaedia Britannica 151, 216
Estonia 15, 18, 21, 22, 23, 24, 26,
28, 29, 30, 35, 36, 38, 40, 42,
45, 47, 49, 54, 58, 59, 60, 65,

66, 70, 72, 73, 75, 79, 90, 92,
    93, 98, 100, 103, 106, 113, 126,
    127, 130, 137, 147, 148, 150,
    157, 159, 161, 164, 165, 166,
    167, 168, 169, 170, 174, 175,
    178, 180, 181, 182, 187, 190,
    193, 200, 201, 202, 203, 215,
    216, 222
Estonian Institute 15
European Court 39, 156
European Parliament 198, 203
European Union (EU) 15, 16, 18,
    19, 35, 40, 45, 49, 53, 54, 77,
    137, 139, 140, 156, 177, 178,
    183, 188, 193, 194, 196, 198,
    199, 200, 201, 202, 207, 208,
    217, 221
Evropa 125
Ezergailis, Andrew 19, 24, 120, 123,
    125, 135, 220

F

Falin, Valentin 24
Ferguson, Niall 182
Finland 12, 14, 16, 18, 22, 23, 25,
    45, 54, 56, 58, 65, 69, 72, 74,
    82, 83, 95, 97, 98, 99, 100, 101,
    103, 106, 108, 110, 134, 137,
    157, 176, 177, 182, 183, 187,
    201, 211
France 14, 110, 116, 147
Fredén, Lars 18, 191
Freedom House 23

Freikorps 27, 90
Freimanis, Jānis 158

G

Gambia 69, 183
Gauss, Christian 189
Gazprom 12
Geneva Convention 39, 155
Georgia 20, 24, 83, 194, 203
Ģērmanis, Uldis 84
Germany 19, 21, 25, 30, 45, 58,
    70, 73, 76, 77, 80, 81, 89, 90,
    91, 93, 99, 100, 103, 107, 110,
    111, 113, 114, 120, 121, 124,
    128, 130, 132, 133, 134, 136,
    140, 143, 144, 146, 156, 158,
    160, 167, 174, 180, 190, 196,
    200, 201, 214, 216
Gestapo 24, 132
Gilman, Aleksandr 61, 160
Goble, Paul 214
Goldhagen, Daniel 115, 118
Goltz, Rüdiger von der 74, 84, 90,
    91
Gorbachev, Mihail 77, 124, 167,
    169, 170, 171
Gorbunovs, Anatolijs 165
Gordon, Frank 81, 135, 220
Göteborgs-Posten 36
Great Britain 15, 25, 108, 116, 123,
    147, 149, 150, 151, 160, 173,
    174
Greene, Graham 37

Guardian 37, 38
Gustavs, Erlands Uldis 220

H

Hague Convention 113, 128, 155
Halonen, Tarja 201
Helsingin Sanomat 11, 21, 53, 194, 201
Henning, Detlef 29, 70, 80
Henricus de Lettis 66
Herder, Johann Gotfried 67
Heunert, Iwan von 113
Heydrich, Reinhard 114
Hilberg, Raul 116
Himmler, Heinrich 113, 114, 119, 127
Hitler, Adolf 26, 27, 36, 42, 74, 76, 80, 90, 93, 97, 100, 101, 103, 114, 115, 127, 128, 129, 130, 132, 133, 134, 136, 137, 138, 140, 142, 144, 146, 156, 159, 175, 176, 190, 196, 200, 212
Holland 15, 183, 221
Hollender, Pål 18, 19
Hollywood 29
Holocaust 15, 16, 41, 109, 113, 114, 115, 116, 123, 127, 134, 135, 136, 140, 169, 220
Höss, Rudolf 27
Hungary 190
Huntington, Samuel 177
Hussein, Saddam 13
Hvostov, Andrei 70

I

Ilves, Toomas Henrik 202, 203
Innocent III 66
Irish Times, The 81, 140

J

Jacob, Duke of Courland 68
Jakobson, Max 203
James, Lawrence 182
Japan 139, 175
Jeckeln, Friedrich 117, 118, 119
John Paul II 211
Juncker, Jean-Claude 199
Jūrmala 38, 60, 158, 167, 173, 209, 218, 223

K

Kalējs, Konrāds 123
Kālis, Mārtiņš 64
Kalniete, Sandra 170
Kalniņš, Ojārs 16
Kalyuzhny, Viktor 79, 95, 146, 181
Karlsson, Klas-Göran 136
Katyn 125, 147
Kaufmann, Max 115
Keegan, John 130
Kekkonen, Urho 211
Kelam, Tunne 54
Kennan, George 194
Kettler, Jakob (Duke Jacob) 68

KGB 29, 30, 63, 94, 121, 125, 135, 144, 163, 194, 207, 211
Khrushchev, Nikita 163
Kirchenšteins, Augusts 104
Kirov, Sergei 105
Klein, Peter 116
Klinge, Matti 14, 73
KM.ru 137
KNAB 208, 218
Kohl, Johann 11
Kolbre, Tiit 201
Kolchak, Aleksandr 84
Kolyma 84
Kozyrev, Andrei 174
Krēsliņš, Jānis 70, 82, 131, 220
Kruglov, Sergej 161
Krupnikovs, Pēteris 117
Kvaternik, Sladko, Marshall 26

L

Lancmanis, Imants 70, 71, 93
Landeswehr 90
Latgale 91, 176
Latvian Central Council (LCP) 131
Lavrov, Sergei 12, 194
Lazda, Paulis 220
League of Nations 91, 98, 108
Legion, Latvian 127, 128, 129, 130, 133, 134, 136, 137, 138, 142
Lejiņš, Atis 213
Le Monde 63
Leningrad 118, 176

Lenin, V.I. 24, 79, 80, 81, 83, 85, 89, 92, 105, 152
Lestene 137, 139
Liepāja 97, 100, 110, 120, 223
Lieven, Anatol 20, 36, 166, 169
Lipstadt, Deborh 116
Lithuania 16, 19, 20, 23, 24, 26, 38, 42, 45, 69, 73, 75, 92, 98, 100, 103, 109, 119, 128, 148, 150, 157, 159, 161, 165, 166, 168, 169, 170, 176, 187, 190, 207, 208, 216
Livonia 66, 67, 69, 70, 72, 80, 90
Lohse, Hinrich 119
Lotman, Mihail 200
Lucas, Edward 95, 178, 214
Luther, Martin 67
Luxemburg 199
Luzhkov, Juri 23

M

Mankell, Henning 29
Mannerheim, C.G.E. 83, 113, 130, 133, 201
Mäntyharju 82
Matisa, Vita 217
Mawdsley, Evan 81
Medijainen, Eero 180
Melenchon, Jean-Luc 19
Merkel, Garlieb 68
Mežs, Ilmārs 44
Milosz, Czeslaw 68

Mitrofanova, Eleonora 23
Moldova 45
Molotov-Ribbentrop pact 100, 147,
    156, 190, 201
Molotov, Vyacheslav 152, 176, 197
The Moscow News 38
Muižnieks, Nils 223
Myllyniemi, Seppo 214

N

Nagy, Imre 85
Narotshnika, Natalia 181
NATO 36, 49, 77, 139, 175, 177,
    178, 193, 194, 199, 221
Nesaule, Agate 25, 26
New Statesman 16
Newsweek 48
New Yorker 31, 73
New York Times 30, 38, 56, 58, 93,
    146, 212
Nicholas II 85
Niedra, Andrievs 89
NKVD 107, 109, 125, 133, 147
Nollendorfs, Valters 220
Norillag 124
Norway 15, 43, 44, 69
Novgorod 66, 178
Nuremberg 120, 121, 126, 132, 136,
    138, 142, 147

O

Oberländer, Erwin 152, 153
Ochsner, Gina 31

Oksanen, Sofi 215
Orwell, George 11, 216
OSCE (Organization for Security
    and Cooperation ir Europe)
    40, 41, 49, 50, 194
OSS (Office of Strategic Services)
    133
Ozoliņš, Andrejs 220

P

Padomju Jaunatne 84
Paju, Imbi 215
PCTVL (Par cilvēka tiesībām vienotā
    Latvijā) 35, 36, 63
Pelkaus, Elmārs 219
Pelše, Arvīds 84, 163
Peniķis, Jānis 19, 220
Pērkoņkrusts 30, 31, 96, 111
Peters, Jānis 165
Peters, Jēkabs 83
Pilsudski, Jozef 83
Plakans, Andrejs 214, 219, 220
Poland 45, 68, 83, 98, 100, 101,
    116, 147, 150, 175, 176, 195,
    200, 203, 208
Pol Pot 23
Potsdam 150
Pravda 97, 197, 215
Priedītis, Andris 220
Pskov 66, 178, 179
Puriņš, Āris 88
Pushkin, Alexandr 77

Putin, Vladimir 23, 35, 41, 42, 47,
    53, 124, 133, 137, 144, 145,
    170, 174, 175, 178, 190, 194,
    197, 199, 200, 201, 202, 203
Pytalovo 179, 184

R

Radzinski, Eduard 85
RCTV Russian TV Channel 141
Reagan, Ronald 40, 170
Reinholds, Vairis 82
Reporteurs sans frontières 23
Repše, Einārs 13
Reuderink, Ronald 162
Reuters 132
Ribbentrop, Joachim von 98
Richter, Hans-Werner 29
Rīgas Balss 87
Roosevelt, Franklin D. 149, 150, 173
Rosenberg, Alfred 27, 74, 82
Rosenfield, Harry 132
Rothko, Mark 20
RTR Russian TV Channel 35
Rumbula 118, 120
Russell, Ken 29
Russia 12, 22, 23, 24, 36, 37, 40, 45,
    46, 47, 50, 51, 54, 63, 68, 71,
    72, 73, 75, 79, 80, 81, 83, 89,
    90, 93, 95, 96, 100, 110, 124,
    131, 133, 136, 137, 140, 141,
    142, 143, 144, 145, 146, 148,
    149, 151, 156, 170, 173, 174,
    175, 176, 177, 178, 179, 180,

    182, 183, 184, 186, 188, 189,
    190, 191, 193, 194, 195, 196,
    197, 198, 199, 200, 201, 202,
    203, 208, 214, 216
Rüütel, Arnold 166

S

Sakharov, Andrei 173
Salaspils 41, 122, 123, 124, 125
Salisbury, Harrison 30
Sanskrit 38, 67
Sazonov, A. A. 24
SD (Sicherheitsdienst) 118, 119,
    120, 132, 134
Sebastian, Tim 52
Serbia 15
Shirer, William 159
Silgailis, Arturs 132
Simenon, Georges 29
Sinn Fein 51
Šķēle, Andris 207, 209
Šlesers, Ainārs 209
Slovakia 208
Šneidere, Inese 145, 155
Solzhenitsyn, Alexander 24, 79, 84,
    175
Soros Foundation 218
Soviet Russia 40, 79, 83, 89, 91, 145,
    148, 176
Soviet Union 11, 23, 24, 30, 42, 44,
    45, 49, 53, 59, 76, 77, 79, 80,
    81, 83, 84, 85, 94, 95, 96, 98,

99, 100, 101, 103, 104, 105,
106, 107, 108, 111, 113, 114,
120, 124, 125, 126, 133, 134,
136, 141, 143, 144, 145, 146,
147, 148, 149, 150, 151, 153,
156, 159, 160, 163, 164, 167,
169, 170, 171, 173, 174, 175,
176, 177, 178, 179, 180, 181,
182, 183, 185, 186, 187, 188,
189, 191, 196, 203, 206, 211,
218, 219, 221
Spekke, Arnolds 26, 76
Spekke, Claudia 220
Spiegel, Der 38
Sruoga, Balys 29
SS (Schutzstaffel) 16, 19, 21, 23, 41,
42, 52, 80, 117, 119, 120, 127,
129, 130, 132, 133, 137, 138,
139, 140, 141, 142
Stahlecker, F. W. 117, 119
Stalingrad 127
Stalin, Yosif 27, 83, 84, 85, 95, 98,
99, 100, 101, 105, 106, 127,
130, 134, 136, 137, 143, 144,
147, 149, 150, 151, 152, 153,
154, 156, 159, 161, 162, 163,
164, 173, 174, 175, 177, 187,
190, 196, 200, 201
St. Petersburg 24, 63, 81, 91, 176,
183
St. Petersburg Times 190
Stranga, Aivars 17, 85, 114, 153
Stricky, Erich von 76

Strods, Heinrihs 153, 166, 189, 215
Stutthof concentration camp 120
Sweden 14, 18, 20, 21, 29, 56, 68,
110, 136, 158, 176, 195, 214
Switzerland 110

T

Tacitus 65
Tajikistan 23
Teheran 149, 174
Teikmanis, Andris 22
Times, The (London) 20, 173
Timoshenko, Semyon 151
Tolstoy, Lev 77
Toynbee, Arnold 177
Transparency International 208
Trenin, Dmitri 80, 201
Trinidad and Tobago 183
Trotsky, Lev 83
Trudeau, Pierre 58
Trūps, Aloizs Lauris 85
Turkey 54
Turkmenistan 23

U

Ukraine 45, 203
Ulmanis, Kārlis 30, 70, 74, 87, 89,
90, 93, 96, 97, 101, 103, 104,
105, 106, 108, 111, 142, 148,
160
UNDP (United Nations Development Programme) 188, 208

United Nations 39, 146, 149, 152, 221
UNNRA (United Nations Relief and Rehabilitation Administration) 132
USA 69, 91, 110, 147, 149, 150, 160, 167, 215

V

Vācietis, Jukums 83
Valdmanis, Alfreds 128
Ventspils Nafta 12, 100, 120, 223
Verne, Jules 28
Versia 190
Vesti Segodna 63, 139
Vīķe-Freiberga,Vaira 77, 194, 195, 196, 197, 202, 205, 206, 210, 219, 221
Vīksne, Rudīte 117, 118, 287
Vilnius (Vilna) 135, 165
Visuri, Pekka 170, 180
Voitkus Lūkina, Maruta 220
Voroshilov, Kliment 100
Vulfsons, Mavriks 147, 152
Vyatlag 124
Vyshinski, Andrei 104

W

Waffen-SS 20, 40, 112, 127, 128, 129, 130, 132, 133, 134, 140
Wagner, Richard 28

Washington 150, 171, 215
Washington Post 25, 38
Weiss, Stephen 132
Welles, Sumner 149
WHO (World Health Organization) 183
Wiesel, Elie 122, 125
Wiesenthal Center 21, 123
Wilkomirski, Binjamin 116
Wilson, Woodrow 89

Y

Yalta Conference 150
Yanayev, Gennady 170
Yekaterinburg 85
Yeltsin, Boris 36, 96, 170, 177, 178, 190, 201
Yourcenar, Marguerite 27, 28
Yudenich, Nikolai 84
Yugoslavia 38

Z

Zatlers, Valdis 221
Ždanoka, Tatjana 156
Zeidenbergs, Gints 220
Zeit, Die 38
Zellis, Kaspars 153
Žīgure, Anna 220
Zubov, Andrei 191
Zuroff, Efraim 21, 123